11 19

MW00390442

# EARL CAMPBELL

# EARL
# CAMPBELL
## YARDS AFTER CONTACT

## ASHER PRICE

UNIVERSITY OF TEXAS PRESS, AUSTIN

Requests for permission to reproduce material from
this work should be sent to:
 Permissions
 University of Texas Press
 P.O. Box 7819
 Austin, TX 78713-7819
 utpress.utexas.edu/rp-form

♾ The paper used in this book meets the minimum requirements of
ANSI/NISO Z39.48-1992 (R1997) (Permanence of Paper).

Library of Congress Cataloging-in-Publication Data
Names: Price, Asher, author.
Title: Earl Campbell : yards after contact / Asher Price.
Description: First edition. | Austin : University of Texas Press, 2019. |
Includes bibliographical references and index.
Identifiers: LCCN 2018052872
 ISBN 978-1-4773-1649-8 (cloth : alk. paper)
 ISBN 978-1-4773-1907-9 (library ebook)
 ISBN 978-1-4773-1908-6 (non-library ebook)
Subjects: LCSH: Campbell, Earl. | Football players—United States—Biography. |
African American football players—Biography.
Classification: LCC GV939.C36 P75 2019 | DDC 796.332092 [B] —dc23
LC record available at https://lccn.loc.gov/2018052872

doi:10.7560/316498

*For my parents and my brothers*

# CONTENTS

EARL CAMPBELL

# INTRODUCTION

Even beneath the supernova-bright lights of the Astrodome, Earl Campbell's eyelids are slipping. It's late in the fourth quarter of a midseason seesaw game on Monday night, and his Oilers are huddling up on the sandpaper-rough artificial turf, stretched thin over a hard concrete subfloor, far below the arena's vast roof. The crowd of more than fifty thousand is a frothy sea of shaking powder-blue-and-white pom-poms, and on the sidelines, the big-haired Derrick Dolls strut in their shiny white boots. Facing Don Shula's storied Miami Dolphins, Earl has already carried the ball nearly thirty times, including on nine of his team's previous thirteen plays. He has gone for three touchdowns, scoring them with power and speed: on one three-yard run, he lowered his shoulder and lifted a defensive end up into the air as if he were a bull flinging a matador; in another, he rammed into a linebacker with his head, leaving his opponent sprawled out on the Astroturf. "Crunching power," Howard Cosell, in his staccato Brooklynese, tells the nearly fifty million Americans watching the game on ABC. Each time Campbell scores, the giant Astrodome scoreboard lights up with a rendering of a bull snorting steam out its nostrils. "Earl Campbell had some head-on collisions with our players," Shula would say after the game. "I think he won them all."

But all that impact has left Earl Campbell wobbly.

"Big fellow, you got one more in you?" Dan Pastorini, Houston's shaggy-haired, perennially beat-up playboy quarterback, asks him in the huddle.

With just over a minute left, the Oilers have the ball and a five-point lead. At second-and-eight from their own nineteen-yard line, all they need to ice the game is a first down. Coach Bum Phillips, the lovable cowboy-quipster riding herd on this resurgent Oilers team, has signaled that he wants to go with Campbell, the reliable rookie, once again.

The play is Toss 38. Pastorini will lateral to a sweeping Campbell, who is to turn upfield behind a leading fullback or pulling guard. It's a routine sequence, one that is deemed a success if it nets four or five yards. Except Tim Wilson, the Oilers' fullback and lead blocker, glances at Earl as the huddle breaks. "I swear, his eyes were closed," Wilson said later. "He looked like he was about to drop. I had to tell him the play, and he barely responded." Campbell has a foggy look from a night of pounding. "It's on two," Wilson tells him, reminding him of the snap count. "Follow me. We're going right."

*Act like you've been there before* goes the old sports chestnut, and Earl Campbell had: only five years earlier, on this very field, announcing himself as the best schoolboy football player in the nation, he had lifted his newly integrated high school football team to the state title. Two years after that, he was back in the same building, leading the University of Texas Longhorns to victory in the Astro-Bluebonnet Bowl.

Happy hoots and whistles rain down from the frenzied crowd, and on the terraced seating levels the dome feels as if it's vibrating, a space-age building about to launch itself skyward. A sign hanging from one of the decks says, "Look Out America, Here Comes Houston." For years, this city's losing squads had played before half-empty arenas, but now, with Campbell on board, the team is 7-4. The marquee *Monday Night Football* matchup feels like a coming-out party. "They've waited a long time for professional football excellence in Houston, and they've got it now," Cosell nasals out. "An underpublicized team, an underappreciated team."

Wilson, squeezing into his stance a couple of yards into the backfield, reaches a hand behind him, lays it against the small of his own back, and flashes an upside-down victory sign—given the timing needed in this football waltz, he wants to make sure Campbell remembers that they'll start on the second *hut*. Behind him, dropped into a frozen stance of his own, is Campbell, all of twenty-three years old, his face and full beard bursting with sweat, his massive thighs—each thirty-three inches in circumference, the size of a grown man's waist—nearly vibrating in anticipation. "We make four sizes of thigh pads," a Houston equipment manufacturer once observed, "small, medium, large, and Earl Campbell."

Pastorini receives the snap, turns over his right shoulder and pitches the ball. Campbell's eyes suddenly widen—"When that ball got in my hands, that leather, it's like I turned into a different human being," he once said. Wilson lands a glancing block in the backfield, just enough to protect Campbell from a loss of five yards. But now five Dolphins, including two speedy cornerbacks, have an angle on the running back. If they can force him out of bounds, they can stop the clock—and maybe give their own offense the ball with one more shot in a high-scoring game.

But Earl Campbell doesn't do out of bounds. He possesses what the writer Willie Morris once described as "the quality of potentiality"—that feeling that at any moment he might go the distance. And so, just as the Dolphin defenders appear to close in on their quarry, Campbell, as if he has rockets laced to his cleats, suddenly outstrips them all. Alfred Jackson, a wide receiver who played with Campbell at the University of Texas, once said he could sense when Earl was striking a big play even as he looked to lay a block downfield: "You could always tell when Earl got in the open because the crowd would roar." Just such a rumble rises out of the Houston crowd now as Campbell sprints down the right sideline past the Derrick Dolls, past the blue-and-white pom-poms, across the Astroturf, all of eighty-one yards for the touchdown.

He gets to the end zone so fast that it seems like a good minute before his jubilant teammates join him to celebrate—mostly Campbell just stands there, hands on hips, sucking air. After half collecting himself, he staggers to the sideline, where Bum Phillips greets him with a big-lipped kiss on his sweat-beaded cheek.

"What you've seen tonight, ladies and gentlemen," Cosell says, in his grandiose way, "is a truly great football player in the late moments take total personal command of a game."

Back in the locker room, Campbell told reporters that even after he got past the first line of defenders he didn't think he had the wind to make it all the way down the field. "Then I saw pure sideline, and I decided to keep running until somebody knocked me down," he said. He had "never been so happy to get in the end zone and get something out of my hand, that football." He was so exhausted, he said, that even getting back to the Houston sideline had seemed an impossible chore. "It looked a mile away," he half joked.

A few lockers down, Pastorini shook his head. "Don't you just love him?" he asked. And sure enough, it was the dawn of what came to be known as the Luv Ya Blue period in Houston, an all-around lovefest in which Earl Campbell would lead the once-woebegone Oilers to the brink of two Super Bowls.

But over in the visitors' locker room, the play that sealed the game had already fixed itself into the mind of Steve Towle, one of the Dolphin defenders, just as encounters with Earl Campbell stuck with so many would-be tacklers. "My career with the Dolphins defines me," Towle once said. "When you play sports from eight years old to the NFL level, it defines everything that I do every day, good and bad. It represents how I wake up each morning. I still miss Earl Campbell every time I chase him down the sidelines and it haunts me."

This is a story about a person, a place, and a time: Earl Campbell; the Texas that Campbell traveled through; and, chiefly, 1970 to 1985, a period when he came of age and dominated American football. It is the Texas of *Dallas*'s J. R. Ewing and sixty-four-ounce steaks, of ten-gallon hats and pitch-black oil, of the Astrodome and Congressman "Good Time" Charlie Wilson, of the Chicken Ranch—the tolerated brothel that inspired *The Best Little Whorehouse in Texas*. It is also the Texas of segregation and desegregation, of the trailblazing politician Barbara Jordan, and of urbanization, as the Marlboro

Men and their kids left their ranches and moved into the swelling cities. Seen from an age in which the bitter divisions of American society play out on football fields across the country—Trump versus Kaepernick, NFL versus CTE (chronic traumatic encephalopathy)—Campbell is an archetype, a modern John Henry, the heroic and tragic figure of a hard-working, plow-straight-ahead man who worked himself into a broken-down condition by giving it his all— his body an atlas of the brutality of the game. Around Earl Campbell moved a transforming, modernizing Texas, one that loved him and exploited him, just as, no matter where we live, we love and leave behind so many of the athletes who labor not only for money but also for our affection.

Campbell's own path, from a small town to big-city lights, mirrors a period of political change in Texas, as Democrats who had so long held control began to see their grip weaken; of demographic change, as hundreds of thousands of Texans began making the same migration as Campbell did, from rural areas to urban and suburban ones; of racial change, during which the long-static balance of whites, African Americans, and Latinos was transformed. (In 2005, Texas became a majority-minority state, one in which people of color outnumber whites.)

As a story about football, it's inevitably, too, about race: if you imagine arraying football cards in front of you from the 1960s through the 1980s, they chronicle a shift from crew cuts to Afros. Eulogizing his black Dallas Cowboy teammate "Bullet" Bob Hayes, who had won gold sprinting for the United States in the 1964 Olympics before playing football, the writer and athlete Peter Gent remembered how challenging Texas was even for an American hero. As late as 1965, Gent writes, COLORED ENTRANCE signs remained on all the downtown theaters, leading to the upper balcony, and there were still two separate drinking fountains. "We trained in southern California because there was no place in Texas that would allow black players to live during camp," remembers Gent. Through at least 1969, Gent's last year of playing on the squad—when Earl Campbell was fourteen years old, growing up in Tyler, an hour and

5

a half east of Dallas—the Cowboys gave rookies a personality test specially "weighted to make certain the blacks could deal with the pressure of living in the South." In Hayes's retirement, Gent wrote, following a turbulent period in the late 1970s that included prison time for a drug-related conviction that was later overturned, he "finally left Texas for the safety of his home state of Florida after Texas beat the shit outta him."

Even though he was handsomely paid, Earl Campbell was a black player toiling, to the point of ruin, for white coaches and white owners. One Orangeblood, as diehard fans of the University of Texas' burnt-orange-and-white-clad athletes are known, whose father was an Austin oil and gas lawyer and a big UT Longhorns booster, tells a story of being invited as a teenager in the mid-1970s into the Longhorns' locker room. There, his father pointed out what he said were unusual back muscles, ones he concluded had emerged during Campbell's upbringing in the East Texas rose fields and made him singularly suited to a bruising running style. The story has the unsettling cast of white people examining black bodies, of seeing those bodies as fit for both field work and football, for labor and abuse.

It's no coincidence that when the aforementioned Chicken Ranch, long accepted (and patronized) by lawmakers and lawmen, was shut down in 1973—an ambitious TV news reporter put together an exposé, much to the chagrin of both blue-collars and blue bloods—only one African American had ever crossed its threshold, and that was its longtime maid, Lilly.

Against this backdrop, we might think of Earl Campbell as a survivalist, in life and on the field, who made use of whatever resources were available to him until they—and he—had been completely juiced. What marked Campbell among the pantheon of great running backs was not just his size and speed but his will, especially to squeeze out that extra yard. Rather than step out of bounds toward the end of a run, he was famous for lowering his shoulder to punish yet another would-be tackler. He leaned forward, almost as if he were looking to pick something up off the turf, and pumped his knees high, leaving little of his body open to direct hits. Campbell, a weary defender once complained, was "all ass and thighs." A University of Texas assistant coach once said that Campbell's running style reminded him of the way Groucho Marx walked—although, of course, opposing defenders viewed the whole thing as desperately unfunny. He wielded not a cigar, but a wicked stiff arm—tutored in the technique by his ninth-grade football coach—the better to slap down would-be tacklers as he trampled forward. "Every time Earl carried the football, we'd have to run a stretcher onto the field to carry one or more of our guys off," the head coach of the Rice football team observed in 1977. "He's a physical, brutal runner. Very hard to stop. I know our defensive unit hurt for three days after the Texas game." Reaching for a way to describe the violence of football, the writer Ta-Nehisi Coates remembered watching Earl Campbell as a little kid: "[He] played offense like he was playing defense. He looked for contact and exacted a price on all who went looking for him."

Earl Campbell's impressive, bone-cracking recklessness was long hailed, with nostalgia, as fearlessness. Writing an appreciation of Campbell in the mid-1980s to mark his retirement from football, the Austin sports columnist Kirk Bohls observed, in a grisly turn of phrase that captured something of the violent, crunching quality of his runs, that Campbell "didn't hit tacklers, he splattered them." He won "the respect of every defensive player who ever had the misfortune to be introduced to his patented stiff arm. He played the game with the subtlety of a sledgehammer." The great sports columnist Jim Murray of the *Los Angeles Times* said Earl Campbell was the best he ever saw: "Put a gun on him and you had a tank." If other running backs crossed the line of scrimmage as if seeking safety, like swimmers paddling past waves and into open ocean, Earl Campbell liked to dive in the breakers. Jim Brown, the rugged, pathbreaking running back of the 1950s and 1960s, put it this way: "It's me first, Earl second, and everybody else, get in line."

In his day, Earl Campbell appeared transcendent, otherworldly, and, especially, invulnerable. After Campbell scored a key touchdown in one of his last high school games, shrugging off would-be tacklers as he led his high school to victory on the way to the Texas state championship game, the losing coach said: "I always thought Superman was white and wore an S, but now I know he's black and wears number 20."

In 1978, the year after Campbell won the Heisman Trophy as college football's best player, the University of Oklahoma's Billy Sims won the award, and Sims's coach, Barry Switzer, was asked how his player stacked up to Campbell: "Earl Campbell is the greatest player who ever suited up," he said. "He's the greatest football player I've ever seen. Billy Sims is human. Campbell isn't."

Even in the pro ranks, where he collected most valuable player awards, his opponents regarded him as seemingly sprung from a comic book. Leading up to his first game against Campbell's Houston Oilers, Cincinnati rookie Greg Bright insisted that he could be contained, even if many called him a Clark Kent in shoulder pads. After Campbell went for 202 yards, Bright was forced to back down. "Earl found a phone booth," he said.

But of course, Superman was a bit of fiction. The comics, after all, show Superman as a young man, never as an old one: no plotlines depict him moving about gingerly with a walker from all the knee surgeries, having trouble shelling pistachios because of debilitating arthritis, or fighting a dependence on pain pills to get through the day. Campbell played before terms such as "concussion protocol" or CTE—the neurodegenerative disease found in people who have had multiple head injuries—became commonplace in sports.

"I was watching basketball on TV with my sons this week in Minnesota," Campbell said in 2018, as he attended Super Bowl festivities. "We watched a pro game and then a college game, and in the middle of the second game, I said, 'Who won that first game?' And they said, 'Dad, you watched the whole thing.' So, there's definitely some of those short-term problems."

His father, Bert, who went by B. C., an alcoholic by turns jolly and stern, died when Campbell was eleven, and it fell to his mother, Ann

Campbell, a motor of a woman, to raise eleven children. Earl, like all his siblings, was a mama's boy. "If they gave out a Heisman Trophy for Moms, Ann Campbell would win it," he wrote in a sweet-minded Mother's Day appreciation in the late 1980s. "My mom's the greatest lady in America. She saw more potential in me than I did." He required the young Los Angeles agent who courted him out of college to travel all the way to Tyler to get his mother's blessing in a house so ramshackle, that even decades later, the man remembered the feeling of the wind blowing inside the walls. Earl Campbell ran for her, and for the men that he lionized—including his father, a missing hero, whatever the man's faults. Other father figures would emerge in B. C.'s stead: UT football's Darrell Royal, whom some players referred to as Daddy D and who, like any great coach, marvelously manipulated players to get what he wanted—and for whom Earl Campbell would be something of a savior as he tried, in the late stages of his coaching career, to repair his reputation as a racist; and Bum Phillips, the Oilers' coach, who pushed Earl Campbell to rush the way a trainer might coax a boxer into the ring. Campbell wanted to impress these men. He had a kind of desperation to please, one that translated into success on the field. "I always thought if I let one or two guys tackle me, I wasn't doing something right. I wanted a bunch of them to get me."

That sort of mentality served Earl Campbell brilliantly on the gridiron. He won a Texas high school football championship in 1973. In 1977, at the University of Texas, he won the Heisman Trophy, given to the best collegiate player, carrying his team to the brink of a national championship. He was Rookie of the Year and an MVP for the NFL's upstart Houston Oilers, the anti–Dallas Cowboys, lifting an otherwise workaday pro football team to greatness. Opponents dreaded having to tackle him: "Every time you hit him," the linebacker Pete Wysocki observed, "you lower your own I.Q."

Football strategy changed because of Campbell. When he was in college, the Longhorns shifted from the wishbone formation, which emphasized finesse, to the power-I, which basically announced that the quarterback would give the ball to Campbell, and just see what

you can do to stop him. The stories about Campbell's physical sac-
rifices are legion, and nearly mythic. How, as far back as middle
school, having suffered a broken arm, Campbell told a friend in shop
class to saw off the cast so that he could play in a rivalry game—he
played, scored touchdowns, and almost passed out from the ache
in his forearm; or how in a game against the University of Houston
Cougars he played with a 101-degree fever and a stomach flu—and
ran for 173 yards.

As with other great professional athletes, there was no off
switch—even in the twilight of his career. The safety Bo Eason, facing Campbell in the great running back's final season, decided to
challenge him in a goal-line stand.

> I hit him square. I mean I popped him face-to-face. After I
> hit him, I couldn't see anything. All I could see was black.
> I thought I was blind. Then I opened my eyes, and I was
> lying on my back in the end zone, and I could make out
> the lights on the ceiling. They were all fuzzy and blurry
> and spinning. I thought I was in heaven. Then I turned my
> head, and Earl was lying right next to me. He reached his
> hand over to help me up, and I said, "Earl, I've got to lie
> here awhile; I think you knocked out my eyes."

Eason realized later in the game, he said, that Campbell had "hit
me so hard that both my contacts flew out. The next day we were
watching film with our defensive coordinator, Jerry Glanville, and
he asked me why I was running the wrong direction the rest of the
game. I told him, 'Coach, I couldn't see shit. Earl Campbell knocked
my contacts out of my head.'"

"You want to know what it was like blocking for Earl Campbell?"
Carl Mauck, an offensive lineman for the Oilers in the late 1970s,
asked. "Go down to the railroad track at night where the freight train
comes through every evening at 9 p.m. Close your eyes and get within ten feet: That's what it was like blocking for Campbell. You hear
that train coming and you better get the hell out of the way."

Campbell sums up his career this way: "I truly believed I was invincible on the football field." He convinced himself that a third-and-three was actually third-and-six so that he would run with an anxious abandon to get that first down. And so the strategy for his coaches became plain: pound Earl. "To appreciate Campbell," Bum Phillips explained in the fall of 1978, Campbell's rookie year as a pro, "you've got to give him the ball 20, 25 times a game. He's the kind of guy who doesn't let up. He'll turn a four-yard run into a 12, or a one-yarder into a four, which is a heck of an accomplishment in this league. I think most of his yardage in college was made after he got hit. Most backs, you block two yards for them and that's what they'll make. But you block two yards for Earl and he'll get four. Do that three times and you've got a first down."

Look at Earl Campbell now and those are wince-worthy words. Sometimes, he says about the simple act of walking, "it seems like something in my body won't let me put my left leg up to the right one and just keep going."

This was his Faustian bargain, trading long-term health for money, fame, and greatness. This book, in a sense, is about why Earl Campbell struck that bargain. Earl Campbell and his wife, Reuna (pronounced Renée), live amid the Spanish-tile-roofed and ranch-style houses in the rolling hills west of Austin. Their kids went to a virtually all-white public school, in one of those districts that became a haven for white suburbanites aiming to insulate themselves after the sort of integration orders that propelled Earl Campbell into the football career that eluded his older brothers, the ones who attended—and went unrecruited at—all-black schools. He has a sinecure from the University of Texas and has licensed his name to a popular brand of smoked sausage.

The arc, from shack to suburbia, reflects a central tension in Earl Campbell. By the time he hit his stride, the major civil rights struggles had ended—fists had been raised in Mexico City, and Martin Luther King had been assassinated. During his junior season in high school, the Vietnam draft ended. And so he occupies a seldom written-about period for black athletes. Nonetheless, as an eighteen-year-old who came of age in desegregating East Texas, he had a profound enough sense of history to tell college recruiters offering bribes: "My people were bought and sold when they didn't have a choice; Earl Campbell is not for sale." In 2017, one of Earl's friends, Ron Wilson, who was in Campbell's class at UT before going on to be a state lawmaker, broke into sobs while recalling the cathartic feeling of watching him trounce anyone in his way. Absorbing all that contact and dishing out that punishment, Campbell, Wilson said, performed "the ultimate sacrifice for his people." But Earl Campbell didn't preach revolt: he genuinely saw himself as a catalyst for racial conciliation, as a messenger handling a football in place of a Bible to bring people of different stripes together. "I was raised not to have negative racial feelings towards the white people of Tyler," he told me. In his optimism, Earl Campbell is classically American, with a deeply felt faith in redemption. One of his sons, after all, goes by the name Christian, and the other Earl named Tyler, for the town in which he grew up, the one with a fraught racial history.

Perhaps Ralph Wallace, a Houston lawmaker and former trucker, best put his finger on the wonder of Earl Campbell's trajectory, that of a man both unloosed and somehow never quite free. Back in 1981, when Earl Campbell, a fourth-year pro at the peak of his powers, was entertaining thoughts about leaving the state for another team, the Texas Legislature did what it could to intervene, decreeing Campbell a Texas hero, an official designation granted previously only to Davy Crockett, Sam Houston, and Stephen F. Austin. Campbell, Wallace told reporters, is "a kind of Horatio Alger, a black man who came out of poverty in Tyler, Texas, out of a segregated community, and he's broken all the chains."

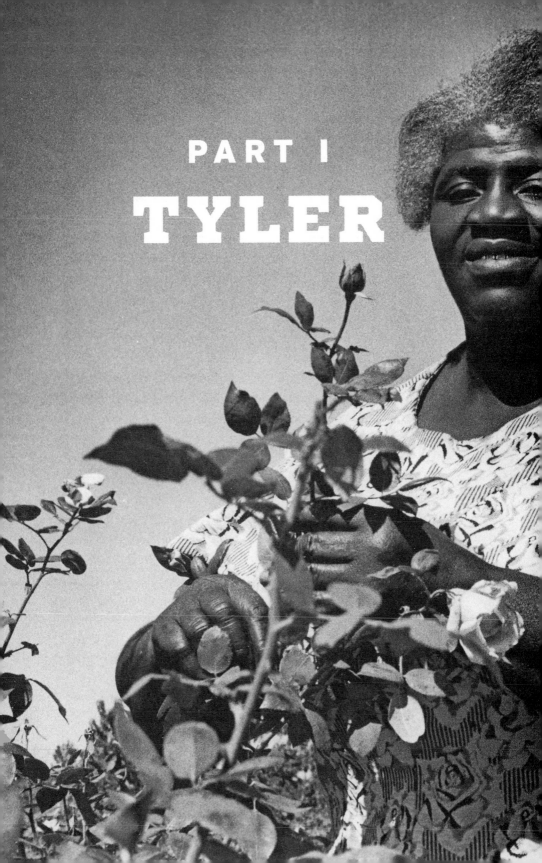

PART I

# TYLER

Earl Christian Campbell, who would become the most famous running back in America and the most beloved man in Texas, was born with a white man's name.

Like nearly all the five siblings born before him and the five siblings after him, he was born in the same bed in which he was conceived, delivered in his parents' tin-roofed home. It was March 1955. Less than a year earlier, the US Supreme Court had struck down as unconstitutional the principle of separate but equal as it applied to public education. But because Earl's parents were poor and black, on the rural outskirts of the deeply segregated East Texas town of Tyler, in a part of the state said to be so retrograde that it has its own time zone—"Set your clock fifty years back," goes the joke—they deferred to the white doctor who delivered their son when it came to the child's name: Dr. Earl Christian Kinzie recommended naming the kid after himself.

Two years after Campbell's birth, when his mother bore identical twins, they met a similar fate. Ann Campbell had wanted to name her sons "Jay" and "James," but Kinzie wrote the names Timothy and Steven—"Bible names," Kinzie later explained—on their birth certificates. When Ann Campbell was well enough recovered from the delivery, she went down to the county clerk's office to have the certificates changed. She returned home, exasperated, announcing to the family: "They wanted to charge me one hundred dollars to change each name on the birth certificate"—a cost the rose-farming family couldn't afford. "So from now on, your brothers will be known as Timothy Bob and Steven Rob."

The story of Kinzie and his forebears says much about the Texas into which Campbell was born. Christian was a family name, handed down through the doctor's clan from as long ago as the 1740s, when Christian Küntzi, a Swiss émigré seeking the freedom to practice his religious pacifism, settled in the Shenandoah Valley. Nearly two centuries later, Earl Christian Kinzie grew up in Kansas in the 1920s, athletic enough to play college basketball. Aiming to escape the Dust Bowl, he trained as an osteopath and eventually moved his family to Texas, to a small town just up the road from Tyler.

Medical care then was still largely segregated. At Tyler's East Texas Tuberculosis Sanatorium, for example, whites and blacks were treated separately into the 1950s. But having come from Kansas, a free state at the outbreak of the Civil War, Earl Christian Kinzie "was kind of galled that he had to have a separate waiting room for black people," his son, Bill Kinzie, a retired doctor, said. Long after the medical practice had integrated, Kinzie plastered one wall of his waiting room with photographs of Earl Campbell.

It's a peculiar fact of the South that the relationships between African Americans and whites, even ones in which African Americans are invariably subordinate, are in many ways more intimate than those in the North, despite the North's sense of self, even today—after its own troubled history of school busing and white flight and racism—as abolitionist and integrationist territory. The adage holds that if you're African American in the South, you can get closer, but not higher; in the North you can get higher, but not closer. It's a central paradox that Tyler and East Texas, a place of deep generosity, general unpretentiousness, and friendliness, could be fairly described by the NAACP's regional counsel, U. Simpson Tate, in 1956, the year after Earl Campbell's birth, as "the meanest part of the state."

"The whole South has a deeper relationship with blacks" than the North, said Henry Bell III, who is white and hails from a leading banking family in Tyler—one that employed Ann Campbell as a maid—and who counted Earl as a teenage friend. "We fished with them," said Bell, now an official at the Tyler Chamber of Commerce who helps organize its annual Earl Campbell football banquet. "We were raised that way."

Sam Kidd, whose family ran a nursery and was just prosperous enough to have a black maid—Zephyr Fears—come in each day to air out the place, tidy up, cook breakfast, and fix dinner, reports that when his parents went out of town, he and his sister slept in her house and went to her church. "It was no big deal whatsoever—everyone knew that those two white children, she takes care of their family," he said.

From the perspective of a black kid, though, the relationship could seem unsettling. "We were in the country when my great-aunt died," remembered Erna Smith, a contemporary of Campbell's at the University of Texas who grew up in the rural Central Texas town of Caldwell. "Anytime you go to a funeral, you see some white people there—that's who they worked for. I was always really creeped out by that. They'd call them by their first name. Everyone else saw it as a sign of respect, and they'd say, 'She was like a member of the family'—and I'd be like, '*Really?*' They'd say: 'Your grandmother never stole. There was never anything missing.' And you'd think to yourself: 'Am I supposed to say thank you?'"

In the doctor's telling of the day in 1955 that Earl Campbell was born, "the family was wondering 'Well, what are we going to call the baby?' I said, 'Why don't you give him my name—Earl Christian?' 'Well, that sounds real good!' And that's the name that went on the birth certificate." But the Campbells owned little: Would they have given away so cheaply the name of their child? Did they worry at all about contradicting the white doctor they obviously liked but also needed?

No less an authority than Andrew Melontree, an African American who formed the civil rights group the Tyler Organization of Men in the late 1960s and who served as a Smith County commissioner, describes Kinzie, whom he met when they served together on a Smith County grand jury, as "a congenial person" in whom he had the "ultimate trust." And yet this story carries inescapable echoes of slavery—of a white man's privilege to name the children of the black men and women he owned. The name Campbell itself was the legacy of slavery. Some time in the past, an ancestor of Campbell's had, like many enslaved people, taken—or, perhaps, been given—the name of his owner. In the book *Tomlinson Hill*, the journalist Chris Tomlinson, who is white, writes about his family's long, intertwined relationship with the family of LaDainian Tomlinson, who is black and whose heyday as an NFL running back came three decades after Campbell's. On property about 140 miles from Tyler, the white

Tomlinsons at one point owned the black Tomlinsons. At the time of emancipation, some of the former slave families took the name Tomlinson as their own, he writes. But that was about all they got: "The (white) family retained ownership of their land and had some key advantages. The most important was the color of their skin."

Even the more forgiving explanations of Earl Campbell's naming carry with them a whiff of buying and selling. "My feeling has always been that it was part of a forgiveness of fees," said John A. Anderson, a Tyler historian who had gotten to know Kinzie through fund-raising efforts for a regional hospital. Kinzie "was very generous with his patients, and this was long before Medicaid and Medicare and all of that sort of stuff."

And yet Earl Christian Kinzie, the man who bestowed his white name on a black child, became a friend of the Campbell family. He had delivered two of the kids born before Earl and at least four others that came after—one of whom the Campbells (or, perhaps, Kinzie) named Margaret, after Kinzie's late wife. Each year on Ann Campbell's birthday or over Christmas, he dropped by bread that he had baked—honestly, it wasn't good bread, laughed Martha, another Campbell sister—and Ann, in reciprocity, baked him a sweet potato pie. Earl Campbell has only warm feelings about his namesake. As he prepared to enter the University of Texas, Kinzie administered his physical. When Earl married his junior-high sweetheart, Reuna, Kinzie was a guest at the wedding. When he was inducted into the Pro Football Hall of Fame, he invited the Kinzies as official guests, and when Earl Christian Kinzie died in 2005, Campbell attended his funeral.

The story of Earl Campbell's name carries a peculiar coda: Earl and Reuna Campbell named their eldest son Earl Christian, after his father—and in a way, after the white doctor who delivered him and the Swiss man who settled in this country so long ago.

Tyler, famously perfumed with roses, carries a lingering scent of its sordid history. Just eighty miles west of Louisiana and, thus, in Piney Woods territory, in catfish-and-bass country, in plantation-home country, it is a city connected by diet and heritage with the darkly forested belt of the Deep South, a city with its roots in slavery—a planters' paradise where a little over a third of the population at the outbreak of the Civil War was enslaved.

If Texas as a whole might be characterized as keen to have joined the Confederacy, Smith County, where Earl Campbell was born, was downright zealous about the prospect. In February 1861, Texans voted by a roughly 3–1 margin to secede from the Union; but in Smith County, home to Tyler, the margin was about 25–1. So eager were Smith County citizens to break with the Union, they sent envoys to Montgomery, Alabama, to help organize the Confederate States of America even before Texas officially recognized secession.

Racial freedom has always come late to Texas, and maybe especially to Tyler. The Emancipation Proclamation went into effect in January 1863, and Robert E. Lee surrendered at Appomattox Court House two years later, in April 1865. But as if news ambled to Texas on an armadillo's back, it was not until that summer that Confederate forces in East Texas put down their arms—and blacks in Texas were not officially informed that they were free until June 19, 1865.

In theory, Juneteenth, as that date is now known in celebrations in Texas and other parts of the country, meant for African Americans like Earl Campbell's family, which had been in Tyler at least as long ago as 1863, not only freedom but also equality and a suite of personal rights. Not so much in Smith County, a territory where subjugation was endemic, where just over a third of households had been slaveholding, including at least fifty families that had owned more than twenty slaves. The freed slaves were barred from walking on public roads or congregating in public without passes from their former owners. And when they were hired to work, they frequently, at the end of the day, found themselves deprived of their wages. The criminal justice system offered little succor. Whites often ignored summonses in disputes involving African Americans. The Smith County sheriff's office refused to serve warrants in such matters.

In one case, a Tyler freedwoman testified that she had witnessed a white employer rape another freedwoman who worked for him. Suggesting that the man's conviction would lead to a race riot in Tyler, his lawyer convinced the all-white jury "not to take the testimony of the Negro"—and the man was acquitted. During his 1868 stint in Tyler, Gregory Barrett, an agent of the US Freedmen's Bureau, a federal office meant to keep the postwar peace, wrote headquarters that whites were overseeing a "reign of terror" and that they threatened to "clean the blacks out." That summer, whites stoned and clubbed black schoolchildren—forcing school to be suspended because the children were afraid to attend. Only the federal presence, Barrett wrote, prevented the freed blacks from facing "a worse condition than slavery."

In the decades after the war, whites held and abused absolute power. Lynchings, each a cruel, sadistic spectacle, persisted in Tyler through at least 1912. After World War I, as returning black veterans began challenging the status quo, Tyler became home to a robust chapter of the Ku Klux Klan. Sundays found the Reverend Albert Sidney Poindexter, the publisher of the *Tyler American*, a Klan newspaper, preaching sermons on racial purity from the pulpit at Grace Baptist Church. Tall, gaunt, and wearing a droopy white moustache and an austere dark jacket over a freshly pressed shirt, he liked to stand on a Bible, the better to loom over his audience, as he held forth on the dangers of equality. On a chalkboard, he would write the salient points of his sermon. Here is one such list, captured in a 1922 photograph:

1. Opposition to Seducers.
2. White Supremacy.
3. Separation of Church and State.
4. One Flag. One Bible. One School.
5. Protection of Virtuous Women.
6. Good Treatment to Good Negroes.
7. Regulation of jitney passenger traffic.
8. Purity of the Races.

9. Here to Stay.
10. Stop the whiskey traffic.
11. Stop Loafing.

That year, 1922, saw the election of a Texas attorney named Earle Mayfield to the US Senate. Known as the Klan senator, he benefited during the campaign from a Ku Klux Klan conspiracy to intimidate supporters of his opponent. After leaving the Senate, Mayfield settled in Tyler. He died there in 1964, when Earl Campbell was nine years old, and was known as a segregationist to the end. For many, many years, the maid for the Mayfields was A. C. Moon, the half sister of Zephyr Fears, the black woman who looked after Sam Kidd, whose home was across the street. ("I was always told to say, 'Good morning, Senator Mayfield' or 'Good night, Senator Mayfield' whenever I should see him," Kidd said.) When A. C. Moon died, Sam Kidd and his sister went to her church funeral service, the only whites there. Naturally, the congregants thought that the Mayfield clan had come to pay its respects. "Everyone there asked if I was a Mayfield"—and he remembered having to shake his head yet again; no Mayfield had bothered to attend.

Driving to Tyler today from the metropolises in the central part of the state—from Austin, for example, a trip that Earl Campbell has made hundreds of times—is like getting lost in Texas's attic. First north to that brimstone, Baptist belt buckle of a burg, Waco, then off east along smaller state highways for a couple of hours, each town more forgotten than the last, each with its grand dilapidated houses, its once-charming Main Street storefronts now given over to antiques stores, themselves full of garage-sale mishmashes, the reliquaries of modest people's estates: Disney shot glasses and cheap aluminum lemon juicers. Hubbard, Corsicana, Malakoff. Here and there, you find old brick warehouses gamely reinvented as artist studios or spruced-up housing, even as each town faces the long, decades-old challenge of losing its most promising sons and daughters to the big cities of Dallas, Houston, and Austin. It's late afternoon on a soggy winter day, and the empty land outside the rain-blurred windows shifts from blackland prairie to post oak savannah. Athens and Brownsboro. Finally, you reach the East Texas Piney Woods and, in the dusk, the trees now just silhouettes, Tyler.

The Tyler into which Earl Campbell was born was—and, in some quarters, remains—nostalgic for the preintegration period. The home of Mayfield, the Klan sympathizer, is now a bed-and-breakfast with the name Memory Lane Inn. (For $159 a night, especially wistful visitors can stay in Mayfield's own bedroom, known as the "Senator's Chambers.") And when, in 1980, the Smith County Republican Women sought the perfect spot for a pit stop during Ronald Reagan's presidential campaign (Reagan said he wanted to plant some Tyler roses at the White House—"A little bit of Texas never hurts," he said), they arranged for his wife, Nancy, to take tea at the old Mayfield house.

Tyler and Smith County were safe territory for Ronald Reagan: the last Democratic president to win the county was Harry Truman. Ralph Yarborough, the famed Texas Democratic senator of the period, who grew up a dozen miles from Tyler, once declared that when you crossed over the Neches River, the sinuous north-south divider that separated East Texas from, essentially, the old American West, "you were in a different world." The only things redder than Tyler's renowned roses, it was said, were its residents' necks.

The year of Earl Campbell's birth, the Tyler Rose Festival queen, Maymerle Shirley, a young woman chosen to serve as the community's ambassador, headed to Dallas for a ceremony in her honor at Robert E. Lee Park. (In Texas, it often feels that just about everything—schools, streets, counties—not named for a Texas Revolution hero is named after a Confederate soldier or officer.) More than five thousand yellow Tyler roses were plastered to the vaulted stone columns of Arlington Hall (the park's replica of the Lee home in Virginia), strewn on the steps, and fashioned into rosebushes. Shirley, a brunette with a toothy smile, wearing a yellow formal dress, white gloves, and a shimmering tiara, marched down the steps amid SMU students wearing Confederate gray. The band played "Dixie"; waving above the whole scene was the Confederate battle flag. You can

see Shirley, and all the other rose queens, each frozen in time, at
the Tyler Rose Museum. Pictures of them, from the festival's start,
in 1933, through today, line the walls. In each photo, a young woman, maybe eighteen or nineteen years old, is situated on the third or
fourth step of a grand curved staircase in the house of a prominent
banking or oil family, usually a Greek Revival with two-story pillars
out front; her back is to the camera, her rhinestone-studded dress
trailing behind her, her shoulders thrown back, her head turned over
her left shoulder, toward the viewer, in a look more doe eyed than
come hither.

None of them is black.

The rose queen pomp is about being "grander than everyday
life," said the oil-and-gas man Ralph Spence. As the 1940 rose
queen, his wife wore a white fur and silver-beaded dress with a train
so heavy that she didn't have to worry about falling forward while
taking the stairs; her motto was "pretty is as pretty does." Their
daughter, Louise, presided as the 1968 rose queen: "It's like fairy
dust is sprinkled on you," she once said. "You realize: 'They really think I'm a queen.'" In 1978, Ralph Spence chaired Earl Campbell Day, when Tylerites turned out to honor the newly crowned
Heisman Trophy winner, known as the Tyler Rose.

And if Earl Campbell's family for some reason had wanted to
visit Dallas that year of his birth, to cheer on Miss Shirley? They
would have had to sit at one end of a Greyhound bus, behind a curtain four rows from the back. "The back of that bus where the hot
engine was—man, that motor ran hot through summer," said Grady
Yarbrough, whose parents, like Campbell's, were black farmers in
the Tyler area, and who still remembers making such a trip as a
twelve-year-old. "Now that was humiliating." Yarbrough still carries wide, thrown-back shoulders and wears some of the same suits
that he wore as a schoolteacher and principal for fifty years. When
he was growing up, he said, there were "certain parameters that the
white community had established"; for example, "You couldn't go
in the front door of any establishment—you went in through a side

entrance or a back entrance. African Americans were not served in white restaurants or in white motels. Most African Americans didn't complain. They recognized it wasn't a healthy environment, they did the best they could do, they tried to make a living, they tried to survive, they tried to provide opportunities for their children and grandchildren."

African Americans' workaday life was ignored by the media. "They didn't want the history of integration recorded," R. C. Hickman, a photographer for the black newspaper the *Dallas Express*, said. "The *Dallas Morning News* wouldn't carry a picture of us unless a black man raped a white woman or maybe if a preacher got run over. We did everything the white folks did. We died, got born, and we got married. We went to school and got degrees, but no one was recording it. You see we were viewed as second-class citizens and we had to prove that we were not."

When members of Earl Campbell's family qualified for college, they were turned away from state-supported institutions. As Laura McGregor, for example, his great-aunt, prepared to graduate from all-black Emmett Scott High School in 1942, she learned that she couldn't apply to Tyler Junior College—or to East Texas State Teachers College or to Kilgore College, the only state-funded institutions of higher education between Dallas and Shreveport. She was black and the schools refused to admit African Americans. "And my parents still had to pay taxes to support the junior college!"—and state taxes to fund the teachers college—she said with a rueful laugh. "Can you believe it?"

In 1955, the year of Earl Campbell's birth, the all-white Tyler school board showed what it thought of the Warren Court's holding in the 1954 *Brown v. Board of Education* case: the board voted to affirm that its integration policy would be the "same as last year"— meaning that total segregation would continue in Tyler schools.

As a boy, if Earl Campbell wanted to visit Tyler State Park, he entered not through the main entrance, the one that led to the nicely manicured white part of the park—with its concession stand, bath-house, diving platform and beach overseen by lifeguards, boat-house, dance floor, playground, and miniature golf course—but via a roughly graded county road to the back entrance, heavily forested and relatively wild, at the far end of the lake, where children played in the water without lifeguards. The legislature had agreed to admit African Americans to the park only after the NAACP filed a lawsuit in the late 1940s. Texas at the time had 57,662 acres divvied up among forty-three state parks: not a single acre was allocated for the use of Texas's African Americans, even though out-of-state whites, who paid no state taxes, could enjoy them.

In the fall of 1956, a year and a half after Earl Campbell's birth, the Texas state attorney general, angered by NAACP lawsuits aiming to integrate parks and schools and seeking a sympathetic venue for his suit to shut down the organization, turned to a Smith County district court in Tyler. Baby-faced, with a high forehead and a penchant for double-breasted suits, John Ben Shepperd grew up less than thirty miles from the Campbell home and had filed a prosegregation amicus brief in the *Brown* case; now he sought to cut the crusading organization off at the knees. In what he hoped would be a template for suits in other states, he accused the NAACP of having illegally "fomented, encouraged, aided and abetted litigation throughout the State of Texas." "For over one hundred years the white and colored races in said State have lived together peacefully and in harmony without strife or litigation"—a sentence that suggests slavery was of a piece with interracial harmony and ignores the efforts of state officials during the previous decades to systematically deny African Americans their basic constitutional rights, including where they could live, how much they could earn, where they could learn, and even where they could use the bathroom in public facilities—"and that, were if not for the activities of the Defendants, they would now and in the future continue to do so." He accused the NAACP, which was represented by Thurgood Marshall, of operating illegally as a for-profit business and thus failing to pay proper taxes; of illegal political activity; and of barratry—litigation for the purpose of harassment. The suit asked that the NAACP be "ousted from doing business in the State of Texas" and that the court dissolve all the Texas NAACP chapters and prevent the organization from soliciting money for the purpose of instigating and bringing lawsuits.

The case was tried in a courthouse eight miles from the Campbell family home. The judge, an old family friend of Shepperd's, went with the state down the line, finding that the NAACP had been "seeking to register students in various schools of this State by a method contrary to the laws of this State, and that such efforts tend to incite racial prejudice, picketing, riots and other unlawful acts and acts which are contrary to public peace and quietude, and that said Defendants, unless restrained, will continue to solicit and incite litigation." Eventually, after Shepperd's term finished that January and he was succeeded by a new attorney general, one more willing to compromise with the NAACP, the organization was allowed to continue its operations in Texas, albeit in weakened form.

Five years after Shepperd's suit and a half dozen after Shirley's Confederacy-themed fête, when a young Earl Campbell, just another little kid, set foot in his all-black, segregated elementary school, Tyler had more $100,000 houses per capita than any other Texas city, sprawling places often built of stone, occupied by executives at Goodyear Tire and Rubber Company, Tyler Pipe and Foundry, General Electric, and bankers and oilmen. Key East Texas gushers had been tapped in the early 1930s, making wildcatters millionaires overnight; their mansions now lined gracious redbrick streets near downtown. It was a wholly different world from the wooden, sagging, seasick quarters in which the Campbells grew up, a gap traversed only by people like Ann Campbell, who served as a maid—a domestic, as they were called—in some of the grand homes. The Campbells were so hard up that after clearing away the picked-over holiday turkey carcass from the family whose house she tended, Ann Campbell would whisk it home to her eleven kids for further scavenging and brothing.

When Earl Campbell was coming of age, a black teen still

couldn't get a burger at the greasy spoon owned by F. B. Brown—unless he bought it by the back door and ate it outside. "We could never understand why Mr. Brown felt we were good enough to haul his hay but not good enough to be treated as equals," Campbell said. At the grocery store, black children knew to put their money down on the counter and push it toward the white clerk—rather than hand it to her directly. "That's just the way it was," said Sam Biscoe, who, as a black high schooler in the 1960s, worked as a dishwasher at Jerry's, a twenty-four-hour Tyler diner that also required African Americans to wait by the back door for their food. "What you felt was, something was wrong. It ought to be righted. We saw protests in different parts of the country, but Tyler was a small city, and we looked to Houston, Dallas for that stuff—we were not as bold." The annual East Texas Fair in Tyler still had a color code: whites only on Mondays, Tuesdays, and Wednesdays; Thursdays, when African Americans were admitted, were known as "Nigger Night."

Growing up in this atmosphere, Earl and his brothers had to do a lot of running. They had to run through the dusk to get home before dark, to avoid harassment from a few of the neighborhood whites who lived between their school bus stop and their own clapboard home in the boonies—these were poor people who couldn't afford to live apart from African Americans. They had to make doubly sure they ran past the houses with white girls, a particularly dangerous source of trouble. They had to run from the police the time a friend of theirs went drag racing on a rural road and ended up crashing the vehicle. Willie Campbell, one of Earl's older brothers, said all that running explains the Campbell brothers' quick feet: "How the hell you going to catch us? We been running our whole lives. White people been running us."

The older Campbell brothers—Herbert and Willie—"were big, strong boys," said Biscoe, who quarterbacked for Willie at all-black Emmett Scott High School. They were great athletes—better, if we are to believe what Earl Campbell says, than he himself was—but were denied a shot at playing competitive big-time college football because they attended Emmett Scott, which had little equipment for organized sports and nearly zero exposure.

But desegregation, which had been plodding along with all deliberate speed in Tyler, got a jolt just as Earl Campbell reached his teens. Disgusted with how East Texas school boards had dodged integration orders since the landmark 1954 *Brown* decision, a federal judge in 1970 finally demanded a more pronounced, forced desegregation. The ruling did not sit well with white East Texans. In Longview, thirty miles east of Tyler, self-described "super-patriots" bombed a parked school bus—the vehicle of integration—in protest; while no one was injured, thirty-three vehicles were damaged or destroyed.

As happened in nearly all school districts forced to integrate in the South (and in many parts of the North), because black schools were in worse shape than their white counterparts or because it was simply unfathomable that white kids would be sent to historically black campuses—or just as an official, sanctioned form of racial harassment and community disruption—it tended to be Smith County's black schools that were closed. "It was a sad day, sad occasion when we got the announcement that the school would be closed," said Donald Sanders, a black Tylerite who would have graduated from Emmett Scott in 1971 and who later became a Tyler city councilman. "None of the white kids were gonna be shipped to Emmett Scott," another former student—a white student—said of that period. "Of course they shut it down." Black coaches, teachers, and administrators, many of them long experienced, typically faced a brutal choice: accept a demotion and be folded into the newly integrated schools—black principals became assistant principals; black music directors now headed just the jazz bands; black football coaches became assistants—or quit. African American parents were naturally apprehensive about sending their kids to white schools. Hoping to assuage their fears, Dorothy Lee, chair of Tyler's Council of Colored Parents and Teachers, wrote a rather touching, encouraging note to all parents of black kids who, like Earl, were due to

27

start attending white schools in the fall, encouraging them to "make a good and lasting impression."

> You will find some of the world's best young men and women in high school today, some black and some white. They are in the school you are entering this year. You have enjoyed good relations with many of these young people at the fair grounds, theaters, in stores and other places. So, they will not be entirely new to you. The student who shows himself friendly will always gain friends, so we trust that you will gain life-long friends during your high school years that will cut across class as well as racial lines.

Still, at Moore Junior High, the first integrated school he attended, and then at John Tyler High, the previously all-white working-class kids' school, named (like the town) for the obscure US president who, following his term in the White House, supported the cause of the South so ardently that he became an outspoken representative of the Confederacy, Campbell witnessed vitriol between white and black kids, snickers, threats, turned shoulders.

Campbell wasn't interested much in the friction. In fact, he was at that age interested in very little other than gambling, petty thievery, and smoking Kools—in sixth grade he picked up a pack-and-a-half-a-day habit. He hustled for cash at the pool hall. His beloved father, who had worked in the fields beside his children by day and had left them nightly after dinner to work at Kmart, had been dead a year, felled by a heart attack brought on by liver failure. Panging with puberty, his father gone, a young Earl drank bootleg whiskey and played dice games at the Sugar Shack—at least once, with the cops calling, he had to rush out the back door and into the pea fields. He would later call this the "bad Earl" phase of his life.

It was his mother, who cleaned houses and farmed roses to keep her children fed and prepared for school, who disciplined him. She scolded him: if Earl's behavior, which verged on the criminal—"I was on the path to the penitentiary"—required her to bail him out, it would be unfair to his siblings, "who didn't make trouble, to take what little money we made and carry it down to the jailhouse and pay fines," she told a reporter for *Ebony* in 1978. "I always told them I would go my limit to get them something to eat and clothes to put on their backs, but I would borrow a dime from nobody to get them out of jail."

Today, a blown-up photo of Earl and his mother hangs in Earl Campbell's office. Earl, along with his brothers and his sons, bears a close resemblance to her: high, soft cheeks, a broad forehead, soft brown eyes, a wide nose, bright smile. The athletic features are rounded out a little now, the hair more salt than pepper. He still wears the full beard of his playing days. He likes to keep his mouth doubly occupied: while he talks, he chews on some barbecue or spits tobacco juice into a red Solo cup or sucks a lollipop.

People have Googled whether Earl Campbell is still alive. And yet, he's right there: popping up to defend the performance of the University of Texas's first black head football coach, waving his hand from a banquet table at a fund-raiser for his son's multiple sclerosis foundation, appearing at a Houston Hall of Fame event, or getting back pats at the "Sober Bowl," an annual get-together to encourage athletes to get clean.

For this book, he offered limited cooperation, making himself available, ultimately, for a pair of interviews—as well as generously providing introductions to several of his family members and friends. The book draws on those encounters as well as on a vast number of firsthand accounts, in-person interviews, boxes upon boxes of memos and long-ago correspondence, faded notes, old newspaper clippings, and other primary-source material about Earl Campbell, Tyler, the University of Texas, the Houston Oilers, and so on. He was perhaps understandably wary of a journalist's capitalizing, however modestly, on his life. The kid who told recruiters that he was not for sale was also savvy enough as an adult to license his name to a successful sausage brand, and hesitant to give it away for free to a reporter. His decision to talk with me about his experiences of desegregation and football, but less so about his wider career, reflects his natural reticence. Despite the Paul Bunyan reputation, Earl Campbell in many ways retains the shyness that marked his youth. He has long been deflective. As a pro, he encouraged reporters cornering him in the locker room to interview the blockers who had opened holes for him. "I don't think I talk enough to be a team leader," he said. "I'm just not that guy." Even as far back as high school, when he was obviously the star of the team, his loyal lead blocker thought of him as a "follower." "Earl had to be led at times," said the high school teammate. "That made me a better ballplayer—I wanted to do a much better job to help him accomplish what he could." Campbell has always possessed a sly, countrified sense of humor. Quiet and self-serious, he wasn't beyond a prank. One night, after his Oiler road-trip roommate Conway Hayman, a 295-pound offensive lineman, had drifted off to sleep, Campbell filled a series of Styrofoam cups a quarter of the way with tobacco juice and placed them on the floor of their hotel room. Then he shut out the lights. When Hayman woke up to use the bathroom at night, Campbell suppressed giggles till he broke out with all-out laughter when Hayman stumbled into the booby trap.

But the public diffidence added to the perception that he was a brawny bumpkin. The embarrassing ravages of football, the natural tightness of his family, a history of panic attacks, the increasing burdens of celebrity—today, at functions, older men constantly regale him with memories of his play, and he generously smiles and extends a warm, knobby hand—and, finally, the man's small-town nature have left him seemingly withdrawn. As if protecting himself and his name, he can be mercurial with journalists, eager to speak up one moment, hard to reach another. "You work to get a status in life," Earl Campbell once said about the isolation of celebrity. "You think, if I could just get this one into the end zone. One problem with getting it into the end zone that nobody ever thinks about, though:

it's pretty damn lonesome after you get it in. Everybody that helped you get it in, eventually you move away from them. You've got to be very careful to keep it to where all of you are like one little family."

Now, underneath that photo of Ann Campbell, he sits at the head of a long oak table in his office in a Craftsman bungalow in central Austin. A mess of posters—he and Walter Payton, both helmeted, enjoying a laugh while walking on a field together, circa 1980—is waiting to be autographed. His secretary, his son Tyler, a handsome, slimmed-down, smaller version of his father—he also played football, at San Diego State, before a multiple sclerosis diagnosis sidelined a potential pro career—won't usher you into his father's chambers until Earl is situated behind the table, his famous, battered legs hidden from sight. A folded walker, tennis balls on the feet, leans in the corner. To maintain the appearance of a dynastic continuity of power, royal courts used to seat a dummy on the throne after one king died and before the next was crowned. *The King is dead! Long live the King!* And as you come in the door, because you haven't seen him take his place and because that face is so familiar, the immediate, instinctive feeling is that a simulacrum of Earl Campbell had somehow been assembled and placed there in homage to a long-ago gridiron hero. Then of course, he speaks, and because of his greatness, because of his shyness, because of the ways his kids guard him and his legacy, you have the idea that you're having an audience with a wide-shouldered monarch who sits in some kind of exile.

"The goal was get out of the rose fields, and not end up at Tyler Pipe," he says now, explaining the very basic aim for a young Earl Campbell.

Was he born with the wrong name—had his parents had some other name in mind for him? "Not that I can figure," he said, as if the notion never crossed his mind.

Even as a twenty-one-year-old college junior, Earl Campbell was savvy about, and, in his easygoing way, floated over, the racial tension that bedeviled his hometown. "The relationships between the different skins are not very good in Tyler, you know what I mean?" he explained to a reporter in 1976. "I've got a lot of friends of both skins. It doesn't take much for me to get along with people. I mean, someone can step on my toes and I continue to get along." Today, Campbell remains shaped by the rural Baptist upbringing that encouraged him to see the best in people. And yet, as a middle-aged African American man who has endured his share of indignities, even as a celebrity, he smarts from his treatment.

He chews on this for a bit. In a discussion of whether his blackness has worked against him, he wonders aloud why his face doesn't appear on billboards in his hometown. "I'd love to do commercials for a car dealership," he says. And then a broad smile: "Let that be known."

He becomes serious again. "You'd think that Earl Campbell has a business in Tyler. They say, 'We'll give you a street.'" There's now an Earl Campbell Parkway in Tyler. "As if it's enough to say thank you. 'That's all you get and be grateful for it.' It's a confusing puzzle for a man sixty years old."

He strokes his giant knuckles across his cheek, like Marlon Brando, and his answers suggest a worldliness stretching beyond the narrow county roads that bounded his childhood neighborhood. "Ninety-nine percent of black men growing up in North Tyler would never have visited Pittsburgh or Cincinnati"—homes of two AFC rivals of the Houston Oilers—"or even Austin," he says. "Goddamn: Most of them wouldn't have gotten out of Tyler."

In a sense, this was Campbell's version of the Great Migration, the same mass twentieth-century movement that saw millions of African Americans head to the cities of the North or the West Coast. In her magisterial *The Warmth of Other Suns*, Isabel Wilkerson sums up the Great Migration plainly: "They did what human beings looking for freedom, throughout history, have often done. They left." "I knew that I lived in a country in which the aspirations of black people were limited, marked-off," Richard Wright wrote in *Black Boy*, his autobiographical novel about growing up in the South.

"Yet I felt that I had to go somewhere and do something to redeem my being alive." The Campbells, tied to their modest plot of roses, coping with the vicissitudes of their lives, were not among those who joined Wright. But Earl Campbell's remarkable ability to run with a ball altered his family's trajectory just as much as any relocation to the North might have. And if he strayed from that path? The stakes were laid out starkly in *The Courting of Marcus Dupree*, Willie Morris's 1983 book about an outstanding high school football player in another part of the South. Morris recounts that a college recruiter told him that if Dupree "breaks his leg this season and never plays again, he'll be just another colored boy from a small town in Mississippi."

Football, which he took up in junior high, and a dose of Baptist church (the family still attends Hopewell Baptist No. 1), where he began singing in the choir, helped straighten out the young Earl Campbell. "If you want to be someplace safe, be in church," his mother was fond of saying. And so as he strode through the campus of the newly integrated John Tyler High as a sophomore in 1971, already powerfully built, sports appeared as a salvation; and though he didn't think about it this way at the time, he eventually came to imagine himself as a divine tool of desegregation. "As we made our way through the racial battleground on our way to the bus each afternoon, I never dreamed the good Lord would choose me to help bring the blacks and whites of Tyler together," Campbell would later say. "The football team was the Lord's answer to Tyler's integration problem, and He handed me the ball."

Of course, it wasn't quite as simple as that.

Campbell, like any great running back, had a lead blocker, in this case a balding federal judge doing his best to keep his weight down, William Wayne Justice. "If it hadn't been for Justice, there wouldn't have been an Earl," said Gary Bledsoe, a civil rights attorney who is dean of the Thurgood Marshall School of Law in Houston.

It was Justice, an activist liberal, who had issued the broad 1970 desegregation order. And it was Justice who, in that first year of the integration of John Tyler High School, just before Campbell arrived, presided over a dispute distinctive of East Texas's mix of race, politics, and football: a case about the John Tyler High cheerleading squad.

This part of Texas was nearly as obsessed with cheerleading as with football. The next town over from Tyler was Kilgore, where the famed Rangerettes, the Kilgore College drill team, were known to kick so high that they could leave lipstick on their knees as their shins brushed the brims of their cowboy hats and who swore by the motto "beauty knows no pain." And the Rangerettes remained, after thirty years, all-white—though their renowned director had sworn she would be receptive to having a black member as soon as a qualified one tried out. ("Can you believe that bullshit?" said the sports columnist Cedric Golden, who was raised in Tyler—his family and the Campbells were friends—and whose wife grew up in Kilgore. "You can't find a black girl who can dance?") Cheerleading was about joy and about community spirit, and there was nothing so warming to some East Texas communities as an unbroken line of wholesome white girls lifting one leg and then the other, a smile stuck on their faces. Of course, cheerleading was also about football, and the two taken together were like Friday-night church.

Historically, white cheer squads had rooted for white football teams, and black squads for black teams. As a consequence of the 1970 desegregation order, Emmett Scott, the black high school, named for a son of former slaves who grew up in Houston and became Booker T. Washington's right-hand man, was shuttered, and most of its students and prospective students—including Earl Campbell—were sent to John Tyler High. About halfway through that first volatile year of busing, the administrators at John Tyler distributed ballots that identified the cheerleading tryout candidates by race—and required that students select four white cheerleaders and two black ones—despite the white-black ratio at the school being roughly 3–2. Incensed at the quota system, African American students staged a walkout. "We weren't going for it," said Linda Campbell, née Hamilton, Earl Campbell's future sister-in-law. "We were sitting around trees on campus. The principals told us we had to leave, so we walked and stopped traffic and went to the Dairy Queen on Lincoln"—now Martin Luther King Jr. Boulevard. Earl Campbell was too young to be involved, but not his brother Alfred Ray—Linda's future husband. About three-quarters of the African American students walked out; Alfred Ray wasn't among them. "He knew my mother would disapprove of his participation in that type of demonstration," Earl Campbell said. "Had I been at John Tyler at that time, I would not have joined for the same reason." Linda Campbell said her family, too, had concerns of the sort that divided families between kids growing up in the 1960s and parents who grew up during Jim Crow. "My father was worried about me, about getting an education"—she said this last part with a little eyebrow raise; he himself was an alcoholic, a womanizer who left her mother, a domestic worker, with seven children, and returned only after she died from complications related to heart trouble and diabetes at the age of thirty-nine. "After a couple of days off, the black radio station told us [it was settled and] to go back." But the administration, determined to stand its ground, decided to suspend all 200 protesters. The students, in turn, wise to the civil rights struggle, sued, claiming they had been unfairly penalized for exercising their rights of free assembly and speech.

William Wayne Justice grew up in the 1920s in Athens, a farming town thirty-five miles west of Tyler, steeped in the law. His father, a politically connected East Texas attorney who was a friend of the future senator Ralph Yarborough's parents, added his son's name to his office stationery when the boy was just seven years old. Pages of the *Southwestern Report*, a legal publication, served as toilet paper in the family outhouse. Justice, who came of age during the Depression, grew to believe it was his job to help the marginalized. A particular incident from childhood stuck with him, one he was determined to address as a judge: a black boy wandering through his neighborhood stopped to play with Wayne, as he was known, and another boy. The mother of the playmate called her child back. "After awhile, he came back out and said that he couldn't play with niggers. This little ol' black kid, he just didn't know what to make out of this. I imagine it just crushed him. He just slunk on home. That angered me."

Yet as a US Attorney, before his judgeship, Justice had, for practical reasons, mostly kept his feelings about race to himself as he cultivated friendships as an overweight, cigar-chomping head of the Tyler Rotary Club—a seemingly run-of-the-mill good old boy. Privately, he supported the landmark 1954 *Brown* decision, he told an interviewer in 1985, but added, "I would not have for the life of me let that be known out in the community, because I suppose that my law practice would have practically dissolved at that point . . . It was a question of economic and social preservation. You couldn't have made it if you'd come out publicly in favor of the decision."

But the federal judgeship, handed to him by President Lyndon Baines Johnson at the behest of Yarborough, for whom Justice had campaigned as a teenager, lent him the cover he needed to express himself. "God-dang, when he got on that bench with a lifetime appointment, he turned into a tiger," his former law partner once said.

By the time of the desegregation case, Justice had presided over a dispute involving a Tyler Junior College rule barring "extreme hair styles." The rule, adopted before the beginning of the fall semester in 1970, required male students to wear their hair above their eyebrows in front and above the shirt collars in back. Beards were prohibited, and sideburns could not drift below the earlobe. Moustaches had to be neatly trimmed. Trouble began when a professor refused to permit a twenty-year-old student to take a final exam in a government class because his hair was too long. Three students were then barred from registering at the college because their hair did not comply with regulations. Several plaintiffs, including a Vietnam veteran and a straight-A student, challenged the rule. The Tyler Junior College president and vice president testified that at educational conferences they had learned that long-haired male students led sit-ins and protests at other universities. ("Some of the administration were not what you would call raving liberals," recalled Robert Peters, who, as a young man, was then teaching US history at the school.) As soon as the lawyers finished their arguments, Justice—who had worn a Beatles wig to court one day as a gibe directed at the defendants—ruled from the bench that the community college rule was unconstitutional. His published decision noted that thirty-seven of the thirty-nine delegates to the Constitutional Convention—the one in Philadelphia in 1776—would have been ineligible to participate under the college rules. The college administration's "rationale apparently was that since long-haired students caused disruptions in other institutions of learning, all long-haired male students are potential troublemakers," Justice observed in his opinion. "I am unwilling to accept a syllogism so perverse and jejune as this to justify the humiliating and demeaning restrictions which this regulation would place on the plaintiffs."

The case exposed how out of touch, how suspicious, Tyler was in those days. Joe Richard Lansdale, the lead plaintiff in the case, remembers that hidebound period: "In a restaurant, I'd get: 'Hey, honey! You give head?' People thought [the hairstyle] was an affront to the American way of life." And the decision marked Justice as an agitator as far as other Tyler citizens were concerned. "He was setting a tone for modern East Texas," said Lansdale—who added that Justice's principle of equal treatment extended from hair length to race. "He was loathed by just about everyone because of the quaint idea that blacks and whites should be treated equally." Quickly, Justice got the cold shoulder from some of his fellow Rotarians. "If someone devised a litmus test for good old boys, Wayne Justice would flunk it," the *Texas Monthly* reporter Paul Burka wrote in a 1978 profile titled "The Real Governor of Texas." The judge, observed Burka, "displayed an astonishing lack of political finesse."

Then came the cheerleader case.

After the walkout, Justice decided the black students at John Tyler High had been suspended in violation of their rights to free speech and procedural due process, and he required the school to immediately reinstate them. "They were tickled and eager to get rid of black students," Justice later said of the high school administrators. And, reflecting a certain late-1960s, early-1970s earnestness, one that also spoke to how hands-on Justice was willing to be to settle matters, he created a local "bi-racial committee" charged with "discussing ways and means of achieving inter-racial harmony and understanding among students, teachers, and patrons"—and ordered the school to choose two more cheerleaders, one white and one black, to better reflect the school's overall racial breakdown.

With that ruling, he gained a new title: the Antichrist of Smith County. When Justice and his wife appeared at the Petroleum Club for dinner, other patrons stood up and stepped out. Workers who had been remodeling the couple's two-story brick house walked off the jobsite. The minister at the First Baptist Church called him a socialist. (Situated on opposite sides of the street, the federal courthouse and the church faced each other "like fortresses across the Rhine," Burka wrote.) Beauticians refused to do his wife's hair. A full sixth of the city's population signed a petition calling for his impeachment. A cousin wrote a letter to a Tyler paper claiming to be ashamed of being related to the judge. Texas lawmakers passed a measure calling for a halfway house for juvenile delinquents to be built next to the judge's home. Death threats ensued; the judge boosted the insurance on his home and stepped up courthouse security. In his early forties, Justice shed fifty pounds and took up taekwondo. "It was a great way to take out my frustrations," he later told the *New York Times*. "You build up a lot of hostilities sitting on the bench all day."

Justice's championing of Tyler's black students didn't stop with cheerleaders. Tyler's Robert E. Lee High School, the school attended by rich and middle-class white kids, sported a Confederate streak—at the school's football games, the marching band wore Confederate uniforms; the drill team was called the Rebelettes; and the football team stormed onto the field beneath a giant Confederate flag "as wide as the goal posts," according to Rostell Williams, an African American who spearheaded a group called Concerned Parents. "Black students at Lee feel the Civil War is fought over and over again each year between September and May," Williams told the Tyler school board in July 1971. "This is of grave concern to the black community and it burns at our hearts." The atmosphere in the classroom was likewise inimical. Bettye Mitchell, one of the black students enrolled at Robert E. Lee after Justice's integration order, remembers that the teacher would write twenty-five words on the board each morning for students to practice their spelling. More than once, at the beginning of class, a white student would enthusiastically wave his hand: "Teacher, teacher: There are 26 words on the board today." Sure enough, one of the students had chalked in the n-word. "She would just say, 'That's not nice' and erase it. There were never any repercussions." In November 1971, at a morning pep rally in the school gym before the big football game against rival John Tyler, white students sang "Dixie" as black students waved shredded Confederate flags and booed. Scuffles broke out, teachers were injured, school was closed down, and police were summoned.

That month, prompted by a new generation of African American activists, especially parents who had come of age in the 1960s, Justice's biracial committee agreed the flag, the fight song "Dixie," and the nickname Rebels should be abolished. Parts of the community pushed back hard. "It is unbelievable that we should be considering the idea of changing the name of Robert E. Lee High School or the established symbols of the school," one N. B. Cooper of Tyler wrote to the *Tyler Morning Telegraph* in a letter following the committee's recommendation. "Robert E. Lee was a man with great compassion and respect for human rights who freed his own slaves before the beginning of the Civil War. There is much being written and said about heritage today, but is it necessary to bury the heritage of the South? We have put to rest the bitterness, the animosities, but must we bury our history?" Sure enough, even after the pep rally riot, the school board rejected the recommendation of Justice's biracial committee. "If the black students had been a little less arrogant, a little less demanding," a board member named Vernon Goss said during the meeting, "compromise would have been accomplished. ... You may eventually get a lot of these things, but is it worth it to polarize and alienate your whole community so that a great number hate each others' guts?" But in December 1971, citing Justice's order that school symbols not discriminate or upset racial harmony, the Texas Education Agency demanded the district get rid of Confederate symbols or lose $800,000 in state funding. The turn of events made Justice something yet worse to the citizens of Tyler—a person who misunderstood the South. "There's a difference between being proud of your Southern heritage and being racist," an indignant East Texas state lawmaker insisted.

As a protest, in the afternoons after school let out, kids from Robert E. Lee "would make the circle around the (federal) building flying huge Rebel flags and honking their horns," remembered a longtime court employee named Myra Rachel.

For all his power—or because of it—Justice was a lonely, unbeloved person in town. After the controversy at the high school, a Tyler politician is said to have spotted Justice having coffee, alone as usual, at an old hotel. He razzed the meddling judge, "How's my friendly neighborhood school administrator?" Unlike other judges who quietly presided over other desegregation cases, Justice would "get your nose rubbed in it," said Charles Clark, a senior Tyler attorney who was, for a time, Justice's jogging partner. (Justice's customary predawn jogging route took him around the Robert E. Lee campus.) "He was not well-liked around here. He didn't care to be." Justice took the pushback with equipoise. "I like Tyler. Here I have found only a minimal amount of personal discourtesy," he told an interviewer years later. To progressives across the state, the judge was a godsend: Justice, the great Molly Ivins wrote once with characteristic wryness, "was bucking for sainthood." He remained in the community through the 1990s, owning a series of houses in the elegant, brick-paved streets of Tyler's Azalea neighborhood, though his last house had louvered canopies over the ground-floor windows—for privacy and security, most neighbors thought.

It was into this stew of race and politics that Earl Campbell stepped as a mere teen, a mess that, one way or another, he would slog through his entire life. Race is an inescapable fact in America, and even more obviously so in East Texas.

Years later, when Tyler hosted a homecoming for Earl Campbell, after he had won glory on the football field, all the town's dignitaries lined up to greet him. They gave Campbell a $10,000 Ford van: Earl Christian Kinzie, the osteopath who had delivered him, handed Campbell the keys. (It carried the license plate RBC 20; Campbell was later asked what it stood for: "Running Back Campbell, I guess," he reckoned. "Hey, when somebody gives you something, you don't ask a lot of questions.") Campbell, in a gray three-piece suit, just shy of his twenty-third birthday, was driven through downtown Tyler in an open-top Mercedes; more than five thousand people—in a town of only sixty thousand—came out to see him, despite near-freezing temperatures and harsh early-February winds.

Afterward, at a banquet that included speeches from the governor and the head of the University of Texas System, 1,200 Tylerites paid $12.50 apiece for sirloin steak, a baked potato, broccoli, and lemon icebox pie. An extra 200 seats had to be set up at Harvey Hall, which backed onto the East Texas Fair, the one that admitted African Americans only on certain days of the week. "We have, as I look out over the auditorium, a true (racial) mixture," Darrell Royal, the coach who had recruited Campbell to UT, said. "And I don't think anyone has done more to achieve that mixture than Earl Campbell. And I love him for it." The only prominent person not serving as one of the official greeters at the event: William Wayne Justice, the judge whose desegregation of the schools had given Campbell the chance to compete on a level playing field and launch his lustrous career. The organizers had made sure not to invite him.

Nearly three decades earlier, a few years after the end of World War II, according to Campbell family lore, a small plane crashed in some farmland northwest of Tyler. The land was tended by Reuben Collins, and as he cleared away the rubble and tried to get help, his heart seized up.

Reuben Collins had grown up illiterate—the 1895 "Assessor's Report of Colored Scholastic Population" for Smith County records that as a sixteen-year-old he still couldn't read—but he had diligently been working this plot of land, giving money each month to the Pattersons, the white family who owned the property, in hope of taking possession of it. This arrangement was itself unusual in the area: whites frequently refused to sell land to African Americans.

But Reuben Collins died, leaving behind a wife, Lizzie Collins, and their eleven children. Collins, a resourceful woman, was a seamstress who owned a Singer sewing machine, and it was by use of that machine that she managed to make some money: show her a picture and she'd cut out a dress. But she could not earn enough to make even modest payments to the Pattersons, who soon repossessed the land. Suddenly, the land that she and her children had hoped would be the family homestead—and all the money they had saved and sunk into it—was taken from them. The change in family fortunes was devastating. One her kids would eventually be killed at gunpoint. But at least one child, twenty-two year-old Ann, had graduated from high school and was married, and with that, the door to opportunity was left just slightly ajar.

Ann Collins and B. C. Campbell had known each other while growing up—their families lived only about a mile from each another, attended the same Baptist church, and had dinner together once a month. Julius Campbell, B. C.'s grandfather—Earl Campbell's great-grandfather—had settled in the Tyler area as early as the 1890s. He hailed from Alabama, and in Smith County he planted pears, plums, and sweet potatoes. Ann had wanted only one child when, in 1942, three weeks out of high school, she married B. C.—a small, thin, mustachioed, "jolly type of fellow," in the words of his sister, Laura McGregor. B. C. served in World War II—journeying all the way to France—and back in Texas, he had an amusing penchant for buying cheap, nearly broken-down jalopies, never owning the same car for much more than a month. But he could also be stern. "He was a tough man," said Donald Hamilton, who played with the Campbell boys on the playground at Griffin Elementary in the early 1960s and was struck even then by Earl's preternatural balance and strength. "Not mean tough, but tough." He also had a taste for white lightning, and he and Ann long engaged in a sort of hide-and-seek: Ann rooting out his stash and him hiding it anew. "All our fathers were alcoholics," said Hamilton, who himself worked a long time to get sober and whose sister married one of Earl's brothers.

When Hamilton's mother died while walking the couple of miles to work as a maid one January morning in 1963—she walked everywhere because she couldn't afford a car—she left behind seven kids, ages eight through sixteen. Their father had long been absent, and her congregation didn't help with the funeral arrangements. For years, after serving in the Marines and working for General Electric, Hamilton said he "carried a bitter root in my heart for the church." But, he said of himself and of the world more generally, "everything that looks dead ain't dead." He holds a luminous smile in a very soft face, one topped off with a Vietnam Vet ball cap; his rounded shoulders sit inside a navy General Electric T-shirt. His story serves as a small window onto that generation of black men's hardship—often marked by addiction, poverty, and the efforts to overcome them—that could have been Earl's lot. Like Earl, he has little time for a certain kind of racial negativity. He explains his lack of resentment this way—"You catch more flies with honey than with vinegar," an adage that serves him well as the minister of a small Baptist church in North Tyler, one that concerns itself with restoring half-lost African American cemeteries. When Ann Campbell was growing old, Donald Hamilton would sit by her bedside to minister to her. They used to play a kind of game, each taking turns recalling their own tough times and announcing, "You ain't got nothing on me."

Ann and B. C. had inherited from the Campbell side of the family a fourteen-acre plot on which they grew peas, corn, and, soon, the cash crop of Tyler—roses. To understand something about the Campbells, about work and race and privilege in Smith County, you have to understand the history of the rose industry in this part of Texas. It was on roses that the Campbell family relied for its meager income. Not for nothing was Earl Campbell nicknamed the Tyler Rose. "Enough thorns stick you," said Sam Goldwater of Lonestar Nurseries, "it becomes part of your blood."

As recently as the late nineteenth century, Smith County was known not for its roses but its peaches. The climate of the area was, as it is now, moist and warm, with southerly winds blowing in heat from the Gulf of Mexico; the soil was acidic; the first freeze came in November, the last in early March, allowing for a lengthy growing season. The trees virtually dripped with the fruit. In 1889, county residents harvested about fifteen million peaches. A few years later, on the southwestern edge of downtown, growers keen to promote the bounty of East Texas opened a white-and-red Victorian convention hall they called the Texas Fruit Palace. At the turn of the century, in the small rural community on Tyler's northwestern fringe that was home to members of the Campbell and Collins families, agricultural agents estimated there were about one million peach trees.

But disaster lurked: a shipment of fruit trees from China to California's Bay Area harbored a destructive insect species that came to be known as the San Jose scale. The scale feeds by sucking juices from twigs, branches, fruit, and foliage—basically, every single component of a fruit tree. And within thirty years of arriving on American soil, the San Jose scale found its way to Smith County; by the outbreak of World War I, the peach orchards of East Texas had been nearly wiped out.

The nurserymen, despondent, had to find another crop.

Several families had done some pioneering work in the rose business: the climate and the sandy loam that had been good for peaches would now lead Tyler to become the rose capital of the country. By the end of the 1930s, more than two hundred companies around Smith County grew roses; in 1936, the year when Tyler crowned its first rose queen, they produced about six million plants. A decade later, they were growing as many as twenty million plants, with names like Radiance, Talisman, Étoile de Hollande, and President Hoover. At home, Tylerites made rose-petal jelly. Each February, the county, or at least some of the white citizens of the county, reveled in the annual rose festival. Tyler was "blanketed with dollar-apiece blossoms," reads an old Chamber of Commerce history of Tyler's Rose Festival day. "The streets were festooned with them. Young women with great armfuls passed out rare buds to pedestrians. Others tossed bouquets into passing automobiles. In the beautiful floral parade, great floats and streams of private automobiles, resembling mobile heaps of multi-colored roses, moved between the dense masses of spectators while low-flying airplanes constantly showered the crowds with rose petals from the air." By 1955, the year of Earl Campbell's birth, Tyler growers shipped out about 250 train cars, each stuffed with 25,000 rosebushes, across the country. Spurred by the *Brown* ruling and the forced integration of schools, among other reasons, white suburbs began blossoming throughout the United States—and many of the new homeowners, it seemed, wanted sweet-smelling roses cultivated by the African Americans of Tyler.

In her testimonial *You May Plow Here*, about growing up black in rural Alabama in the early twentieth century, on land not much different from the kind the Campbell family tended, Sara Brooks remembered, "We never was lazy cause we used to really work. We used to work like mens." Rose work was especially miserable. "It's skilled, back-breaking work—uncomfortable work," said Sam Kidd, whose family ran one of the largest rose farms in the area and who, as a high school junior, preferred the dreary, ceiling-fan-cooled work of printing out and affixing labels for office mailings to toiling outdoors in the rose fields. "Nobody ever liked working in the roses. It was hard work in the sun, and it was mostly blacks doing it." Decades later, in a demonstration of how she and her siblings had worked, Martha Campbell crept, half squatting, half crawling, along the living room of the one-story brick ranch house she shared with her sister, Margaret, the one Earl had constructed for their mother Ann with money from his first professional contract. Rose raising depended on a horticultural surgery called budding: the operating theater was a furrow; the patients—thousands upon thousands of them—were thornless stems called cuttings; the equipment consisted of a small beaten wood-handled paring knife and small rubber ties; the light was an already-hot mid-spring sun; the nurses, in the case of the Campbell family, were a line of kids bent double, each younger than the one ahead.

Budding involved grafting eyes taken from mature rosebushes onto small green plants called cuttings, which were planted each January in bedded fields. Once spring rolled around, the Campbell kids each morning would line up at one end of their property and, stooped, spend hours making their way through the furrows. The first person in line grafted the eye—or bud—to the base of each young cutting. Without this eye, the cutting would end up a thornless plant with a few scraggly white blossoms—essentially, a wild rose. The eyes were taken from bud sticks, cut from two-year-old rosebushes the previous November just before harvest and kept in cold storage until budding season. Each bud stick, about nine inches in length, had about seven eyes—enough to graft seven rosebushes. The bud sticks were marked according to variety—there were about fifty varieties altogether, at least a third of them some shade of red—and were de-thorned for easier handling during budding season.

This was the procedure Margaret mimicked, practically on all fours, as a wide-screen TV nearby played MSNBC and her younger sister, Martha, laughed from a La-Z-Boy. The rich smell of a baking chocolate pecan pie wafted from the kitchen. Like a surgeon whose fingers were still fluent in a procedure—even if she hadn't been in an operating room for years—Martha cut, de-eyed, grafted, and tied a series of imaginary rosebushes. "Oh, brother, how I remember them days," she said. During school hours, the kids spent early mornings in the rose fields; when there was no school, they worked on their knees from six in the morning to six at night.

Earl joined his family crew at the age of five. He had shown a precocious physical prowess from infancy. His brother Herbert remembers that when Earl's twin brothers were born, Earl, less than two, still in diapers, managed to run to a neighbor's house to alert some relatives. But the family joke was that for all the praise heaped on Earl as a football player for his hard work, he had never been keen to toil in the rose fields. "He was always the laziest hand we had," Ann Campbell once laughed to a reporter.

By age five or six, a Campbell would qualify as a "tie-er," securing the newly grafted eyes in place with "bud rubber," a four-inch-long strip of rubber-band-like material. The Campbell kids earned positions as budders through seniority and hard work. Later, using his special budding knife, Earl would make a small slit on the lower stalk of the foot-high cutting. He would then part the bark slightly and slide in the eye he had sliced off the budding stick. "They do it so fast you don't know what they're doing," said Bill Kinzie, who watched as a kid while rose growers pressed through the furrows, one rosebush at a time. As the year went on, a tame bud would appear and the Campbells would return to the fields the following spring to trim off all the wild bush above it. Then the eye would sprout into a full-fledged rosebush. Earl and his family probably prepared as many as sixty thousand plants a year; 65 percent of them would survive the budding process and become rosebushes.

Eventually, two years after budding, a tractor would make its way through the furrows, digging deep beneath the bush and shaking off the sandy soil. The Campbell family would sell most of their harvest to a wholesaler, who dipped the roots in hot paraffin to seal them for shipment. And beginning in the late 1940s, Ann Campbell manned a wooden roadside booth not far from the house, selling roses from her farm. "I've been on this corner for thirty-two years," she told a reporter in 1979, "and all my life I never had to file an income tax return, never had no money in a bank. What little we made on the roses we spent right here."

The horticultural manuals are rich with florid language: cuttings were to be stored "in moist sphagnum moss or shingletow." Beware "heavily callused cuttings," J. C. Ratsek, a researcher with the Texas Agricultural Experiment Station in Tyler warned in 1933, and "do not bury in soil where they may become infected with crown gall." But the reality was much earthier. At most farms, the white owners slouched in lawn chairs, as if on the porch of a modest plantation home, and shaved thorns from bud sticks while the budders, frequently African American, wearing long sleeves and bonnets, grafted in the field.

A 1988 Tyler newspaper story recounted how one set of black women—the Beasleys—had worked in the fields of a white family, the Moores, for four generations. "Her mamma's taught her just how to tie," the latest Mr. Moore told a reporter as they watched twelve-year-old Tomekia at work. "She wraps two times below, then three to four above, then ties it off with a good knot. Look how fast she is." When harvested, the sixty-five thousand or so surviving rosebushes brought in just more than $1 each; the Beasleys—Mrs. Beasley and her four daughters—got a nickel for each bud they grafted, and could do about two thousand plants a day. "I sometimes wonder how many pretty flowers I've made in all these years," Mrs. Beasley told the reporter. "I wonder how many rose queens really know, really see, how much work goes into making roses."

But the Rose Festival is about fantasy, and it's an all-white one. A. W. "Dub" Riter Jr., a civic-minded banker who served as president of the Texas Rose Festival Foundation, once said: "If I had to say one thing that makes the festival run, it's a spirit of cooperation." In truth, many African Americans—and working-class whites—were not much interested in lining the streets of Tyler to wave to the new white queen. "I think my babysitter took me once," snorts Cedric Golden, the black sports columnist who grew up in Tyler. And the event doesn't benefit anyone except, perhaps, the tourist industry. "It's not about benevolence," said John A. Anderson, the (white) Tyler historian who once served as a fund-raiser for a major hospital in the area—a tough task during Rose Festival preparations, when tens of thousands of dollars is spent by leading families on gowns, crowns, and accoutrements. In Tyler, Anderson said, "between September and December, if you're trying to raise money, you're dead meat."

By working the rose fields and taking odd jobs around town—B. C. worked at Kmart, and Ann spent Saturdays as a maid at the lake house of Henry Bell, a prominent Tyler banker—the Campbells earned a couple of hundred dollars a week, always enough to eat, even if the food remained basic. Breakfast consisted of a baked potato. Dinner might be canned salmon—jack-mackles, the Campbells called it. Another standby was canned sloppy joe meat, stretched with flour, eggs, and cornmeal to satisfy the hungry family.

In 1966, the Campbells were a family of thirteen—two parents and eleven kids, including Earl, an eleven-year-old with a mischievous streak. They lived in a creaky, cramped cottage with peeling linoleum floorboards. A rough dirt driveway led to the front door; across the road sat a junkyard. The backseat of an old automobile served as the porch bench. The family would wake up cold in the winter, even though they nailed quilts to the walls as rudimentary insulation. "You'd walk through that house and you might step through the floor," is the way a high school classmate of Earl Campbell's described the place. Alvin Flynn, whose family owned the land once worked by Reuben Collins, and whose father would drop off hand-me-downs and fresh deer meat for the family, remembered that the cracks in the wooden frame house were so wide that you could see outside. Rain leaked through the roof. The bathroom was an outhouse. Three or four kids crowded into each bed, and whoever slept with the youngest kids sometimes woke up to a wet sheet.

That year, B. C. Campbell died, his alcoholism having caught up with him. He had been forced to go to the hospital, where he soon succumbed to organ failure. Naturally, the episode deeply affected Earl Campbell. After games, he once said, "I'd bust out of the locker room, and I'd be happy until the time I hit the door. Then I'd feel real sad because I'd see all my friends going off with their fathers." When, at the age of twenty-two, Campbell was summoned to New York City for the presentation of the Heisman Trophy, he opted to take a taxi from the hotel instead of the limousine ordered for him: the limo reminded him too much of his father's hearse. Even thirty-five years later, when a reporter asked him about his upcoming induction into the NFL Hall of Fame, his thoughts trailed to his father: "I have to be honest and say the one thing I hate most of all is that although my father will be there in spirit, I wish my father would be sitting there," the words of a son searching for fatherly approbation. "I think he'd be very quiet, but I think he'd say, 'I always knew my son could handle it.'"

Ann Campbell, stricken but indomitable, took stock of a suddenly dire situation. She had all of two dollars in cash. Her youngest child was just three years old. She began clothing the kids—Willie, Evelyn, Ruby, Herbert, Alfred, Earl, Timothy Bob, Steven Rob, Martha, Margaret, and the baby, Ronnie—in Salvation Army castoffs and made sure to give them as much loving as she could muster, without playing favorites. She kept the house neat, and visitors remembered it as full of family pictures. The wood-frame home is "not much to somebody coming in," Earl said his senior season, when he was the most heavily recruited schoolboy in the state of Texas. "But to me, it's the world. We don't have much but we're happy with what we've got. I'm happy and I'm loved. That's all I want. Without love, you're nobody."

Despite that pride, he could still be a self-conscious teenager about his home. Embarrassed that his girlfriend, Reuna Mozell, who grew up in a relatively middle-class household and who would later become his wife, might see where he lived, he purposely gave her wrong directions to his house. Finally, keen to celebrate Earl before a key high school homecoming game, she asked his sister Evelyn the way. Reuna, as a surprise, decorated the house with balloons and streamers and wrapped the house in butcher paper that said: "Let's go Lions! I love you Earl!" How did Earl Campbell meet this show of enthusiasm? Mortified that Reuna had seen his home, he demanded to know which of his siblings had given him away—and he avoided Reuna for at least a day.

Self-reliant, Ann Campbell baked bread, churned butter, made plum and pear jelly, canned peach preserves, and each spring slaughtered a calf or a hog. At one point, when Earl was a young teen, the family had a pig named Arnold that had earned the kids' affection. (The pig was named for the swine on the TV show *Green Acres*.) "I said to Mama, 'I don't want to eat that poor thing,'" said Margaret. The reply was succinct: "Y'all are going to eat that pig."

In many ways, the life of the Campbells was not unusual for African Americans in the South. In 1975, the year after Earl Campbell graduated from John Tyler High, 13.5 percent of white Texans lived below the poverty line; among black Texans, the figure was nearly 28 percent. (Today, a fifth of black Texans live below the poverty line.) The annual income for white men was about $41,000 in today's dollars; for black men, $27,000. Extra money came to the Campbells in the way of $20 every month and $100 every Christmas from Laura McGregor, Ann Campbell's sister-in-law. After graduating from Texas College, the all-black school in Tyler, McGregor saw no opportunity for herself in that town. A moment of humiliation from 1941 stuck with her after she left college, as it still did, fresh with pain, in her brick ranch house in 2017: she was seventeen and taking a city bus to see some friends when a white man ordered her to the back before slipping into her seat. She found her way to Los Angeles, where she taught elementary school, outliving three husbands before eventually making her way back to Tyler. Added to regular small gifts of cash from one of Ann Campbell's sisters in Houston, McGregor's contributions were received like remittances from a shiny, far-off land.

McGregor, childless, saw Ann Campbell as a hero. Her kids thought of her that way, too. They took to calling her the First Lady. "When God took that rib from Adam to make a woman," Campbell wrote in a Mother's Day appreciation in a now-defunct Austin paper in 1989, "I believe he gave some of that rib to my mother, because she's such a strong woman." Even when her kids were grown and she had long occupied the brick home that Earl bought for her, Ann remained resourceful. The Tyler attorney Charles Clark, who has represented members of the Campbell family, including Earl, remembered visiting the Campbell place for a cookout around 2003. It was hard for Ann to get around, and she sat on an elevated chair frying hamburgers in an iron skillet. Clark started talking with her about the burgers and noticed that she was mixing oatmeal into the burger meat. "I said, 'That's unusual.' 'It will make it go a lot further,' she told me." When Ann Campbell died, in 2009, her pallbearers included Earl Campbell and her other sons. "Not a day goes by we don't think of Mama," said Margaret.

Earl Campbell was always a big kid—a "nice-sized fella, even in his grade school days" is how his fifth-grade flag football coach, Thorndyke Lewis, described him. Lewis grew up in nearby Henderson, the son of a school principal who believed that athleticism was next to godliness. Lewis decided to show his charges the fundamentals of football and baseball after school each day. He taught hand movements and speed drills. Even at a young age, Earl Campbell had more drive, more speed, more size, than the other kids. Lewis even made him a kicker—"he had a big leg." Lewis is a religious man—he said he survived the humiliations of segregation by adhering to the Christian edict "have neither envy nor malice in your heart"—and so his words carried special heft when he said that "watching Earl Campbell play football was almost as good as going to heaven."

But though as a child Campbell was superior—in the way that parents can pick out the top athletes in their kids' little league basketball and baseball games, and even the kids themselves know who is fastest and strongest—he was as yet no star. A man at a tire shop on the Cut, once the central boulevard of African American life in Tyler, now a mostly boarded-up set of storefronts, said he worked it out later that he had played against Campbell early in high school—no reputation had yet preceded him.

Campbell wanted to play defense in those early years—he was bowlegged like his hero Dick Butkus, the hard-nosed linebacker for the Chicago Bears who appeared on the cover of a 1970 edition of *Sports Illustrated*—when Earl was fifteen years old—with the caption "The Most Feared Man in the Game."

As he emerged into teenagehood, Earl Campbell had the sort of revelation that all great athletes have—an early self-awareness of some welling-up of ability. The great basketball skywalker Julius Erving once said that as a kid, in the early 1960s, he had felt "these different things within me, certain moves, ways to dunk." Athletes articulate this moment of self-knowledge in different ways; Campbell characteristically couched it as a near-religious epiphany. "When I got to the ninth grade"—at Moore Junior High—"that's when I began to realize that God gave me a talent that he didn't give Johnny down the street," he once said.

Others began witnessing, voluntarily or not, Earl's greatness. Andy Dillard, a pro golfer from Tyler whose ten minutes of fame came when he birdied the first six holes of the 1992 US Open at Pebble Beach, was asked once how he got hooked on the sport. "Earl Campbell got me interested in golf," the story goes. "Oh, really? I didn't know he golfed." "He doesn't. I was playing football in junior high and I tried to tackle him one day and right then and there I decided to take up golf."

It was in ninth grade at Moore that Campbell began to date Reuna; she first spotted him in the yard of the junior high. "My cousin kind of liked him, too," said Reuna, the daughter of a machine operator and a hair stylist, "but I decided I'd go after him." To some extent, their match, too, could be laid at the feet of William Wayne Justice. It was the first day of busing in the Tyler school system, and the authorities had ordered Earl Campbell to Moore Junior High, all the way across town. "That first day, when he stepped off the bus, there was this halo over his head," Reuna Campbell remembered.

At Moore he started learning formal football technique from Butch LaCroix, who was black. He partnered with Ann Campbell to focus Earl on football. Campbell once described LaCroix as "someone I'd have wanted my father to be like, if he were alive." Years later, when LaCroix died prematurely from a heart attack, Campbell decided not to attend the funeral—training camp obligations, he explained to LaCroix's widow. "Earl simply couldn't handle burying someone who had become another father to him, not at that stage of his life," Ann LaCroix told a reporter.

But in 1971, Campbell's ability had not yet fully revealed itself, especially not to Corky Nelson, the thirty-three-year-old first-year head coach of the John Tyler High football program. Campbell, the big sophomore linebacker, missed early season workouts and appeared uninspired when he did show up. Thrust into a new school, Campbell said he suddenly "felt a lack of passion" for the game. He was homesick, in a way. Like other African American students, he had been flushed into a foreign-feeling high school, one that was still trembling from the cheerleader discrimination episode and subsequent African American walkout the previous year. And unlike Butch LaCroix, Corky Nelson was a white guy who drove a green Volkswagen and hailed from San Antonio—a completely foreign part of the state. Nelson, who had shown up with an all-white staff, launched a charm offensive, sending each assistant to have dinner in the homes of varsity players. "In the heart of north Tyler," Michael Johnson, a black receiver at John Tyler, once told ESPN, "that was pretty bold." African Americans and whites on the team had little to say to one another on or off the field: 1971 and 1972 were "two years of what you might call close encounters," Nelson, who died in 2014, once told a *Dallas Morning News* reporter. "There weren't too many people—black or white—who liked integration. It was definitely a time of turmoil." In the book *Silver Rights*, about the integration of schools in Mississippi in the early 1970s, a white math teacher, Ruby Nell Stancill, describes the period this way: "We had our little boat that was going along and integration rocked that boat. It was frightening to the white people and to blacks because what we had been accustomed to was changed—two separate ways for all these years and then everything changed—just ruined—is the way most of us felt." When the black and white schools merged "we were really afraid."

This, at least, was how white teachers and coaches perceived the turbulence of integration. What was it like for a black teenager? For Campbell, a feeling of discombobulation, compounded by going from being the oldest kid in school to one of the youngest, and having to prove himself now as a teen, manifested itself as a kind of indifference. Nelson was unimpressed. Campbell was still undisciplined: because he wanted to play with his brothers on defense, when he was occasionally trotted out as running back in practice, he would intentionally fumble the ball. And in the fall of 1971, in his tenth-grade year and his first at John Tyler, Earl Campbell, destined to be one of the great football players of all time, was relegated like other newbies to the junior varsity team. In a sense, this liberated Campbell; he was not under the direct thumb of Nelson and could assert himself on the field. He flourished. With Campbell leading the squad, the B team began the year 5-0; the varsity went 0-5. Then, midway through the season, the starting varsity linebacker went down with an injury, and Nelson called up Campbell.

In his first game, against Longview, Campbell notched eight sacks. "No one knew who he was," said David Barron, who was ahead of Campbell at John Tyler High and was at the game to visit friends still in the band. You didn't go to John Tyler games at that point to watch football as much as to hang out—if you went at all. The previous season, the squad had notched a 3-7 mark—and that, in turn, was better than the 2-8 record from the year before that. "Our band was much more accomplished than our football team," said Barron, who had played trombone. Before desegregation, "there was not a lot of talent coming into John Tyler." But now, in the stands, Barron saw something he had never seen before, something that made him sit up and stop palling around. "Somebody was getting across the line of scrimmage at the snap and getting to Jeb Blount"—the Longview quarterback, who was good enough to one day play in the NFL—"who was still pulling back from center." Barron happened to be witnessing the first public glimpse of one of history's most dominating football careers. Campbell was such a better athlete than the kids he was up against that he passed through the opposing offensive linemen as smoothly as a current of water washes through weeds. With Campbell on board, the varsity squad finished 4-0-1; despite playing only five games, Campbell was honored as the region's newcomer of the year.

If not for desegregation, Earl Campbell and his younger twin brothers, excellent football players themselves, would have played at Emmett Scott—if it had still existed—and John Tyler surely would have remained mired in mediocrity. "White [high school] coaches were privately salivating at integration. They wanted to have all that athleticism and speed," Michael Hurd, the author of *Thursday Night Lights*, a history of black high school football during segregation, said. "All of a sudden schools that couldn't score a touchdown were winning a championship."

The following fall, his junior year in high school, marked Campbell's maturation as an adult and as a player. He reached his full height, five-eleven—not quite tall, but certainly muscular. He had the head of a Roman senator—big, imposing, large featured. And he was strong; his teammates shied away from trying to tackle him in practice. "We decided to see if he could carry the football without fumbling it," said Leon Van Alstine, one of Nelson's assistant coaches. The "only two people who would really hit him were [his brothers] Tim and Steve."

Nelson had made him a two-way player, which at first further alienated Campbell, who was bent on being a defensive great. An episode off the field led Campbell to think more closely about his commitment to school and football. One Thursday, following a morning pep rally ahead of the big rivalry game against Robert E. Lee, Campbell and some teammates skipped class to hang with friends in another part of town. Nelson decided to hold them out of the game—and gave them a tongue-lashing for their irresponsibility.

It was a complicated moment: conventionally, of course, a coach chews out his players, but Corky Nelson was a white coach—Campbell's first white coach—and here he was admonishing a handful of black teenagers, including the team's star. But something about Nelson's straitlaced ways—"If you score a touchdown, people are going to know it," he had once told Campbell; "You don't have to show out"—fit Campbell's workaday approach. On a cold, rainy Friday night, the team squeaked out a 6–0 victory even without Campbell, but he felt some guilt. He had let down the John Tyler Lions, the twelve thousand fans who had come to the rivalry game to see him play—and his mother. For her part, Ann Campbell told Nelson that it was his right to suspend Campbell, but to leave the lecturing to her. "Momma Campbell, she kept tight rein on those kids," said Van Alstine.

Ultimately, the team finished 8–2, missing out on the playoffs. That summer, in an astute move that recognized that an inspired Campbell could be the star player on the team, Nelson hired La-Croix as an assistant. Earl later said he considered the hiring of his mentor part of God's plan; Tyler fans would come to think of the choice as heaven-sent.

If you wander into Tyler Commercial Kitchens, a restaurant supply business that sits just past the Walmart Super Center as you head west out of town, you will invariably find a hefty sixty-two-year-old man with wild shoulder-length hair matted beneath a camouflage gimme cap and a silvery goatee on his chin, wearing a denim blue shirt and cargo shorts. His shoes rest on the foot flaps of his decked-out electronic wheelchair, and he plies a little joystick as he spins along the aisles full of chrome-plated appliances. Running vertically up both his knees are three-inch purple scars. This is Lynn King. When I talked to him on the phone, I was honestly not sure whether he was a black man or a white man, and was too embarrassed to ask—he told me about growing up working class and country in an area not far from Swan, the small community that was home to the Campbells, and I had been told by a former coach that the best way to learn about Earl Campbell and John Tyler football was to talk to King.

He is white. In his pine-paneled office in the back there is a hospital bed crammed in across from the desk. The only decoration on the walls is a single framed black-and-white photo, cut from a magazine, of two young men executing a running play in a football game. One, Earl Campbell, is clutching a football with two hands; ahead of him, an even larger person plunges upfield, looking, evidently, for someone to clobber. "Power football," reads the caption, "as supplied by the blocking of fullback Lynn King and the big thunder of super back Earl Campbell, pays off big for Tyler."

When you tell King that you have come to talk about Earl Campbell, he warmly grasps your hand with both of his and stands up out of his wheelchair as if he has been called again to block. He shows you that picture in the back and tells you that he never asked for Earl's autograph. You take the framed photo off the wall and look at the back. A flowing script says: "To My Friend, Lynn, Peace and Love, Earl Campbell." "Earl had the quickest feet," says King, whom Tylerites described at the time as "the white guy blocking for that black boy." "There was no sweeter feeling than setting a block, hitting the ground, rolling over, and still see him running," he says.

On the face of it, King and Campbell could not have been more different. King was a hell-raiser and goat roper whose friends were mostly into Future Farmers of America. When he wasn't playing football, he was prepping for the rodeo, riding broncos and bulls. "Lynn King was the epitome of the redneck white guy and Earl, of course, was on the other end of the spectrum," Nelson once said. In some ways that is obviously true. But Campbell was country, too—everyone who lived poor outside Tyler knew something about handling hay. King and Campbell had spent all their football time together during their junior year, and as senior year approached, they became close friends off the field, too. King began giving Campbell lifts around town in his Pinto and then eating meals at Ann Campbell's place—he even stayed overnight sometimes. Nelson said the friendship was key to the team's success, making it easier for uneasy people to get together: "A strong bond developed between them, and that was the turning point for our team. That's when the team came together."

Ahead of the fall 1973 season, Campbell's senior campaign, the team was taken lightly by pigskin prognosticators. John Tyler was returning just six starters, so *Dave Campbell's Texas Football* magazine, the state bible for all things gridiron, picked the team to finish fourth in its district. But under the radar, the team was gelling—bonding on the field as the players sweated together through late-summer two-a-day practices, and off the field as teammates gave Earl Campbell and his younger twin brothers rides. "No big thing," said King. "They just weren't fortunate enough to have a vehicle." Not only could Ann Campbell not afford a car for her teenage sons to share, but the boys didn't even have luggage. When Earl and his brothers prepared for away games, they packed their uniforms into Brookshire's supermarket brown paper bags.

His teammates had come to realize there was something special about Campbell. "Earl wasn't Earl until his senior year," said King. He and Campbell roomed together on the road, the only black and white players to do so. But that August, during the swampy summer two-a-days in the Pit—the John Tyler High practice fields—Nelson decided that Campbell would play only offense during the upcoming season. The decision appeared to make little sense—Campbell was the team's best defensive player. A University of Texas defensive coordinator who had been sizing Campbell up for recruitment called him the best high school linebacker he had ever seen. "He could have played at any college or university or pro team at middle linebacker," Leon Van Alstine recalled, still sounding a wistful note about the havoc Earl Campbell might have wreaked. In his junior year, Campbell weighed a muscled two hundred pounds. "He would body-slam a ball carrier," said one high school opponent.

"He was so strong he would just pick him off the ground and throw him down. There wasn't a back who could outrun him, so he was all over the field." But Nelson wanted him to be crisp on offense. "He couldn't score points on defense," Nelson observed.

Earl was unsure: "I didn't like Corky before my senior year," Campbell joked in 1979, when he was a pro football player, back in Tyler to dedicate a new gym. "He came to my house and told me they were going to switch me from middle linebacker to running back. Thank God for Corky Nelson, he was smarter than I was. He knew my future was at running back, not linebacker."

The playbook was shorn down to two plays, said John Tyler High quarterback Larry Hartsfield: "Earl left; Earl right." It was hard for other players to get the ball—even as defenses put virtually all eleven players on the line of scrimmage to stop Campbell. "I'd be so wide open, I'd do jumping jacks in the end zone," Johnson, the wide receiver, told a reporter years later. "It would be on the film. Corky would say, 'If you do another jumping jack, you'll never play another down for this football team.'"

Campbell played special teams and in goal-line defense situations, too: the team blocked an astonishing thirty punts that year. Tim Alexander, who played for rival Robert E. Lee, remembers that as the upback in the punting formation—the guy who is a kind of firewall between the center and the punter—his job as soon as the ball was snapped was to "run straight at Campbell like I was in heat": "We figured that was the only way to stop him from blocking punts."

As the team racked up wins, Tylerites, black and white, began piling into the stadium to cheer on the Lions. It's impossible to overstate how important football was (and remains) in this part of Texas. Basketball was still the precinct of the Lakers and the Celtics—no Texas team made it to the NBA finals until 1981—and major league baseball was relatively new to Texas. Football was king. The University of Texas Longhorns had won the national championship in 1969, and the Dallas Cowboys had won their first Super Bowl in 1972.

This corner of East Texas was especially football obsessed. Jeb Blount—the quarterback Campbell had sacked eight times in his varsity debut—claimed to have developed his passing accuracy while herding cattle on his parents' ranch. He would frighten the lead bull by nailing him in the forehead with a football, causing all the other cattle to follow. That John Tyler team "was something for us whites to be excited about," said Sam Kidd, whose family ran a prominent Smith County rose nursery. Before that 1973 season, perhaps the last time Kidd had been at the school district football stadium—today named for Earl Campbell—was for a James Brown concert in the late 1960s with his wife. They were among the few white people at the show. But now, in a sign of what Earl Campbell and the Lions meant to Tyler, fully mixed crowds were showing up to games. Even people who were opposed to the desegregation order came out to cheer. "Everybody in Tyler, blacks and whites, got behind Earl Campbell," said Kidd. "He was our hero. It was a weird feeling to have a black hero. He was the first one." The observation echoes what Yarborough, the senator, had once said: "People in deep East Texas have told me, 'Ralph, football's the main thing here that's done more to end friction between whites and blacks, and more to bring about integration of schools, than all of the courts put together.'"

After the sting of missing the playoffs the previous year, the 1973 John Tyler squad worked desperately to close out each regular season game. Against Texas High, for example, Campbell threw a seventy-three-yard option pass to ensure a 21–16 victory. Before the season-ending game against John Tyler, coaches at Robert E. Lee, studying 8 mm game film, found the Lions had a tell: the spatial relationship between King and Campbell in the backfield as they got into their stances was a tip-off about which way Campbell would take the ball. "We knew the plays they were about to run, and we still couldn't stop him," said Alexander, who also played linebacker for Lee. John Tyler ended up crushing its rival.

As Earl was gaining his stride on the football field, his academic career plodded along. He struggled to a C average through much of school. One coach for an opposing program grumbled that Campbell "can't read, can't write, and can't fail." "My mother asks me if it hurts to hear that," Campbell told a reporter while still in high school. "I just tell her Jesus Christ had it worse than me. He died on the cross." It's a remarkable—and, in its winking irony, self-deprecating—rejoinder, and one that speaks to how he was approaching deification in the town of Tyler. Campbell learned at an early stage to speak about himself with the third-person remove of a celebrity athlete: "[Academics] didn't always interest me a great deal. I played a little too much. I can make it in college. The only thing Earl has to do is apply himself to his studies like he does on the football field."

Top college football programs appeared unworried—he had plenty of offers to tour campuses. Campbell's performance in the playoffs further ramped up interest. In the district championship game against Plano, Campbell gained 219 yards on twenty-four carries, including one in which he carried six Plano players on his back fifteen yards before finally falling under their weight. Campbell scored three times, and John Tyler won 34–0.

Before the regional final against Campbell and his squad, Coach W. T. Stapler of Conroe High had decided "to ignore the pass and put nine people on the line to challenge him." For most of the game, the strategy worked well for Conroe—the top-ranked team in the state—and Campbell was even knocked unconscious early in the second half, missing most of the third and fourth quarters. But with his Tyler team down 7–3, he came back for the last drive—this was a time long before "concussion protocol" became a phrase known even to casual watchers of the game. Of the final nine plays, Campbell got the ball eight times. On one third down, he threw an eighteen-yard pass to Hartsfield, his quarterback. Defending near its end zone, Conroe stacked the line of scrimmage to stymie Campbell. It didn't matter: from the five-yard line, Stapler observed afterward, "he carried my whole team into the end zone." Later, Stapler and his staff studied films of the run. "It took 10 different hits to put him on the ground. I'm not saying all 10 tacklers hit him. But they did have shots at him. He ran past two tacklers at the line of scrimmage. Then he spun and bounced around till somebody else got a shot at

him. I know it sounds impossible, but we've got the film to prove it."
Campbell's performance in the Conroe game made him the consensus top running back recruit in the country.

"Every Monday morning during the playoffs," said Van Alstine, "there'd be scouts there from all over. The further we went along, the more people were there Monday morning. Kids didn't even want to talk to news media or anybody else. They'd go the other way." The postseason tear continued, even as teams were determined to stifle Campbell. In the quarterfinals, Tyler beat Fort Worth Arlington Heights 34–12, with Campbell logging 189 yards on eighteen carries, including four touchdowns. In a sense, Fort Worth's gang-tackling was successful—until Campbell made it into the open field. Two of his eighteen carries totaled 138 yards.

Among that game's spectators was Ray Renfro, a former Cleveland Brown wide receiver whose son, a speedster named Mike Renfro, was playing cornerback and wideout for the Arlington Heights squad. On one play—one that would make Ray Renfro realize that Campbell had not only power but also speed—Campbell got loose up the middle, leaving it up to his son Mike to make the tackle. "Mike hesitated for a moment and lost his angle on him," he later told a reporter. "Earl was gone. No one caught him. I thought then he had the potential to be one of the best." What he saw that day put Ray Renfro in mind of his old teammate Jim Brown—at that time the greatest running back in the history of the NFL. "Jim was more of an upright runner and he didn't punish tacklers like Earl does," he said, in what amounted to an extensive scouting report. "He's the most punishing runner I've ever seen. Jim seldom ran over defensive backs if he didn't have to, but Earl runs over anybody who gets in his way—backs, linebackers, or linemen. Jim had sprinter's speed, but he didn't have Earl's power. At the same time," he added, "a lot of people don't realize how quick Earl is."

The streak continued. In the semifinals, played in Waco, Arlington Sam Houston fell to John Tyler 22–7; Campbell went for 166 yards, including one giant run in which he basically walked over a player who would become an all-conference defender in college. New bumper stickers began appearing around Tyler: "Thank You, Mrs. Campbell."

The state title game, against Austin's John Reagan High—named for the postmaster general of the Confederacy—was in December, just before Christmas, at the Houston Astrodome, the very same stadium in which Earl Campbell would star, less than five years later, on his way to being named NFL Rookie of the Year. J. B. Smith, a part-time bus driver for Continental Trailways trying to supplement his income as a police detective, drove the John Tyler band to all the playoff games. "Campbell would say, 'Yes, sir' and 'No, sir' even to the bus drivers," said Smith, who was in the stands for the championship game. "He was always humble."

The week ahead of the game, Lynn King got so banged up in a rodeo that he missed two days of practice. "A bull stepped on my head and put a big old knot on it," he said. "Couldn't get my dang helmet on." Still, he made it on the field—and Campbell was not to be stopped. He ran for 164 yards in the 21–14 victory, including a run off left tackle in the fourth quarter that went for fifty-seven yards and, with fifty-three seconds left, the winning touchdown.

It had been a remarkable playoff performance: more than 850 yards and eleven touchdowns in five games. One journalist said it was like Sherman's march through Georgia. The newspapers dubbed Tyler's unlikely championship win the "Rose City Miracle."

It was the only title game Campbell would ever win, and, perhaps, in his eyes, the game with the most social import. "I looked up into the stands and saw a sea of people, blacks and whites together, jumping up and down, cheering wildly hugging one another—celebrating their football team," he once said. Whites certainly saw it as a confirming moment about harmony in their community. Nelson Clyde IV, the scion of a Tyler newspaper business, whose wife, mother, grandmother, and daughters have been anointed Rose Queen, and who himself served in the Cannoneers, the successor to the Robert E. Lee Rebel Guard, likes to call Tyler "Mayberry on steroids." That integrated championship team, led by Campbell, "had a great impact on how we saw our community," he said. Joan Brooks, an African American woman who taught business at John Tyler, described that championship run in a slightly different way: "We got used to a bunch of white women hugging us that year." The victory "was able to at least paper over some of the hard times that followed the desegregation order," said David Barron, the former band member who was just ahead of Campbell at John Tyler High and who later became the managing editor of *Dave Campbell's Texas Football* magazine. "But as time passed, things pretty much went back to the way they were."

That night, the team got home about ten. Lynn King and the team manager headed over to Earl's for a party—the only two white guys there. "We even had some beer, and Mama didn't fuss about the drinking," said King. "I guess she felt it was a special occasion. As well as I remember, Earl didn't drink much, but I know I did."

The next day, December 23, 1973, the Campbell boys squeezed into King's beat-up Pinto to go Christmas shopping. People wanted to give them things for free. And what all of Tyler now knew, that Earl Campbell was arguably the best football player to pass through those parts, was about to hit all of Texas. Six days later, the new issue of *Texas Football* magazine was published, with a picture of Campbell rolling against Arlington Sam Houston. Over the previous summer, he had received only a brief mention, deep in the pages of the magazine; now he was touted as "the most coveted schoolboy back" in the country. Among the scouts and coaches from major football programs at the Astrodome for that championship game was a charming forty-nine-year-old with a boxy face. Darrell Royal, the storied head coach at the University of Texas, realized that he had less than a month to convince Campbell to become a Longhorn—and for all Royal's success, he knew his own redemption depended on it.

# PART II
# AUSTIN

One afternoon in the fall of 1966, Ken Dabbs, the thirty-one-year-old assistant football coach at Sweeny High, situated in a speck of an oil town a little over an hour southwest of Houston, was giving Elmo Wright, his star receiver, a lift home in his green '39 Chevy pickup when he asked him where he would like to go to college.

Wright, the second oldest of seven kids, had had no expectation of attending university. Neither of his parents had gone to college, nor had his older brother. And he genuinely didn't think of himself as a football player, let alone one good enough to get a scholarship. Before his junior year of high school, he hadn't played a single down; he had played saxophone in the school band and piano at church, and his only dream was to perform in a jazz club in New York City. "I was just going to be happy just to finish high school," he said. But after getting crosswise with the band director at Carver High School, the all-black school he was forced to attend through his junior year, he took up football, persuaded by a friend who used to cut Elmo's hair and then play catch with him. He found, to his coaches' delight, that he had breakneck speed on the field. Wright thinks he ran so fast only because of a deathly fear of being injured by a tackler. That terror, of a slender musician suddenly in a football helmet, pushed him to greatness. Wright set high school touchdown records; in one game, he scored five of them, three on offense and two on interceptions returned as a defensive back.

Sweeny High, named, like the town, for a Tennessean who had settled the area 130 years earlier with his 250 slaves, was newly integrated and undefeated, and would go on to win the state championship—thanks, in large part, to the talent and work of Wright and other black players who joined the team their senior year. There were thirteen of them, and every one of them got a scholarship to play football in college. Not that there weren't adjustments. Dabbs remembers that the new players at the start of the season tended to wear their shirttails out, and football protocol at Sweeny called for the players to have their shirts tucked in. So one day Dabbs, who is white, talked to an assistant principal—Everett Gee, who had been principal at Carver—to ask his advice about how to approach the players. "He said, 'Coach, listen to me. You set the standards. You keep the standards where you want them, don't ever lower your standards for our people. We've worked all of our lives to get across these railroad tracks, and we ain't going back. You want them to wear a coat and tie on game day, they'll find a way. Don't worry about it: they want to be here.'" All their lives, their all-black school bus had made a left at the Y as it headed into town, into the poorer black community, to a beloved school that lacked a good field, first-rate instruments, or current textbooks; now it took a right at the Y, into the white neighborhood to Sweeny High. As at Earl Campbell's John Tyler High, the story goes that as the Sweeny team began piling on victories, black and white fans who once sat apart started huddling together in the middle of the grandstands.

Wright, who grew up in a modest house by the Brazos River, his father a construction worker and a lay minister, could have played college ball anywhere—he had already received offers from as far away as Notre Dame. But as a top-notch student, he had been up to Austin the previous summer for Boys State, a camp run by the American Legion to inculcate impressionable kids in the workings of government, and had liked the place immediately.

"I'd love to go to the University of Texas," he told his coach that day in the pickup. "I'd like to be first Afro-American to play there."

The following morning, Dabbs went to his boss, head coach Ed Wagner, and told him what Wright had said.

"Why don't you just call Darrell Royal?" the head coach said.

"Well, why don't you call him?" said Dabbs, intimidated by the prospect of phoning Royal, the head coach of the UT Longhorns. At the time, Royal, a thin, square-faced, dimple-chinned man, forty-two years old, had twice won the national championship. His photo, with his lake-blue eyes and softly parted hair, had held the cover of national magazines, and across football-crazed Texas he was worshipped.

"No, why you don't call him?" Wagner responded. He made it sound like it was as easy as asking a neighbor for a cup of flour, though he was clearly daunted himself.

And so Dabbs called Royal's office in Bellmont Hall on the University of Texas campus, and his secretary came on the phone. "I'd like to talk to Coach Royal about a recruit," Dabbs said, and knowing that locating a top-notch recruit was like striking oil, she put Dabbs through to Royal. Five decades later, at a café north of UT, Dabbs still remembered the particulars of the conversation: "I told him who I was and what I was calling about. 'Coach Dabbs, I'll tell you this: We'll certainly evaluate him and we'll check on him, and I will get back to you.'"

Royal quietly brought Wright up to Austin to look him over. It was the end of a long day, and Wright remembered the hallowed coach as strikingly noncommittal, even unenthusiastic, though the coach was clearly considering the prospect of integrating the team. "I come into his office, and he's a little ragged, slouched down in his chair. I was wide open. He explained to me that it's going to be tough. 'You're going to have to be like Jackie Robinson.' To which I said: 'Who is Jackie Robinson?'"—Wright laughs at this point in the story, at his own lack of a sense of the moment as a teenager. "I wasn't into baseball or football or black history; I was into Miles Davis." Of Royal, he said, "I didn't get the impression he was really trying, compared to Notre Dame and all the other recruiters." For decades, he looked back at that meeting and thought perhaps Royal's indifference had nothing to do with race: "Maybe it was just because he was tired," he remembered thinking.

In fact, Darrell Royal—or maybe the institution or its donors—was unprepared to add a black player to UT's showpiece football squad. And so, a few weeks after Dabbs initially contacted Royal, the Longhorns' head coach called the young coach back: "First of all I want to tell you that what you described to us is outstanding. He'll have an opportunity to make it somewhere. He's the real deal, grades and everything. But unfortunately, at this stage of the game we're not ready to take that step."

"I remember having to tell his mother," said Dabbs. "I told them: 'I just don't think they have a scholarship available.' I didn't lie. That was a political way to do it. They probably knew. But he was never bitter." Dabbs drove Wright to Houston to visit the Astrodome and arranged for him to play at the University of Houston—he suggested to Wright's parents it would be helpful to go to school not too far away. As it happened, Wright's first start on the Houston varsity football team was against the Longhorns. He remembered getting a handoff on a reverse: "I was zipping and zapping, and I bounced outside at the line of scrimmage. And it was weird. I remember I was kind of looking for Coach Royal. And then, as I went up the field, I remember thinking, 'This is some nice grass, right here.' We never had grass like that at Carver." That 1968 game ended in a tie, 20–20.

Wright, who would be named an all-American receiver with the Cougars, gained fame for his practice, first in college and then in the pros, of high-stepping his way into the end zone. "This was after 1968, the year Martin Luther King and Bobby Kennedy were assassinated," Wright said.

> We had just integrated our team, and you can imagine playing against Georgia and Ole Miss. So when I started to dance, there was this mindset of a lot of people at the time, and my teammates were telling me, "You're crazy. You're going to get assassinated." That wasn't the protocol. You were supposed to act like you've been there. But I was just so happy to score. It was the culmination of a lot of hard work . . . We were studying *Don Quixote*, and he saw things differently. So when I was in the end zone, I was thinking, "The fans love me." They were throwing things at me, but I pretended as if they were throwing flowers. They had never seen anything like that. I was just so happy to be in the end zone, and I had so much conditioning in my legs, so that's what I did.

Eventually, Wright starred professionally for the Kansas City Chiefs, and after his football days were over, he worked as a policy aide in Houston-area government. If ever there was a person, in other words, who had the composure, talent, and smarts to integrate football at the University of Texas—a modern Don Quixote who could dance to the end zone before hostile crowds—it was Elmo Wright. And on paper, Darrell Royal could have taken that step— in 1963, the UT Board of Regents authorized the "full integration" of the university's dormitories and athletics programs. But the UT Longhorns remained white: his 1969 squad was the last all-white team to win a national championship, and Royal's varsity team remained free of African Americans until 1970.

Dabbs, however, had not heard the last of the famed UT head coach. Seven years after informing the small-town football assistant that he would not take Wright, Royal called again. Dabbs, it turned out, had an important role to play in the integration of Longhorn football, the illustrious career of Earl Christian Campbell, and nothing less than the salvation of Darrell Royal.

From the white-and-gray reading room at the University of Texas's Dolph Briscoe Center for American History, you can see the north end of Darrell K Royal–Texas Memorial Stadium, bulging like a giant cruise liner coming into port. And even in the comfort of the air-conditioning on a summer day in Austin so hot it feels as if you could bake chocolate chip cookies on the pavement outside, even as the stadium shimmers in the distance, reading confidential memos outlining how, over the years, UT resisted integration leaves you with a dizzy, time-warp feeling, as if suddenly being struck with heatstroke.

At the University of Texas, there was no conspicuous blocking-the-schoolhouse-door moment, of the sort involving governors in other states that played out on black-and-white televisions. Instead, in a scheme nefarious in its bureaucratic smarminess, a steady, quiet stream of paperwork stymied the admittance of African Americans to the university and, when the institution's hand was forced by the courts, the participation, at every stage, of African Americans in student life. The very last bastion of whiteness at UT to integrate was the football team. In their starkness, preserved on beautifully fragile pieces of onionskin paper, carbon copies that were part of the machinery of segregation, the documents make you lean back from the desk to which librarians bring boxes marked "UT President's Office Records" containing ancient folders marked "Negroes," and whisper, to no one in particular: "Jesus."

The missives and memos run back and forth between the nine members of the board of regents, the all-white, nearly always male overseers of university policy. Wealthy oilmen, attorneys, and bankers, they were the appointees of, and typically the biggest campaign contributors to, segregationist governors whose political constituency tended to be the conservative, traditional precincts of the state. Authors of the correspondence include the university chancellor, hired and fired by the regents and charged with executing policy across the far-flung state university campuses; the university president, who likewise served at the pleasure of the regents and who watched over the flagship campus in Austin; other university officials, including deans of admissions, chairs of departments, and so on, who posed questions about the ins and outs of integration; progressive students and faculty intent on pushing the regents to liberalize their policies; and finally, alumni and other residents of Texas who generally wrote in to oppose, in cranky and hateful language, the presence of African American students on campus, in their old dorms, or on their beloved football team.

These records reveal regents who appear more concerned with not getting ahead of public opinion or overstepping the expectations of the legislature, which provided money for the operations of the university, than with promoting any genuine educational ideal or the university's role in encouraging free conversation—those interests appear not at all. Instead, in a moral cop-out, the university administrators couched their anxieties as a desire to avoid civil unrest.

On the face of it, the chronology is simple. The correspondence travels quickly through the 1930s and 1940s—when African Americans were barred from taking classes at UT—to 1954, when the Supreme Court ordered integration with "all deliberate speed," to 1956, when the first African American undergraduates were admit-

73

ted to the university, through 1963, when the regents ordered dormitories and athletics to be integrated, through 1970, when the university finally admitted a black player to the varsity squad, to 1974, when Earl Campbell stepped on the field while his fellow black students complained of being marginalized on campus. The excuses used to bar African Americans from the football team, long after the school had been forced by courts to integrate, illuminate what we might think of as the rationale and logistics of apartheid. In its details, the justification of the racist, two-tier system was characterized by banality, almost practicality: regents argued that integration would leave students unhappy; segregated housing and eating facilities were too big a challenge for traveling teams; no decent African American athletes were also good students; having integrated teams would make it harder to recruit good white athletes; UT had an agreement with other Southwest Conference schools not to integrate. "That racism was subtle," said Nick Kralj, who attended UT in the early 1960s before serving as an aide to Governor John Connally and as a confidant to Frank Erwin, the powerful regents chair of the 1960s and 1970s who was one of Royal's chief allies. "It wasn't the Ku Klux Klan. These were country-club types. And they didn't want their country club integrated—or their football team or their school."

In many ways, even as its leaders managed to avoid a showdown with federal troops, UT was a conventional institution of the South, one whose early patrons rued the Confederacy's Civil War defeat. In 1933, a little over two decades before Earl Campbell's birth, the university commissioned a memorial to Jefferson Davis: to the men and women of the Confederacy, read a dedication plaque—one not removed till 2015—"who fought with valor and suffered with fortitude that states rights be maintained and who not dismayed by defeat nor discouraged by misrule built from the ruins of a devastating war a greater South."

Six years later, in 1939, George Allen, a life insurance salesman in Dallas, became the university's first black student when he decided to enroll in a few graduate business courses; to beat Jim Crow, he registered by mail and telephone. When he appeared on campus two weeks later and his race was detected, he was pulled out of class and his registration was canceled. "Negro Discovered in Class at U.T." said one headline. Evidently anxious about the prospect of integration, the regents resolved in 1944 that buildings on campus "shall not be used for any public meeting or entertainment attended by members of the Caucasian Race and the Negro Race, until and unless definite arrangements shall have been made in advance of the meeting or entertainment to segregate completely the members of the Caucasian Race and the Negro Race to be seated in the audience." One of the regents, Orville Bullington, announced, "There is not the slightest danger of any Negro attending the University of Texas, regardless of what Franklin D., Eleanor, or the Supreme Court says, so long as you have a Board of Regents with as much intestinal fortitude as the present one has."

As if taking Bullington up on a dare, Heman Marion Sweatt, a civil rights activist and mailman from Houston, a slight man, un-Campbellian in stature, applied to the University of Texas Law School in 1946. When UT declared him ineligible because of his race, Sweatt sued; a trial judge allowed the state to establish a temporary law school. It initially consisted of two attorneys in Houston teaching courses near their offices. "It is fairly obvious that the Negroes are determined to make it as embarrassing as possible and as expensive as possible for us to maintain separate institutions for the two races," UT president Theophilus S. Painter wrote in 1948 to D. K. Woodward Jr., a Dallas attorney who chaired the UT Board of Regents. "In the end, the financial burden will be extremely heavy to the State, and, as you have often said, it is the price we pay for segregation." The state attorney general, a dairy farmer named Grover Sellers, promised that Sweatt would "never darken the door of the University of Texas." But in 1950, the US Supreme Court, in a case that anticipated *Brown*, ruled in favor of Sweatt, holding that the faculty, reputation, and facilities of the all-black law school were unequal to those at UT. The Equal Protection Clause, in short, required Sweatt's admission to the University of Texas. (One of Sweatt's attorneys was Thurgood Marshall.) Upon Sweatt's enrollment, one law faculty member ceased his custom of addressing students by an honorific in order to avoid having to say "Mr. Sweatt." That October, during Sweatt's first semester, a wooden cross covered with kerosene-soaked rags was set aflame on the law school grounds. W. Kirk Astor, a contemporary of Sweatt's who hoped to do graduate work in political science, ran a similar gauntlet. He was finally allowed to take classes on campus—as long as he sat in a specially assigned seat in the back of the classroom with a metal ring on the floor around his desk-chair "so that his blackness wouldn't rub off on the white students," the historian Joe Frantz wrote in his *Forty Acre Follies*. "Kirk was abased, the other students were embarrassed, and eventually the barrier came down."

It wasn't until 1954, in *Brown v. Board of Education*, that the Supreme Court declared that the doctrine of separate-but-equal educational facilities violated the Equal Protection Clause. The very notion of separate but equal was an impossibility, the justices held, because to separate children in public schools "from others of similar age and qualifications solely because of their race generates a feeling of inferiority as to their status in the community that may affect their hearts and minds in a way unlikely ever to be undone."

The *Brown* decision prompted at least two decades of attempts by the regents and university administrators to maintain an apartheid system—one meant to prevent African Americans from fully participating in the life of the university, especially on the football field, even as courts technically allowed them to be on campus. Less than two weeks after the *Brown* ruling was handed down—about a year before Earl Campbell was born—H. Y. McCown, the admissions dean, dashed off a note to the university president with a proposal to "keep Negroes out of most classes where there are a large number of [white] girls." In one internal letter after another, McCown, a decorated retired US Navy man who had commanded a destroyer in the Pacific during the war, comes across as decidedly anti-integration, regularly cloaking his segregationist tendencies in concerns about bad publicity and about public feeling generally. "If we want to exclude as many Negro undergraduates as possible," began McCown in his 1954 memo, the university should require African American students seeking admission to undergraduate professional programs to first spend a year taking mandatory courses at Prairie View A&M or Texas Southern University, both black schools. Essentially ignoring the thrust of *Brown*, the regents adopted the proposal.

An episode that unspooled over the summer of 1954, just after the *Brown* decision was handed down, illuminates how far the regents were willing to go to keep the football team free of African Americans. That June, Marion Ford, a sixteen-year-old from Houston who was a top student at his black high school, and who in his young life had already worked as a newspaper carrier, a truck driver, a lifeguard, and a columnist for the school newspaper, applied to the university. Known by the nickname Big Drip, he was a talented kid, counting himself a saxophonist and creative writer. He belonged to an engineering honor society. He said he wanted to major in chemistry. McCown, citing the policy he had devised to keep African Americans out of UT, wrote Ford that he could major in chemistry at Texas Southern, and therefore he was refused admission to UT. Ford responded that he in fact wanted to study chemical engineering, a major not offered at Texas Southern. He suggested he was getting the runaround—"Southern Discrimination," was his phrase—and wrote, "I am not interested in living in your dormitories or becoming socially prominent with the Caucasians, but I do want a chance to get the best formal training in my state." In a condescending letter of admittance in late July, McCown wrote to Ford, "I hope that you will do well in the University and that you will get over your inferiority complex and the idea that you are being discriminated against."

Finally, all appeared set for Ford and six other African American men to become the first class of black undergraduates at the university. Ford arranged for housing in Austin. In mid-August he submitted a rushee information card to UT's Interfraternity Council, still on file in a warehouse of university records. He wrote that he planned to join the ROTC program, and in a sign of his eagerness, he asked that a copy of the *Fraternity Handbook* be sent to him.

But there was a problem: Ford, who was a brawny five-ten-and-a-half and 209 pounds and had been a varsity swimmer and all-state lineman at his all-black high school, told a *Houston Chronicle* reporter in August that he hoped to play on UT's football team. The reporter, in turn, contacted UT regent Leroy Jeffers, a Houston attorney, to ask for comment. Jeffers said the regents hadn't considered the prospect but that it would be weighed "from all angles for the best interest of the university." Privately, he was alarmed. The following day, Jeffers sent a copy of the article—headlined "Houston Negro Seeks Grid Tryout at Texas"—to the members of the board of regents and the chancellor. It was one thing to admit African Americans, another to allow them to play on the football team. (Or to perform on the football field in any capacity at all. On the very day, August 25, 1954, that Jeffers sent the article to the regents, Arno Nowotny, the widely beloved dean of student life at the university, wrote to UT president Logan Wilson about the problem of black students who wanted to study at the university and also participate in the school band. "An undergraduate Negro student, J. L. Jewett, has inquired about playing in our Longhorn Band in the fall," Nowotny wrote. "I hope we continue to admit Negro students only when we have to do so. I could wish that young Jewett had chosen the symphonic band or some other less spectacular student activity; but I plan to have a real conference with him, and stress the importance of his showing real humility in his band participation.") Five days later, on August 30, the regents chair asked the state attorney general whether, even if the law required UT to admit African Americans, the university was required "to permit such negro students upon admission to participate in such extracurricular activities as band and football or other intercollegiate activities." That same day, McCown wrote to the UT president that African Americans, were scheming to figure out courses of study that were not offered at black schools, taking "a more calculated approach" in their applications. "They are now carefully advised and are constantly probing for programs of work not offered at one of the Negro institutions," he wrote.

In a memo marked "personal and confidential," UT Board of Regents chairman Tom Sealy, a Midland oilman, informed the other regents that after a "full investigation," the university had determined that black students could take at least their freshman classes at black institutions. In other words, even if Texas Southern did not have a chemical engineering major, it had freshman offerings that mirrored UT's. The plan was essentially a delaying tactic, meant to buy the University of Texas at least another year in which to figure out how to prevent black students from enrolling.

And so, less than a week after Marion Ford had told the *Houston Chronicle* he wanted to try out for the football team, after the university president, the regents, the university lawyers, and the state attorney general had huddled together, letters were sent to him and the other incoming African Americans, explaining that their admission had been rescinded. The full weight of the Texas government and the University of Texas had come down on this teenager—and a half-dozen other African American admits—because of the mere notion that he might step onto the football field.

Ford was refunded the $20 deposit for his room at a blacks-only dormitory (the dormitory had been established for black graduate students first admitted in 1950); at McCown's direction, he was informed that the rooming contract was "now voided." The sacrosanct football program remained unsullied, and some Texans who learned about the university administration's about-face were pleased. J. L. Shanklin, a dentist in the Hill Country town of Kerrville, wrote McCown "to congratulate you on your very sane stand in re—the case of Marion G. Ford Jr.": "The problem is not one of racial, religious, social, or political, but is one of our Constitutional rights. . . . If Democracy is the best form of government and is to survive, we will have to fully subscribe to the theory that the majority must supersede the wants and claims of the minority. Surely the majority of Texans does not want to accept racial equality, nor do they want to foster a situation that will surely lead to social and sexual homogeneity."

Apart from a one-sentence story in the *Informer*, a Houston black newspaper, that noted Ford had been "rejected then accepted and rejected again," a line that in its weariness suggests something of the condition of being black in America, there was little mention in the press of UT's backtracking. But the university had been shaken by the prospect of an African American trying out for its football team. The admissions department put a one-year moratorium on accepting Negroes (the word it used) while it figured out a long-term strategy.

In June 1955, university administrators convened, for the first time, the four-person Committee on Selective Admissions. The committee members suggested, in a report delivered to the university president and marked "not for publication," loosening the graduate student application process so that "the University would be in a position to plead that it is acting in good faith to bring an end to segregation and it should have some bearing with the courts in any attempt to postpone the admission of Negro students at the undergraduate level." The committee observed that if 2,700 freshmen were admitted, 300 would be black, according to state population proportions—more than the administrators could stomach. The University of Texas had long admitted (nonblack) students based on how well they did in high school. But the report, laying the groundwork for standardized testing as a pillar of admissions, showed that UT freshmen had significantly higher aptitude test scores than incoming freshmen at three Texas black colleges. "Cutting point of 72 would eliminate about 10% of UT freshmen and about 74% of Negroes," states one footnote, speaking of a standardized test cutoff. "Assuming the distributions are representative, this cutting point would tend to result in a maximum of 70 Negroes in a class of 2,700." And so in 1957, UT became among the first public universities in the country to require entrance exams.

Athletics, and football in particular, presented UT with a logistical conundrum: even as it was resisting integrating its student body, would the university bar other schools from bringing their black athletes to UT's fields and tracks? In October 1954, UT was scheduled to play football against Washington State in Austin. Among

Washington State's players was Duke Washington, a black running back. No African American had played football in Texas Memorial Stadium, and a 1953 UT regents policy barred the "participation of Negroes in football games." A few weeks before the game, UT athletic director Dana X. Bible called Stan Bates, his counterpart at Washington State. Less than a month earlier, Marion Ford and the other African American students had seen their admissions to UT rescinded. In the 1980s, Bates recounted the September 1954 conversation for a book on the history of Washington State athletics.

> He sort of hemmed and hawed around a little, and then said, "Ah, Stan, I understand that you have a black player on your team this year."
>
> "That's right," Stan replied. "Duke Washington, our fullback. And he's a good one."
>
> "Well, ah, Stan, you know we don't have black players in Texas, and we'd like you to leave him home when you come down here. It might be better all around."

Bates told Bible that if Duke Washington couldn't play, Washington State wasn't coming.

With the matchup two weeks away, Washington State president Clement French, relaying a similar message, tried a cheery tone with UT president Logan Wilson. "I don't know whether the Austin papers carried the account of our Southern California game of last Friday night, but if they did you know that we not only got walloped but that the outstanding bright spot for our team was the young man who has been the center of our discussion," he wrote. "Therefore, unless he is injured and unable to travel, there is no question but that he will be in our traveling squad and will play." UT acceded, but university officials in Austin drew up a memorandum of understanding. "Whether Washington State College plays the Negro boy here will be regarded by The University of Texas as their business and not ours," the memo, which can be found in the UT archives, states. It continues: "There may be a hotel or housing problem. Mr. Bible and others will do what they can to assist in finding suitable housing, but the attitude of The University of Texas will be that the problem is essentially that of the visiting team." Wary, once again, of the prospect of negative press coverage, the memo concluded: "Insofar as it can be avoided, there is to be no publicity at either end."

Ultimately, Duke Washington made the trip with the team and ended up staying at the home of a black family while the rest of his team checked into an Austin hotel. The Longhorns won, but Duke Washington scored a touchdown on a seventy-three-yard draw play. In his great memoir *North Toward Home*, Willie Morris, who graduated from the University of Texas in 1957, recalled the "entire student section rose spontaneously and applauded."

Two years later, with the University of Southern California, which had long been integrated, scheduled to play football in Austin, UT officials deliberated over how to handle the prospect of black fans showing up to the game. "One can visualize (with a shudder) the disturbance arising because a Negro attempted to sit next to or near a white person who had definite adverse feelings in such matters," Lanier Cox, the assistant to the UT president, wrote to the chair of the board of regents in early July 1956, two and a half months before the game. Warned Cox: "Since the University of Southern California has a star Negro fullback, it is entirely possible that his parents or friends from California may make the trip to Austin. It would be difficult to control the sale of tickets by visiting schools. Therefore, it would appear that little could be done other than to admit Negroes holding tickets in the visiting team section." As for other African Americans seeking to buy tickets, he said: "It is recommended that the Negro section in the stadium be continued and that all Negroes who ask for tickets be sold a seat only in this section. This should reduce substantially the possibility of Negroes sitting among the white spectators in the west stands and thereby creating a situation of possible ill feeling or even violence."

In the end, USC's Cornelius Roberts, nicknamed the Chocolate Rocket, ran roughshod over the Longhorns, racking up 251 yards and three touchdowns. UT lost 44–20 en route to a 1–9 season. Among the spectators at that game was Marion Ford. He had played for Illinois before coming back to Austin as a transfer student, among the first black undergrads admitted in 1956. After the game, Ford approached UT head coach Ed Price to again float the idea of walking on as the university's first black football player. "Ed," Ford said, "you need me. I can help you." ("I was a cocky son of a bitch," Ford later told Dwonna Goldstone for her excellent book *Integrating the 40 Acres*—the UT campus is nicknamed the Forty Acres after its original footprint.) Price, who had not had a winning season for several years and who must have known he was likely to be fired at the end of the season, gave no real consideration to Ford's proposal. "He was very amiable," Ford, who died in 2001 after launching a successful dental practice in Houston, later told a reporter. "He knew he needed help. But he said, 'It's out of my hands.' . . . It would have been a good stroke for Texas, a beautiful opportunity for a premier university to forge ahead and a hell of a rallying point."

Perhaps Price told administrators about being approached by Ford. Later that week, in a confidential memo, McCown, who as dean of admissions had tried to thwart Ford's admission in the first place and who was now the dean of student services, reassured the UT president and vice president that Bible, the athletic director, "feels that the coaches will have fairly positive control over Negro participation in the contact sports in selecting their teams."

University officials moved swiftly. Less than a month later, in mid-October 1956, UT president Logan Wilson issued a confidential memorandum titled "Concerning the Participation of Negro Students in Intercollegiate Athletics." Acting in "the best interests of colored as well as white students," considering "long-established traditions in this region," and aiming to "minimize frictions which might develop and which might be expected in extracurricular areas," the regents had decided that even while "complying with the mandate of the Supreme Court by providing full educational opportunity to Negro students . . . it would be unwise at this time to extend the interpretation to include all areas of student life, many of which are not directly educational in character."

That same month, Clinton Givans, an air force enlisted man who planned to enter the university under the Korean GI Bill, wrote to Bible, the athletic director, about trying out for the football team. He wanted to go to UT, he wrote, because as a native Texan he would not have to pay out-of-state fees and

> because there are no Negro schools that rate as high . . .
> in subject matter or intercollegiate athletics and since
> I've been in service the competition was rather stiff that I
> had formed a small ambition in my mind and to make the
> University's football squad was one of them. . . . I do not
> wish to make any national scandal or bring any bad rep-
> utation upon the school by a matter of racial segregation,
> but I really want to get a chance to try to make the varsity
> squad of the football team.

Bible rebuffed him. In the coming season, Bible wrote to Givans, UT had games against Georgia and Tulane, "neither of which will permit its team to play against integrated squads. Furthermore, our Conference has not taken any action along this line. And it is our plan to continue to schedule teams in the South and Southwest. So the picture is most uncertain at this time."

These questions clearly preoccupied UT officials. The same day that Bible wrote Givans, McCown wrote to UT's vice president to ask the university to establish a policy "concerning Negro participation in intercollegiate sports, particularly football." The university reiterated that African Americans could not participate in intercollegiate sports. There were holdouts: Sterling Holloway, a regent, argued in a letter to UT president Logan Wilson in 1958 that UT was a diminished university for not allowing African Americans to participate in athletics: "Provincialism, of which total exclusion of Negroes from athletics is an expression, is not the hallmark of a university destined to pay a crucial role in the intellectual life of the free world."

Tellingly, Holloway suggested at least allowing them to participate in track and field because "no bodily contact is involved." This sort of thing lurks in the correspondence among university officials in the 1950s and into the early 1960s—an explicit anxiety about physical contact between whites and African Americans, especially between black men and white women. In the wake of *Brown*, university officials eliminated intramural wrestling, ordered separate hospital wings for black and white students, demanded that lab partners not be of different races, canceled an annual coed swimming competition, and ended mixed-race dancing. "We will try to avoid embarrassment by not scheduling dances such as a Paul Jones"—a kind of square dance—"where a person has little or no choice in selecting a partner," according to one confidential memo.

It was one thing to talk with people of another race and another to touch them. It's no wonder that the football team and the dorms— that is, areas of campus life that involved the intimacy of human contact—would be the last areas of the university to be integrated. Students, by and large, were instigators of integration. In October 1961, as they weighed a nonbinding referendum on the question "Do you favor allowing participation of capable athletes of all races in the University's athletic program?" an undergraduate named John B. Holmes Jr. argued for the "no" faction in the pages of the *Daily Texan*. Holmes, whose father was an oilman who gave Darrell Royal the use of his personal airplane for recruiting visits and who himself would go on to a twenty-year career as a district attorney in Harris County, winning a reputation for convincing juries to sentence black men to death, claimed that integration would harm recruiting and the performance of the Longhorns.

But there was evidence of just the opposite—that segregation was harming football recruitment. In March 1961, Junior Coffey, a top high school athlete in the state, the soft-spoken son of a farm laborer in the Panhandle town of Dimmitt, announced he would like to play for the University of Texas if the Southwest Conference allowed African Americans to compete.

> Coffey said he wouldn't mind being the first Negro athlete to play for a Southwest Conference school but he also

85

thinks it will be a while before Negro athletes are allowed to participate. "It all depends on the people—your people," he said. "Some of them might not understand and accept it. I know it would make things rugged for everyone if it came now. I am going to have enough trouble with my studies. I understand the problems involved. I guess they (the Southwest Conference) knows what they are doing but they're losing a lot of good Texas boys."

Unable to play in the Southwest Conference, Coffey ended up leaving the state for the University of Washington in Seattle, and later had a successful NFL career.

With many African Americans wanting to stick closer to home, some say the best college football program in Texas in the 1950s and into the 1960s was not at the University of Texas but at all-black Prairie View A&M. The school, a two-hour drive east of Austin, won five national championships between 1953 and 1964. "Back in the good old days, before integration"—Michael Hurd, the author of a history on black football in Texas, is half joking as I interview him; he raises his eyebrows here and widens his smile—"there was a pipeline from black schools to black colleges." Of course, UT never played Prairie View. Was it because UT was afraid of losing? Was it that African Americans were perceived as pollutants? "Don't overthink it," Hurd says. "A black person in Austin wasn't even allowed on campus. They wouldn't think of having a game between the schools."

In the end, students at the University of Texas in the fall of 1961 passed the referendum by a margin of 5,132 votes for integration to 3,293 against it. The regents shrugged off the result. In a bit of fuzzy math, one of the regents told reporters the board would ignore the referendum, since "only about 20 percent of the student body" voted in favor of integration. "To me," the regent W. W. Heath told radio station KTBC, "that would indicate a great majority of students are satisfied with the situation." The board issued a statement, claiming, self-seriously: "[We have] a heavy responsibility to perform, and we respectfully ask you to trust our judgment. We do not feel that any substantial changes should be made in the immediate future, but we shall continue to move forward with due and deliberate speed as we think advisable under all the circumstances which exist from time to time."

That phrase—"due and deliberate speed"—was, of course, a purposeful echo of the language in *Brown*. The regents wanted to suggest they were abiding by the ruling even as they continued to do everything they could to forestall the integration of the school and its football team. As a member of the all-white Southwest Conference, UT "should not take unilateral action," Thornton Hardie, the chair of the regents, argued in the early 1960s. (Another conference team, SMU, managed to unilaterally integrate in 1966.)

In his memoir, Willie Morris wrote that he found the mix of politics, racism, and education in Texas "tawdry and suffocating." What he chiefly noticed as an undergraduate were "the boorish remarks of Regents, who could make the most reflective and charitable monk in the most isolated cloister want to bite back, the mindless self-satisfaction of most of the students, and politically, the general hardening of the arteries after the Supreme Court decision of 1954."


Where was Darrell Royal amid all this? He had grown up poor in Oklahoma—perhaps as poor as the Campbells. Born in 1924 in the town of Hollis, a packed-earth sort of place just east of the rolling red hills of the Texas-Oklahoma state line, he was raised in hardship. The *K* in Darrell K Royal honored his mother, Katy Elizabeth, who died of cancer when he was just four months old. The family had a little house with a milk cow and chickens and a garden; the place was right by US Highway 62, and as a young teen, with the Depression taking hold and the creeks around Hollis choking up with sand, Darrell would keep an eye on the cars and trucks, water jugs hanging off the sides, driving off to the West. At night, he slept with a damp rag over his face to filter the dust. He took to sports early—he was basically a hyperactive kid—and when he wasn't playing one sport or another, he was working: early jobs included shining shoes, feeding newsprint into the presses, and pulling cotton. "He was smaller than a lot of 'em," his father, Burley Royal, once said, "but he could do a day's work with the best of them."

The summer after his freshman year in school, with opportunity hard to come by, he and his father and brothers struck out, in their loaded-down blue Whippet—a beaten-up sedan that looked not unlike a Ford Model T—for California. "What furniture we couldn't sell we took with us," Royal told *Texas Monthly* in 1974. "That old Whippet would barely make it through the mountains. We had some of those canvas water bags tied to the side ... They were supposed to keep the water cool, but the water was as hot as the sun." In the San Joaquin Valley, he worked as a fruit picker and painted figs with olive oil, which was said to ripen them faster. It was an unhappy time. He was ridiculed by other workers as an Okie bumpkin, and the whole family was squeezed into a shack.

And so when the fall rolled around and he was deemed too young to play on the local school's varsity football team, he decided he had seen enough of California. He hitchhiked back to Hollis, wearing his government-issued overalls and carrying little more than a ball and a mitt in an old Victrola box. He led his high school football team to a state championship, and after a stint in the military, he ended up playing for the University of Oklahoma. As a player, he was rough and scrappy—just the kind of qualities he would long value in his recruits. Leading Oklahoma as its quarterback, he had a stretch of seventy-six passes without an interception; on defense he set an Oklahoma record for career pickoffs. He notched an eighty-one-yard punt and a ninety-five-yard punt return—both OU records. As in high school, he led his college squad to an undefeated record and a championship.

A decade later, at age thirty-two, he was hired by the University of Texas, at an annual salary of $15,000, to take over the beleaguered football program following the firing of Ed Price, the coach who had just turned down Marion Ford's offer to try out. He had had short coaching stints at Mississippi State and the University of Washington and up in the Canadian Football League, but the once-storied UT team, coming off a 1–9 season, figured to be his toughest assignment yet. In Royal's first season, he turned the team around for a winning record of 6–4–1, including a victory over tenth-ranked Arkansas and a Thanksgiving Day upset of fourth-ranked Texas A&M, quickly winning the hearts of the Longhorn faithful.

Royal had overseen integrated teams at Washington and with the professional Edmonton Eskimos—he reportedly chewed out white players for directing racial slurs at black players—but the Longhorn team he inherited was all-white. Even as students and some faculty members pressed for change, Royal appeared uninterested in joining them. "Last Saturday a Negro football player from the University of Oklahoma made 135 yards rushing against the University of Texas football team," wrote the UT student association president, Frank Cooksey—who would later become mayor of Austin—on October 15, 1959, to university officials. "I dare say that the coaches on the Longhorn staff would be quite ready to accept the services of any one who could play football as well as Mr. Prentice Gautt did on Saturday afternoon."

Perhaps not. On November 10, less than a month after Cooksey's letter, McCown sent a confidential memo to UT president Logan Wilson to brief him on "the feeling of our coaches concerning Negro students participating in intercollegiate sports." Royal "has coached Negro students but says they create problems," McCown wrote.

> White players particularly resented Negro boys coming in their room and lounging on their beds. Darrell was quite pronounced in not wanting any Negroes on his team until other Southwest Conference teams admit them and until the housing problem is solved or conditions change.

McCown continued:

> The coaches wouldn't want to have their players housed in different places. On the other hand, it would be un-

thinkable to assign a Negro and white student as room-
mates. If we were the only Southwest Conference team
with Negroes it would be ruinous in recruiting. We would
be labeled Negro lovers and competing coaches would
tell a prospect: "If you go to Texas, you will have to room
with a Negro." No East Texas boy would come here.

McCown suggested that in the meantime, the university should
"continue our delaying tactics. In my opinion, we are not ready for
integration in Intercollegiate Athletics at the present time. Neither
is our public."

Did that kind of thinking trickle down to the players? A few
months later, on New Year's Day 1960, the 9–1 Longhorns squared
off against top-ranked—and integrated—Syracuse in the end-of-
season Cotton Bowl. Syracuse was led by Ernie Davis, who would
become the first African American winner of the Heisman Trophy.
Just before halftime, a fight broke out. After the game, which the
Orangemen won, Syracuse players said Texas players ignited the
brawl with racial slurs. A Syracuse player said a Texas player, Larry
Stephens, called Syracuse tackle John Brown "a dirty nigger." "Oh,
they were bad," said the Orangemen's black fullback, Art Brown.
"Talk about high standards and scholarship. One of them spit in
my face as I carried the ball through the line." Royal countered that
Syracuse players had said "some pretty uncomplimentary things"
to Mexican American Longhorn halfback Rene Ramirez, known as
the Galloping Gaucho. The New York team, he said, "was more concerned about the race question" than his own.

Written nearly three years later, an internal regents letter from
November 1962 gives another glimpse into Royal's thinking on integration—which might be described, generously, as pragmatic.
Heath, the regents vice chair, wrote that at a meeting earlier that
year, head coaches

unanimously agreed that they did not feel that the time
had come for us to integrate athletics. Several, including

Darrell Royal, said they had no objection to integration of
intercollegiate athletics as such, but were greatly concerned about the effect it would have on our recruiting
and that even though we might obtain a few good colored
athletes, unless the other schools integrated at the same
time, inevitably in their recruiting, they would use the
fact that our colored boys were living in the same athletic dormitory and associating closely with the rest of the
team in their recruiting efforts with the white boys and
their parents who might object to such a system or prefer
to live, socialize and play with white boys.

But late in 1963, facing lawsuits from their own students over
segregated dorms and newly crusading powers in Washington, the
regents finally cracked. Heath, a politically connected insurance
attorney from East Texas and now the regents chair, was widely
known as a segregationist. But an old friend, Lyndon Baines Johnson, prompted him to change direction. With passage of the Civil
Rights Act on the horizon, Johnson told Heath that UT was in danger
of jeopardizing its federal funding. Heath admitted that he "came
on the board with a lot of prejudices" and did not realize that "on
federal research grants, you get cut off a lot of places if you're not
integrated." Publicly, Heath couched the regents' change of heart
that November—just days before the assassination of John F. Kennedy in Dallas—as the latest manifestation of the body's judicious-
ness. "Under our oaths of office to uphold the Constitution of the
United States, our only choice has been that of timing the 'deliberate
speed,'" he said. "Some feel we have been too slow, others that we
have been too fast."

Immediately after the board's action doing away with race-
based student restrictions, Royal, cornered by reporters following
a football game with Baylor, was asked whether he was currently
interested in black high school prospects. "No," he said. But Royal
also said that any student who met the university's academic requirements and could make the team could play for Texas.

That answer left the team's door ajar to African Americans, causing some Texans concern. One Longhorn fan from Houston, an engineer named A. Rogers Mielly, reading Royal's remarks in the newspaper, wrote straight away to the UT chancellor to register his concern. Royal

> is an ambitious young man who's [*sic*] dream is to pro-
> duce a football team second to none, and surely he is to
> be commended for this viewpoint, but when he has in
> mind searching the nation for negro football material to
> strengthen his team has he given thought to the neces-
> sity of absorbing these negroes in the social life of Texas
> University where they will be placed on a pedestal before
> young women at dances, and other social events which in
> due course brings on marriage.

Mielly wrote that on November 19, 1963—eleven years before Earl Campbell joined the Longhorns. His inquiry continues: "Also can the star negro of a future Texas football team be taken home and accepted over weekends in some of our best homes?"

Chancellor Harry Ransom replied to Mielly and copied Royal: "You can be sure that Coach Royal and his staff will pursue a moderate, wise, and equitable policy in the conduct of all athletic affairs at the University. I am quite certain that the Regents did not intend and Coach Royal does not intend to 'search the nation for football material' with any such purpose as you have in mind."

Yet not all regents were roadblocks to equality. Wales Madden, who, at the age of thirty-three, was the youngest-ever regent when he was seated in 1960, pushed for the integration order—he was partly inspired, he said, by a memory he still carries with him. As a five- or six-year-old in Amarillo in the early 1930s, he persuaded his parents to let him go to church with the black couple who worked for the family; he can still recall the smell of the dirt and straw beneath the tent and the "simplicity of equalness." From the law office he still visits, at age ninety, in Amarillo, he said, "I can assure you about my views and Darrell Royal's views on giving anyone a chance who had been proven fit for the position—color did not matter. I was pretty broad-minded, as you can imagine, and Darrell was just not prejudiced against the black people."

Whether or not you believe Madden's assurances, that November 1963, after the regents announced their decision to integrate university athletics, the education reporter Anita Brewer of the *Austin Statesman* observed: "Just how soon the backfield will be integrated depends now on athletic director (and football coach) Darrell Royal."


The Longhorns did not put a black player on the varsity team until 1970. In that long, seven-year period between the regents' nod to Royal to bring on black athletes and the day he finally did—a biblical span, equal to the length of time Joseph sequestered food in the great warehouses of Egypt ahead of the seven years of famine— the beloved coach had, in some quarters, earned a reputation as a racist holdout.

How much of that long stretch—a stretch that included the slighting of Elmo Wright, the speedy wide receiver from Sweeny whom Ken Dabbs brought to Royal's attention in 1966—can be blamed on Royal and how much on the regents, boosters, and university officials remains an open question, even to the people who played for him. "Royal, at the end of the day, was the whipping boy, if you will, as it relates to carrying the banner for discriminatory practices at UT," said Alfred Jackson, who played wide receiver for the Longhorns, roomed with Campbell for nearly his entire stint at the university, and went on to play in the pros. Even after the regents rescinded the prohibition on black athletes, Gary Cartwright observed in *Texas Monthly*, Royal faced resistance from the "Orange Coats," "that splendid assortment of dentists and bankers and contractors and Regents who hired Royal in the first place, then attached themselves to the UT football program like ticks on a bird dog. Those were and still are your racists, your true orange-blood bigots." They "made it clear that the first black Longhorn had better be two steps faster than Jesus and able to run through a brick wall." The 1963 decision, absent a mandate, "was like handing Royal an anchor and telling him to swim with it," the *Austin American-Statesman* sports editor Lou Maysel said.

Royal appears to have made a calculation—call it shrewd, call it cynical—not to get ahead of the regents. "When I first came here, one of my friends told me, 'if you play your politics right, you'll have a long career.' I told him right quick that I wasn't a politician and didn't intend to be a politician; I was going to coach the best I could and hope that would be acceptable," he once told a *Texas Monthly* reporter. "That turned out to be a naïve, immature approach. You're just ignorant and dumb if you don't know who the Regents are and the chain of command."

Politically speaking, Royal had the clout to integrate the football team. He had earned the fealty of the regents and major donors by delivering a national championship in 1963; having already appointed him athletic director, the regents in the championship's aftermath named him a tenured professor. His support was sought by the governor. And so, in 1966, he could have called Ken Dabbs back and told him that he was pleased to take on Elmo Wright. Decades later, speaking about general foot-dragging on integration, Julius Whittier, Texas's first black varsity football player, said Royal "could have had the courage to stand up in the main mall and yell, 'Look, you assholes, you've got to do this.'"

But publicly, at least, Royal did the opposite. The same year that he privately passed on recruiting Elmo Wright, Royal offered three reasons why African Americans weren't on UT teams: the athletes were not interested in the university; they were not talented enough; and they failed to meet entrance requirements. And so, as in every previous season, there were no black players on the 1967 varsity football squad. That season, the group Negros Associated for Progress picketed home football games with signs that read: "Orange and White Lack Black." During one 1967 game, in a reference to the UT mascot, forty black students in the end zone bleachers held up cards that said: "Bevo Needs Soul." Campus police asked them to leave.

Nor were there any black players on the 1968 varsity team. The previous year, a black student named E. A. Curry made the fresh-man team as a walk-on, and in the 1968 season, he was allowed to suit up, but never took the field as a varsity player—a stacked Long-horns squad and weak grades kept him from playing and from trav-eling with the team. In a devastating 1972 series by a pair of Associ-ated Press reporters examining racism in the UT football program, Royal bristled at criticism that he had tried to mock Curry. "So lo and behold the blacks on the East Side said I just suited him up to ridicule him, put him on the bench, exhibit him, not let him play, embarrass him, when really I was trying to reward him." During that season, 1968, Royal offered the first UT football scholarship to a black player, a linebacker named Leon O'Neal. But he, too, failed to make the varsity squad after grades forced him to leave school.

In 1969, a student questionnaire administered by the univer-sity's counseling department, its results marked confidential and "not for circulation," found that most black students felt they were unwelcome as participants or spectators at sports matches. "The black student on this campus obviously feels very alienated . . . due to the racist attitudes and policies of many organizations, e.g. so-rorities, fraternities, the whiteness of the sports scene, insulting politics of University housing facilities, and the presences of rac-ist faculty and staff members," observed the researchers Ira Iscoe and Jess Preciphs of the UT Psychological Counseling Center. (Just over 20 percent of black respondents felt they were treated unfairly during classroom participation and activities; 18 percent felt they were graded unfairly.)

The journalist (and, later, Hollywood screenwriter and direc-tor) James Toback, just twenty-five years old, journeyed to Austin on assignment for *Harper's* in the fall of 1970, when, finally, Whittier joined the varsity. "Why, I want to know, is UT lagging?" he won-dered to a group of black football players, some still in high school, some at college, assembled in an Austin bar. Even conservative schools—SMU and Baylor—were outpacing supposedly progressive UT in the area of integration.

One of the players pointed to the chairman of the board of regents, the imperious Frank Erwin, known around campus for his burnt-orange Cadillac and the moment in October 1969, when, wearing a hard hat and brandishing a bullhorn, he ordered students to unchain themselves from the live oaks and pecan trees that Erwin had directed be bulldozed to make way for a 15,000-seat stadium expansion. As the protestors sang "God Bless America," Erwin demanded that campus police arrest twenty-seven of them on charges of disorderly conduct.

Erwin "don't like black folks and he *loves* that Texas football team; so he wants to keep it lily white," one of the players told Toback. "And he can do it, too, because he's the man that can pressure the coach out and hire a new one. The coach will be doin' whatever Erwin wants him to." Another blamed it on "the players": "You get a cat like the star running back who went to high school in Bridge City, the whitest town in Texas, and he said, 'I'll never play football with a nigger.' Who wants teammates like that? Better to go to a worser school or out of state." Another player pegged it to the coach: "Darrell Royal. He's the man. Darrell Royal is *the Man*. He could be Governor of this state tomorrow if he wanted. He don't have no use for no *nigger*. He wants a 'colored' boy. A proper Christian, a Boy Scout. And you won't find many of them around anymore, even in Texas."

Larry Goodwyn, a white historian of populism who had studied at UT and helped organize the get-together, told Toback that Royal was "no racist": "At least no more than the Northern liberals or half-liberals who also claim not to be. He's subject to a lot of pressures. Quiet pressures. Some people who hold power in the university don't figure there's any reason for having a black player when the team's winning all the time."

Another of the players interrupted Goodwyn, asking, rhetorically, why Royal hadn't recruited more black players.

"He'll say they're too dumb, they can't get in, their SAT scores are too low. I'd like to get a list of the SAT scores of some of those white morons he carries every year."

"Right on, brother. And there's another thing. He doesn't want no black *stars* on his team. A black cat's got to be better than a white cat to get an even break but he can't be *too* good. He doesn't want any black boy *dominating* the game. It's part of the whole attitude."

After the 1968 game against Houston—the one that saw Elmo Wright handling the football in Austin—ended in a tie, Darrell Royal did not schedule another game against the Cougars. "You ask Royal why he doesn't schedule Houston," one of the players told Toback. "You know why? Because he's afraid Houston would whip his ass and Houston is nearby Texas with black cats carryin' the team! He'd be humiliated. It would bust his whole white-supremacy thing. You just ask him!"

Royal, game for an interview on race, picked Toback up at a hotel and drove him over to a Mexican restaurant. One of the first things Toback asked about was the Houston scheduling theory. "'Bullshit, bullshit!' His face reddens. 'Look, I can see people who haven't made it becoming bitter, using all kinds of excuses to explain away their mediocrity. . . . Houston's not in the Conference and that's all there is to it. Do you think that just because Notre Dame had Negroes I'd have been any madder last year at having lost to them than I would have been at having lost to Arkansas which was all white? It's ridiculous."

"This whole race question is very complicated," Royal said over the meal, during which the headwaiter came over and asked the coach to autograph some menus.

"A bunch of Negro boys came to me a while ago and said I could solve all possible difficulties by hiring a black coach. Now that would be fine for them but I've got to look at the other side. I'd have a whole lot of white boys on the team coming to me saying they couldn't play for a black coach. The family atmosphere of the team would be destroyed. And don't kid yourself. A lot of these Northern teams—professional and college, in all sports—that brag about their integration aren't getting along at all. Once the club harmony and spirit begin to deteriorate, I don't care what kind of talent you have, you won't win."

"Is it important to you that you have Negro players on the team?"

"No."

I wait again.

"Listen, I know a lot of black people think I'm a racist. But what am I supposed to do, run around denying it? That's incriminating in itself."

His own culpability was something that Royal wrestled with his entire career—and his public statements always carried a flavor of defensiveness. "The proper thing—and the true feeling, too—is that we should've done it a lot sooner," Royal told John Wheat of the University of Texas's Center for American History in the 1990s, long after he had retired. "But, you know, no one school is any more racist than the other, or any less racist than the other. They rap the University of Texas, saying it's more racist because they were the last to integrate, and that's not true. But that's recruiting talk; that's stuff that they put on you."

Michael Hurd, the historian of black Texas high school and college football, said as a kid in the late 1950s and through his teenage years in the early 1960s, he used to lie in the grass outside his Houston home in the working-class black neighborhood of Sunnyside—his mother was a teacher, his father a welder—tune his transistor radio to a black station, and root for the Longhorns. Then he encountered one of those disillusionments of adolescence: "I remember learning from someone that 'Darrell Royal doesn't want black players' and feeling really sad about that."

When, on an icy early-January day in 1974, Darrell Royal, handsome and seemingly self-assured in a William Shatner way, stepped into the modest Campbell abode, determined to convince Ann Campbell that her son ought to play football for the University of Texas, he might as well have descended from the starship *Enterprise*. He was among the most famed coaches in college football: still shy of his fiftieth birthday, he had already presided over three national championship teams. He had never once endured a losing season; at one point, his Longhorns won thirty straight games. He was voted "Outstanding Coach of the Sixties" in a poll conducted by ABC Sports, beating out Bear Bryant of Alabama, John McKay of USC, and Woody Hayes of Ohio State.

And yet when Darrell Royal showed up in Tyler, less than two weeks after John Tyler High had won the state championship, he was a vulnerable man. In many respects, the meticulous order that Royal had built for his family and his program was crumbling. He was still reeling from the death of his twenty-seven-year-old daughter, Marian, a talented artist, in an automobile accident in Austin that April. She left behind two young children who were in the car with her when it collided with a University of Texas shuttle bus.

In a separate, professional key, he had grown sick with concern about his most hated rival, Barry Switzer, the bright, loud, upstart coach of the Oklahoma Sooners. Royal thought Switzer was a cheat and a son of a bitch who had been stealing recruits and secretly filming UT's practices—as indeed, Switzer later admitted in his autobiography, he had.

And at that very moment, when Royal was at the peak of his fans' adulation, he felt keenly that his legacy was in jeopardy. President Nixon had sauntered down to the locker room to declare the undefeated 1969 Longhorns the national champions after a thrilling 15–14 victory over second-ranked Arkansas, another all-white team. But in that increasingly self-aware period, Texas and other schools of the South stood out for their whiteness. And now, as Royal approached the Campbell home, black players, though finally allowed onto the varsity, found much to criticize in the UT program. In the autumn of 1972, a little more than a year before Royal journeyed to the Campbells, his first half dozen black players had told a pair of Associated Press reporters about their alienation from the team. "Nothing out in the open," said sophomore linebacker Fred Perry about racism among Longhorn coaches. "Just their overall attitude." Across Texas, black players and their parents, long ignored by the state's flagship institution, assumed, with some justification, that the Longhorns' head coach was a through-and-through racist; the second part of the five-part AP series began, "Darrell Royal's image is so bad among some blacks that they suspect he even taunts and mistreats his maid." Separately, a former player of Royal's, Gary Shaw, a white offensive lineman, had recently published a tell-all book that painted Royal as two-faced—charming and uncaring. Royal and his aides were quick to dismiss the book, *Meat on the Hoof*, as the work of a disgruntled bench warmer. And yet, buried in *Meat on the Hoof*, which sold more than 350,000 copies, was a damning scene. Shaw recalled how, after he had popped a dummy in practice, Royal approvingly said, "Shaw, if you keep playing like that, we might have to start treating you like a white man around here."

The book put Royal on the defensive, and the AP series had stung. Together, they appeared to confirm the football team's earned reputation as one inhospitable to African Americans. Alfred Jackson, who was Earl Campbell's freshman roommate at the University of Texas and who, like Campbell, was the middle kid of eleven children and grew up black in rural Texas before heading to UT on a football scholarship (the similarities to Campbell stop about there) remembers an uncle warning him not to attend the university: "Don't go to the University of Texas. You're going to be discriminated against. And Darrell Royal doesn't like black players. You're never going to make it there. You're not going to get a chance to play."

Jackson keeps an office in Austin, on the very top floor of the Frost Bank Tower, a Gotham-like, iconic glass-and-steel building that towers over much of downtown. That aerie offers him a panoramic view from which to describe the relationship between the stadium and the rest of the university. He favors pinstripe suits with pocket squares, of the type former NFL players on the Sunday pregame shows wear. Still broad shouldered, with an athlete's purposeful gait, he has naturally gone a little soft in the belly, and today, amid all this luxury, he worries whether his private-school-educated kids, even as they face the inevitable slights of growing up black in America, will understand the struggles their parents and grandparents faced. The stories about Royal, he said, were "also circulated by all the other coaches in the Southwest Conference and outside the conference." But Jackson pushes back on the narrative, crediting Royal with setting up a mentorship program to help black athletes think about a professional life after football. "I was an unexposed black kid who didn't know anything about zero," he said. "Royal was very fair to me in an era in which there was not a lot of fairness around."

Royal found the AP series confounding. He had given his blessing to interviews with the black players about race on campus, and now he was learning in newsprint about their unhappiness. The black players, either because they didn't recognize themselves in the journalists' work or because they were worried about their status on the team or for some other reason, quickly told Royal that their remarks had been taken out of context, and they apologized. But the whole thing was especially bewildering to him because it came just as his thinking about race—and, especially, his responsibility to push for equal opportunity—was evolving. Wearied by the inexorable expectations placed on his team, and privately weighing the prospect of retirement, he wanted to land one final recruit to rescue his reputation.

In football stadiums in the South, change came about not because the whites in power suddenly grew compassionate, but because they wanted to compete. Consider the parallel case of Alabama and

Coach Paul "Bear" Bryant. From its inception through the 1970 season, Alabama football, like Texas, was all-white. If you visited a Dairy Queen in Tuscaloosa back then, said one Tide fan, there were two separate, unlabeled windows—one was for African Americans and one was for whites; everyone knew which one to use. Conventional wisdom holds that Bryant, like his friend Royal at Texas, had enough clout to integrate the football team. "Bear Bryant was big enough to have taken on [George] Wallace," Howell Raines wrote in a 1983 reflection about the coach in the *New Republic*. "If he had offered one clear-cut public gesture of condemnation, who knows what might have been spared that benighted state?"

But their biographers paint Bryant and Royal as swimming against a strong segregationist current. "Bryant was a football coach," Keith Dunnavant, the author of *Coach: The Life of Paul "Bear" Bryant*, said. "He was not the governor, not the king—he could not make segregation go away with the snap of a finger, any more than any businessman in Alabama at the time could have." And as long as Bryant was winning, said Don Keith, another biographer, "I don't think he saw a need for pushing that too hard."

Through the end of the 1960s, it was almost as if there were two divisions in college football: the Big Ten and the Pac-8 had the Rose Bowl, and the southern schools had all the other bowls. The teams in the South "could never face a black player and win a national championship," said longtime Austin sportswriter John Maher. During the 1970 season, Alabama hosted USC, the first integrated team to play the Tide on its home turf, and Alabama got hammered. Sam "the Bam" Cunningham, a seldom-used African American fullback, scored two touchdowns and rushed for 131 yards. Kentucky coach Jerry Claiborne, in what feels like a facetious swipe at the civil rights movement, said that Cunningham did more to integrate Alabama in sixty minutes that night than Martin Luther King had accomplished in twenty years. "They had never seen anything that big, that fast, that color coming at them before," USC linebacker John Papadakis once told a documentary film crew. "And believe me, that's a neon experience."

As with Alabama, the prospect of losing prompted Texas to integrate. "Everything starts with winning," Royal was fond of saying. "I don't see how a competitor can enjoy the parties and things if he gets beat."

Royal "came to realize he wouldn't be as successful in his career if he didn't get them," said Kralj, the friend and adviser of regents chair Frank Erwin, speaking of African Americans. The regents figured it out, too. "Let's face it," Royal told the *Boca Raton News* in 1973. "It's a fact that when I first came here, Texas wasn't integrated. Then . . . the Regents said we could start integrating, but they meant that we didn't have to push it or worry about it. After a few years, they were, 'All right, we really meant it.' Then they progressed to 'Gawl-dog, let's really go out and make the effort to integrate the school, totally integrate athletics.'"

But when Royal finally directed that African Americans be recruited, he found that his miserable record on race put him at a competitive disadvantage. The long delay in integration, he had to admit, had "become a stigma." Mean Joe Greene, who, as a contemporary of Elmo Wright's, went to high school in Temple, sixty-five miles up the interstate from Austin, and who is enshrined in the NFL Hall of Fame as the anchor of Pittsburgh's Steel Curtain defense, did not even consider UT because it appeared uninterested in black players.

The experience of Kirby Sams, a talented black running back from the coastal city of Corpus Christi, suggests how and why African Americans were suspicious of the UT program. In December 1966, about the time Royal gave Elmo Wright a once-over, the head coach invited Sams and one of his white high school teammates for a campus visit. It was Sams's first time on an airplane. As soon as they landed in Austin, the teammates were separated. Sams was shepherded to a library on campus and left alone for a couple of hours to take the SAT. He didn't even know what the SAT was, let alone that he would suddenly be sitting down to an exam during a football recruiting visit. And instead of tagging along with his high school teammate, who was hanging out with members of the all-e

white football team, Sams was assigned a black UT track athlete, James Means, as his escort around campus. Means, then a senior, an Austin native from a politically involved family, was UT's first black letterman, but even as he clocked faster times than his teammates, he was the only member of the track squad to whom the university had not offered a scholarship.

"He was very, very, very angry," said Sams. "It surprised me they set me up with him." Means warned him not to come to UT. "He told me, 'They just want the white boys. If you come here, they're not going to give you a slot, they're not going to give you a shake. It's all just lip service. You're going to be treated disrespectfully.'" UT put Sams up at the Villa Capri, a motel near campus, and when Sunday morning rolled around, he strode into the hotel lobby and finally met Darrell Royal.

> The first word out of his mouth was "boy," like a greeting, and right there, after hearing all of that anger from James, all I wanted to do was eat my breakfast and get home. I've thought about it since—maybe that was the way he talked to everyone, but the moment I heard that word come out of his mouth I wanted to get out of there. He said, "Boy, you're set to be the first colored boy to play for the University of Texas." I just wanted to get back to Corpus.

Sams ended up attending Michigan on a scholarship; an injury early on ended his football career.

Sams wasn't the only black Texan picked up by a Michigan school. There's a story that Michigan State coach Duffy Daugherty was in Beaumont, in southeastern Texas, to recruit the African American standout Bubba Smith. Michigan State not only was the first major college team to have more black starters than white, but also had a black university president about the same time UT had its first black varsity player. The story is that Daugherty, who led Michigan State to the national championship in 1965 and 1966, saw

Royal in Beaumont and said, "Darrell, what are you doing in my neck of the woods?"

"This has hurt me in recruiting and has hurt me with just straight friendship of blacks," Royal told Denne H. Freeman for his 1974 book *Hook 'Em Horns*. "It has made them very leery to be around me. They might like what they see and might like what they are experiencing when they are with me in person, but they still have it in their head that this is a devious, slick SOB we're dealing with."

The early black players he managed to land found the program to be cold, even hostile. Whittier said that his teammates would invite him to join them for a burger but never dared to ask him to go out with girls, and he was never invited to parties. They even refused to room with him—except for one, Billy Dale, a senior, who volunteered to be Whittier's sophomore-year roommate and was promptly shunned by his own white friends. ("Senior years are supposed to be special," Dale said, "mine was not." He still today declines to elaborate on how his teammates betrayed him.) Whittier, who died in 2018 after suffering from Alzheimer's disease, told the AP reporters that African Americans don't get "chill bumps" when they hear the UT fight songs. "Since when have you seen orange (or) red, white and blue doing us a favor?"

There was something tone deaf, history blind, and maybe a little defensive about Royal's response. "How can he say that the orange has done nothing for him?" Royal said. "He's been here on scholarship. He's been exposed. He's getting an education preparing himself where he can do something to contribute to his race. What has his country done for him? I wonder if he knows what other countries have done for blacks?"

Some Texas papers, in a show of Royal's continued popularity, refused to run the critical AP series, instead publishing editorials in praise of his system. "These newspapers have faith in Coach Royal whom we know to be a man of the highest integrity, dedicated to his coaching career, and to the men who play football under him, regardless of race, color or creed," read one. But the damage was done:

in 1972, not one black player signed to play with the Longhorns.

Royal laughed off the recruiting miscues. "We batted zero last year so anything we do is a gain," Royal told a reporter in February 1973, just about six months before the start of Earl Campbell's senior season at John Tyler. But evidence suggests he was deeply affected by the criticism, and now, in what turned out to be the dusk of his spectacular coaching career, his own thinking on his responsibility to affect race relations was changing, thanks to an unusual friendship that had lately developed with Lyndon Baines Johnson. During Johnson's White House years, he and Royal kept up a kind of smiling, mutually beneficial benignity toward each other. Johnson wasn't much of a football fan—"He couldn't tell you who was playing left guard or tailback," said Larry Temple, who served as Johnson's White House counsel—but Royal's popularity made him a useful ally. As early as January 1964, less than six weeks after JFK's assassination, an influential Houston attorney wrote the White House to recommend Royal for vice president. The top Johnson aide Walter Jenkins wrote back, suggesting, playfully, that the idea was intriguing, but out of the White House's hands. Of course, the notion was ridiculous, but the episode suggests how popular Royal was—and underlines the White House's savvy with top Democratic donors. (Royal was on the list of dignitaries scheduled to meet Kennedy on his arrival in Austin, following his visit to Dallas; an invitation to Royal on White House stationery is among the material in his files on the UT campus.)

Mindful of that popularity, according to records kept at the LBJ Presidential Library, Johnson welcomed Royal and his wife aboard Air Force One in 1967. Their relationship deepened after 1968, when Johnson opted not to run for reelection and began spending far more time at his ranch outside Austin. In May 1971, Royal gave Johnson, now more than two years out of office, a gift of cuff links and a belt buckle. The following March, the Royals were guests of LBJ and Lady Bird during a vacation to Acapulco. And that November, Royal gave the president a watch. "You have been responsible for many enjoyable Saturday afternoons, but having lunch with you, and those fine young men you brought with you, was an exceptional and most enjoyable treat for me," Johnson wrote Royal.

The conversations between Johnson and Royal were far from superficial. In some ways, Royal was Johnson's final project—a last attempt at helping, in some small way, heal the great racial wound in America. In the quaint, uncomfortable phraseology of the time, patronizing in a way that suggests he genuinely thought he wasn't a racist even as he had kept doing racist things, Royal told the journalist Jimmy Banks in 1973, "I think I've always had, basically, a lot of compassion and feeling for the blacks."

> But it's like President Johnson told me: he said, "You know, I never had thought I was prejudiced, and I still don't believe I was, but I just wasn't as concerned about their problems as I should have been."
>
> That's what got me to thinking. I hadn't done anything to hurt 'em—but neither had I done anything to help 'em. Any fair-minded person would say that things had not been fair, and I knew they hadn't been fair. I knew blacks weren't being treated equally and I knew they weren't being given an equal chance. But I really hadn't worried about it, 'til then...
>
> That feeling came partly from spending a lot of time with President Johnson. If there's one thing he talked on, during the time I was with him, more than anything else, it was the race situation. Equal opportunity. The deprived. For many years, the deprived. Far too long, the deprived. This entered into our conversation a lot of the time when we were together.

The last time Royal saw Johnson was at a civil rights symposium at UT in December 1972. Johnson, concerned that his Great Society achievements would be overshadowed by his acceleration of the Vietnam War, had convened a meeting of civil rights leaders to commemorate passage of the Civil Rights, Fair Housing, and Voting

Rights Acts. Staving off chest pains—he at one point popped a ni-troglycerin pill before the audience—Johnson worried aloud that he had not "done enough" to promote equal rights. The moment must have resonated with Royal: Gary Shaw's book had been published earlier that year, as had the five-part AP series about the alienation of black football players at UT. At the symposium, Royal would have heard Johnson say that the country's objective "must be to assure that all Americans play by the same rules and all Americans play against the same odds."

> Yesterday it was commonly said that the black problem was a southern problem. Today it is commonly said that the black problem is an urban problem, a problem of the inner city. But the truth is that the black problem today, as it was yesterday, is not a problem of regions or states or cities, or neighborhoods—it is a problem, concern, and responsibility of the whole nation. Moreover—and we cannot obscure this blunt fact—the black problem remains what it has always been—the problem of being black in white society.
>
> To be black—to one who is black—is to be proud, to be worthy, to be honorable. But to be black in a white society is not to stand on level ground. While the races may stand side by side, whites stand on history's mountain and blacks stand in history's hollow.

As if speaking directly to Royal, there in the audience, Johnson called on a football metaphor:

> Not a white American in this land would fail to be out-raged if an opposing team tried to insert a twelfth man in the lineup to stop a black fullback on the football field. Yet off the field, away from the stadium, outside the reach of the television cameras and the watching eyes of millions, every black American in this land—man or woman—plays

out life running against the twelfth man of a history they
did not make and a fate they did not choose.

A few weeks later, Royal spoke with LBJ for the last time, following a New Year's Day come-from-behind Cotton Bowl victory over
mighty Alabama. "I get the feeling that you and Edith are waiting for
an invitation before you'll come out here to see me," Johnson said,
in his folksy way. "But I want you to call me just like you'd call your
momma, and say, 'We're coming out to see you.' If I'm busy, or have
to be somewhere else, I'll just say so and we can make it another
time. But I don't want you waiting for an invitation. I really think
we ought to get together more often." He yelled so much during the
tight game, Johnson told Richard Nixon the following day, that he
had suffered "heart pains all night" and had had to summon doctors.

Less than a month later—on January 22, 1973—LBJ was dead.

Royal was on the road in East Texas when he heard the news on
the radio. He immediately steered the car back to Austin. As Johnson lay in state at the LBJ Presidential Library, Royal was among
those who volunteered to take a two-hour shift to stand by the cas-
ket. He still had time to transform his own legacy on equal opportunity, to change his reputation from the man with three all-white
national championship teams.

And so, in mid-August 1973, seven years after Royal had told
Ken Dabbs he was not ready to offer a scholarship to Elmo Wright,
Royal tracked him down to ask him for a peculiar kind of help. It
was nearly one o'clock on a Sunday, a couple of hours after church.
Dabbs was by then the head coach at the new football program at
Westlake High, in a fast-growing suburb on Austin's western fringe,
and Royal asked Dabbs to come by his house. That old feeling of intimidation crept back. "I was nervous, I was scared, but I went over
there," Dabbs said.

Royal offered him a job as freshman backfield coach—and then
he asked Dabbs to recruit in East Texas and South Dallas, areas with
high concentrations of African Americans.

"And he asked me, 'Do you have any questions?' And I said,

'Yes, sir, I have one: When you can hire anybody in the United States of America, why would you hire a nobody coach from Westlake?'"

"I'll be real honest with you," Royal told him. "If I had listened to you in 1966, I wouldn't be in the mess I'm in now."

Read generously, the line amounts to a private confession. Less charitably, it was a weirdly self-involved and self-pitying sentiment coming, as it did, from a powerful white man considering issues of race and equity. Thinking back on it, a black coffee in hand in the corner of a café north of UT, a leaky heart valve recently replaced and his nose sounding stuffy, Dabbs said that Royal, intent on recruiting African Americans in the sunset of his coaching days, turned to him for a simple reason: "I don't think anybody on that staff had even coached blacks in *high school*."

Royal's final instructions for him were these: "There's a kid in Tyler, Texas, named Earl Campbell, and I want you to get him for us."

When Royal called him that August, Dabbs had not heard of Earl Campbell. But after catching one of his early games that season, he remembered thinking: "That's the most dominating running back I've ever seen." Campbell was fast becoming the most hotly recruited football player in the nation—during his senior year, more than 250 scouts would travel to Tyler to see him play—and Royal had told Dabbs to do whatever it took to get Campbell to commit to Austin. Campbell had been offered bribes ("inducements," the recruiters called them—a brand-new shotgun stuffed with hundred-dollar bills, a suede coat, a car, a job—these were the sorts of goodies offered to players or their relatives), but had rejected them: "I'm not going to be any sold black boy," he told a reporter in January 1974, less than a month after he led John Tyler to the state championship and two months before signing day. "I won't be bought. Money doesn't excite me. I don't have a car, and a car doesn't excite me. I'm interested in what schools can do for me in the classes. Can I get any help? I'm going to college for an education first and football second."

A few years earlier, as an African American athlete in the South, Campbell would have had many fewer options—either play below the radar for a black college or journey far from home to play at a place like Michigan State. Now, though, all the big schools were gunning for Campbell, and for elite African American athletes of his generation, whatever the draws of a historically black school might have been, little consideration was given to playing for Prairie View A&M or Grambling. "There was much more exposure" at the newly integrated athletic programs, explained Michael Hurd. "You'd be on TV on every Saturday. You'd be on a big campus. You were scouted better by the pros; the black colleges didn't get that kind of respect." Soon, that became a kind of self-fulfilling prophecy. In 1968, the NFL drafted eleven players from a single historically black college—Jackson State, in Mississippi. Eleven years later, after Texas, Alabama, and other schools finally integrated, the entire Southwestern Athletic Conference, a constellation of black schools that included Jackson State, had only five players selected.

When Dabbs first approached the door to the dilapidated Campbell property, the famed football coaches Bill Yeoman of the University of Houston and Barry Switzer of Oklahoma had just emerged, and Dabbs thought to himself, "Oh, Lord, how am I going to make this work?" He had been entrusted with one real task by Royal, and it appeared unlikely that he would be able to pull it off. But a modest bit of spontaneous wit helped ingratiate him with the family. Ann Campbell, inundated with recruiters, asked Dabbs how she could remember him. He told her about a hair-styling cream advertisement with the catch phrase "A little dab'll do ya." "Well," Dabbs said, "just add another b and an s, and you've got Dabbs." A week later, Dabbs, persistent, stopped in again at the Campbell home. One of the girls answered the knock, saw Dabbs, and shouted, "Mama, Coach Brylcreem is here." Down-to-earth and friendly, Dabbs made a quick connection with the family—even today, he can quickly name all ten of Earl Campbell's siblings, in birth order. "Ken Dabbs was the sort of coach that if he were with you in your living room and you went off into the kitchen to fix something up, he went into the kitchen with you," says Elmo Wright. "He didn't do this because the man was uninformed about etiquette. He did this because Dabbs was Dabbs." He was, in other words, genuinely interested in the people with whom he was dealing. "If I sold myself and they believed in me—I already had the University of Texas by my name," Dabbs told me. "You sell yourself not only to the parents, but to the coaches, the superintendent, the principals"—anyone, in short, the player might turn to for advice.

He flattered, calling Ann Campbell one of the best cooks in America. And he was persistent, making himself a fixture around Tyler. During one stretch, Dabbs spent seventeen nights in Room 164 at the Ramada Inn, paying a dozen dollars a night for the pleasure. "Coach didn't want me to leave till I got him," Dabbs remembered. "You don't get too many of that size, that speed, that power, that grace, that character." Sometimes, because collegiate recruiting rules allowed only a certain number of visits to a player's home, he would meet Earl Campbell in a room on the second floor of the Bell home, where Earl's sister, Evelyn, was a maid. Young Henry Bell, who was a student at Robert E. Lee and a member of the school's Rebel Guard and is today the genial chief operating officer of the Tyler Chamber of Commerce, remembers coming home from Lee High School and no family member greeting him at all—"Did anybody know I was home?"—and seeing a strange forty-something man in the room painted all burnt orange. He said to Evelyn, "There's a man in there." "Oh, that's Coach Dabbs."

(Many decades later, just before Dabbs underwent radiation treatment for prostate cancer, he got a call from an East Texas number. "We were watching television around eight o'clock and this number comes up, a 903 number, and my wife said, 'Who is that?' And I said, 'If I didn't know better, I'd say that's Earl Campbell's high school phone number.' And then I hear on the phone: 'Coach D, this is your eighty-five-year-old girlfriend, Ann Campbell.' And she says, 'I talked to Earl today, and he told me you're having some health issues. Tell Miss Marguerite'"—Dabbs's wife—"'you have nothing to worry about, because I'm praying for you morning, noon, and night to the good Lord, and he's going to take care of you.' I got misty-eyed crying.")

Even as Dabbs got close to the Campbell family, a kind of secondary recruiting effort developed as universities interested in Earl deployed African American coaches to mine whatever connections they might have. Royal summoned Bill Lyons, a twenty-five-year-old black former UT basketball player and native of Tyler who had shown himself adept at straddling two very different worlds—cultivating powerful patrons (including Frank Erwin and Barbara Jordan) and calling on his ties in African American communities far and wide to convince ambivalent young black men to attend the University of Texas. A few years earlier, for instance, he was dispatched to San Antonio to convince Julius Whittier and his father, a medical doctor who knew Lyons's family, to attend UT.

Now Royal directed him to the Campbell family. "Help me sell the program," Lyons says Royal told him in the fall of 1973. "We got to have someone tell our story." Hair parted, dressed in a navy blue jacket with a Longhorns lapel over a V-neck sweater and button-down shirt, Lyons at age seventy still looks charming, as if he is preparing to have his ninth-grade school picture taken.

Even as Lyons called on family ties to steer Ann Campbell to Texas—his father's mother knew the Campbells—he deliberately went about examining which of the wealthy white families that Ann Campbell worked for had UT connections, "I said, 'Let's see who Mrs. Campbell knows,'" he recalls, and deputized them to encourage the Campbell family to pick Texas.

But it was Darrell Royal who was the closer, like the queen played from the back row late in a chess match. And so, a couple of days after Texas beat Nebraska on New Year's Day in 1974, Dabbs and Royal set out from Dallas on frozen I-20. It would be the head coach's first meeting with the coveted recruit, and the pair hoped it would clinch the deal, as it had for countless other young men, most of them white, around Texas.

Royal had always been a three-yards-and-a-cloud-of-dust operator, favoring a bruising, grinding running game to an aerial assault.

"When you pass," he liked to say, "three things can happen—and two of them are bad." He "scorned passing because it was art, not muscle," the journalist Jan Reid once wrote in profile of the coach in *Texas Monthly*. "It introduced randomness to the game. The rushing game, on the other hand, forced one-on-one confrontations, strength versus strength. By running the football, you not only defeated people, you established your physical dominance. The victims remembered. And word got around." No one could better deliver that message, Darrell Royal had concluded, than Earl Campbell.

With Dabbs at the wheel, they made their way carefully to Tyler, passing no fewer than a half-dozen tractor-trailers that had skidded off the road. Finally, they swung off on US 69 and stopped at a supermarket on the outskirts of Tyler. They picked up groceries so that Ann Campbell could make everyone a steak dinner; they thought she'd like to show them hospitality, but they didn't want her to have to shell out for food. Back on the road, they took a left at the old Tyler Pipe Company onto the blacktop of County Road 492 and, hard by an auto salvage lot, drove up to the Campbell place. When Ann Campbell apologized for the state of her house, Royal gently waved it off: "Mrs. Campbell," he told her, "I grew up in a house not near as nice as yours." The comment immediately relaxed her. But Earl Campbell appeared aloof. Dabbs was accustomed to a warm reception—he was on genuinely good terms with the Campbells—but this time, with Royal on hand, something felt awkward, especially with the young man they had come to court.

Given UT's history of segregation and the recent newspaper series about alienated black Longhorn athletes, Dabbs had a sense of what was wrong. It didn't help that nearly four years earlier, the Associated Press had reported that at a meeting of coaches in Washington, DC, Royal told a group of black coaches that "the black coach has not reached the point where his coaching is as scientific as it is in the major colleges." The meeting never actually took place, and even if it had, Royal was in Austin that night accepting an award from Lady Bird Johnson. "Such thoughts are not in my heart and

I could not have made those statements," he said after the article appeared, in a University of Texas news release. "The whole thing is a vicious invention." The wire service ran a retraction, but the episode, fairly or not, cemented the feeling that Royal and his program were hostile to African Americans. "Every black athlete that Royal has attempted to recruit since 1970," the journalist Gary Cartwright reported in 1974, the year Darrell Royal and Ken Dabbs showed up at the Campbell family home, "has heard the story (though not the retraction), and most of them have received laminated copies of it, courtesy of rival recruiters." Royal considered suing for libel, but decided to let it drop—a decision he forever regretted.

It was in this atmosphere that the relationship between Earl Campbell, then all of eighteen years old, and Darrell Royal began frostily.

"I understand you don't like black people," Campbell finally told the famous coach.

Royal was stricken, but composed. "No, Earl, that's wrong," he said. The coach told Earl and his mother that he wasn't going to talk about what other people had said about him, but that he would tell them anything they wanted to know about his own thoughts and feelings and about the University of Texas. "I asked simply that they not let other people taint their impressions of me," he once told the journalist Sam Blair. "They seemed to like that attitude."

Earl Campbell told him that his dream was to be able to buy a new house for his mother someday—and Coach Royal told him and Ann Campbell about his own mother's early death, how his grandmother looked after him when he returned to Hollis as a fifteen-year-old, and how he always regretted that she died before he had grown up and was able to help her.

A relationship that had started off chilly began to warm.

The coach went on the offensive. He told Earl that even though his abilities were impressive, he would have to prove himself to earn playing time.

And then, in a savvy move, he addressed the "inducements" that he suspected were being offered to Campbell. These were the early days of under-the-table "scholarships": only a couple of years later, Texas A&M boosters gave Eric Dickerson, a Texas running back from Sealy, a Pontiac Trans Am, which he drove to Dallas to accept an offer to attend SMU—to the chagrin of the A&M supporters. The seedy recruiting hijinks of his competitors wearied Royal, who claimed to run a clean program, and they eventually played a role in his decision to retire from coaching. (Unbeknown to him, his underlings were making efforts of their own. The UT recruiters had one rule, Lyons said—don't tell Darrell Royal about any untoward activities, thus preserving his plausible deniability.)

In a sense, Royal outmaneuvered Campbell. Just as the player had tried to confront him at the beginning of their meeting, Royal now tried to call him out on the possibility that he would be tempted by inducements. "Earl, if this is a factor, and that is what you want, please don't string me along," he told Campbell. "Some way or another, let me know you're not interested in us if you're going to go for that kind of deal."

Now it was Campbell's opportunity to show his faithfulness to the civil rights struggle, and he framed it in a strikingly self-aware way: "Coach," he told Royal, offering a line similar to the one with which he had rejected bribes, "my people were bought and sold when they didn't have a choice. Nobody is going to buy Earl."

That might have been the decisive moment in the recruiting battle to land Earl Campbell, but Royal still had to convince Ann Campbell. "Mrs. Campbell," Royal told her, "we are here to tell you that we are offering Earl a good place to earn an education and the opportunity to make the Texas football team." The emphasis on education, and her fast affinity for Royal, clinched the deal for Ann Campbell. "We're coming to Texas," she told Royal and Dabbs. In the end, the coach and his lieutenant ended up staying two hours. "The atmosphere was cold when we came in," said Dabbs, "but extremely warm when we left."

Privately, however, Earl continued to be dogged by an indecisiveness he rarely exhibited on the field. "He stopped me in the hall one day in school," Van Alstine, the assistant coach at John Tyler

High, remembered. "'What do you think I should do?' 'Earl, you're
going to have to make up your own mind,'" Van Alstine told him.
"'But if it was me, I'd go to UT because you will get an education,
and Darrell Royal will see to that.'" Still, weeks later, just as it appeared Campbell was a lock to go to Texas, Dabbs learned that he
had taken a trip to Norman to meet with the Sooners:

I thought it was over. I knew if they picked him up, they
had to have him back by noon on Saturday [because of
NCAA rules]. About eleven or eleven thirty, a single-
engine red-and-white plane lands. He gets off it. He's
carrying—he doesn't like me telling about it—he was carrying pictures of the [famed Oklahoma football players]
Selmon brothers and Joe Washington. He had an Oklahoma shirt on. I picked him up—he didn't have a way home.
I'd been there three hours, I think. Well—he won't talk.
He just answers questions: "Fine." "No." "Hm-hm."

And I say: "I'll come out and see you in the morning at
church." "No." He was totally confused and didn't want
to talk. Well, I went back to the Ramada that Sunday
night, I sat there, I sat there, I sat there. I was frustrated.
I didn't know what to do. I guess it was about five or five
thirty that afternoon I said to hell with it. I got in the car
and drove out there.

She was in the back room on the old couch, in bed, with
a red handkerchief.

And Earl came in, and I started all over again like it was
the first day.

About that time the phone rang.

And he goes up over there to pick it up. "Yessir.' 'Yessir.'
'Yessir.'

"Mama, this is Barry Switzer on the phone. He wants
to know if he can come by tomorrow night and visit with
you."

And she raised up out of that bed just like the good Lord

raised her up, and she said: "Earl Christian Campbell, we ain't lost one thing in the state of Oklahoma. And you know good and well you're going to school with Coach Dabbs at the University of Texas.'

And he just turned around and said: "Coach Switzer, I'm going to the University of Texas."

It appeared to be a victory, but Campbell, at least the way he tells the story, remained unsure through the eve of signing day. He decided to do as he had been taught by his parents whenever he had a dilemma—he prayed: "God, if it's your will that I should attend the University of Texas, then I'll get up during the night to pee. If not, if I sleep through the night, then I'll know your choice for me will be the University of Oklahoma." That night in March 1974, Dabbs and Royal returned to Tyler, bunking down at the Ramada where Dabbs had virtually camped out through the fall. After a morning coffee, they headed over to the Campbell place. There, Campbell could be found, quiet and calm, on the family's sole couch—the lion in repose. Here was a great man, it seemed, judging by all the people pressed into the house—and yet he was only eighteen. He was shy about the attention he was getting from these adults, pleasantly smiling now and then as the Reverend J. H. Williams of the Hopewell Valley Baptist Church No. 1, or the bank president, Henry Bell, and his wife, Nell, presented a hand to shake. There was hardly room for Earl's many siblings, all of whom were on hand, all of whom had come back to pay witness to the moment when their family's trajectory promised to shift. Campbell said he mostly couldn't wait to put his shoulder pads on again, to prove to the University of Texas that he was worthy of their commitment. "I liked what I saw, what I heard," he said of Texas. "The campus looked beautiful, and the people were friendly. They offered to help me get my education. Texas did not buy me. Blacks are through selling themselves, or at least I'm not going to sell myself. Texas offered me everything legal, and there was none of this stupid talk of cars and money."

The reverend made an invocation. Darrell Royal praised his star recruit and compared him, of course, to Roosevelt Leaks—a Longhorn running back who had just rushed for 1,415 yard in his sophomore season and had finished third in the Heisman balloting—one of the few other black players on the team. "He will get a fair chance to prove himself. Everyone who starts for me has to prove they are worthy," Royal announced. "But in view of personal appraisal, sure, Earl has the ability to play his first year." Royal handed Campbell his pen, and Earl cracked a small grin and raised his hand to flash the "Hook 'Em Horns" sign, an index finger and pinkie finger raised upward. He was a little afraid of leaving home—and, especially, of leaving his mother. Ann Campbell was asked to say a few words on the occasion. She said, in her loving, proud, and stern way: "Here at home there has been a wonderful relationship between mother and son, and I know that wherever Earl goes, he will not give anybody any trouble."

There were still a few wrinkles left to iron out. When it appeared as if Campbell might fail a class at John Tyler—and thus fail to qualify for UT—Lyons made a deal with the teacher: UT would offer a full scholarship to another student in the class if she would pass Campbell.

"She was conciliatory in her grading," he said.

A few months later, in July, with Earl Campbell delivered, Royal arranged for Lyons to be hired full-time, as an assistant athletic director, even as he was finishing up at the University of Texas Law School. UT paid Lyons $25,000, more than the school's head baseball coach earned. A jotted note by one of UT's public relations specialists, charged with putting together a press release announcing the hire, reveals one of Lyons's mantras that proved helpful as he faced pushback from black families—he was called an Uncle Tom, he said—for working for the university.

"When people ask him about black and white," says the note, "tell only color that matters is orange."

When Earl Campbell unfolded himself from young Henry Bell's

Chevy coupe after the four-hour drive from Tyler to Austin in August 1974, all his belongings fit into the supermarket bags he used as luggage. "When we first moved into dorms, some guys might take a half a day to get their stuff in their rooms," Rick Ingraham, who would be a key lead blocker for Campbell at Texas, told me. "Earl had two pairs of jeans, a couple pair of underwear, and some T-shirts—and that was it." The NCAA gave him $15 a month to pay for laundry. Reuna, putting herself through Tyler Junior College as a legal secretary, occasionally sent him a few dollars in her daily letter. He was so poor compared with his classmates—as the flagship state university, UT was the school of choice for well-to-do Texans—that he once walked into First City Bank to ask for a ten-dollar loan. "When school started, I was amazed at that many people," Campbell told the university alumni magazine years later. "Where I came from, we didn't have a thermostat on the wall where you could walk over and turn it to 60 and it'd get cold. I had my own bed. I had eaten good food before but not on a constant, everyday basis. I'd hear some of the guys whining about staying in Jester"—a dorm so massive it was said to have its own zip code—"but to me, it was Cadillac style."

He had declared the campus beautiful after a UT booster flew him to Austin for an earlier campus visit during his recruitment—his first plane ride. He was so nervous that he asked Dabbs for some of his Red Man chewing tobacco. Now he would learn that there were, in a sense, two Austins: the dreamy, blues-playing capital of Texas, the center of the counterculture in the Lone Star State, and the Austin of officialdom and tradition, whose emblems were the pink granite dome of the state Capitol and the Tower, the administrative headquarters of the University of Texas.

For all its progressivism, Austin had (and continues to have) its own race problems. Covenants on the books since the early 1900s prevented African Americans, Latinos, and Jews from buying homes in well-to-do neighborhoods. In the early 1960s, a new city-owned power plant went online right in the middle of the town's Mexican American neighborhood. When Tommy Wyatt, the publisher of *the Villager*, a weekly, black East Austin newspaper, moved to town in 1962, he could go to the Scarborough's department store downtown, but—because he was black—he couldn't try on a hat before buying it. "If it touched your head," he told the *Austin American-Statesman*, "you bought it whether you liked it or not." And a gentleman's agreement that neatly skirted the Voting Rights Act held that powerful business leaders would decide which African American and which Latino won the unofficially designated minority city council seats. (That agreement remained in place until 2014.)

Through the late 1960s, Don Weedon, owner of the Conoco Station at 34th and Guadalupe, just off campus, was known for refusing service to or insulting African Americans or people he deemed hippies. Weedon, thin and bow-tied, had played football for UT in the 1940s and was among a coterie of boosters for the program—Royal and his assistants often repaired to the filling station after practices for a few beers.

One Saturday night, in late April 1968, only a few weeks after the Reverend Martin Luther King Jr. had been assassinated, Weedon settled onto a bar stool at the Lemon Tree Club to watch a televised championship bout pitting the white boxer Jerry Quarry against the black boxer Jimmy Ellis. He started asking other bar goers whether they would like to place a bet on "the nigger"; he was willing to back the white fighter. He then began to direct his comments toward a black UT undergrad named Leo Northington Jr. Northington had just finished playing a set with an otherwise all-white band at the club. "Where you from, boy?" he kept asking Northington while making loud remarks about "dirty niggers." Northington ignored him. Weedon, in a rage now, attacked. Northington flattened him. "He looked surprised after getting hit," Northington said. "He looked like he didn't expect me to retaliate . . . Like he expected me to say, 'Please Mr. Weedon, don't hit me no more.'"

By that Friday, the Student Nonviolent Coordinating Committee and Students for a Democratic Society had organized a boycott of Weedon's station. They handed out flyers: "We can no longer afford to see black people mistreated by honkies without retaliation."

In the early afternoon, more than 130 people gathered, aiming to prevent cars from turning into the gas station. The police showed up; thirty-three people were arrested. The local alternative paper, the *Rag*, declared that Weedon, a friend of Royal's and a devoted Longhorn, "is a racist (as well as an all-around bigot who has attacked persons wearing beards)."

It was a clash of two Austins, which were often divided generationally and culturally over issues of race and war. By the early 1970s, the vibe emanating from the university campus was decidedly tie-dye and granola. The *LA Free Press* described Austin as a "hippie Palm Springs," and it grew famous as the birthplace of the cosmic cowboys, country-and-western fans who embraced the counterculture. Nothing Strikes Back was a black-light ice cream joint, open every day except for John Lennon's birthday. At the Octopus Garden you could get cold fruit juices and "cosmic munchies." The Delta Diner served up healthy helpings of vegetarian cuisine; "bring yer plate, bowls, glass & implements of destruction," read an ad. The whole area around the campus had a brown-rice feel. The head shop Maharani sold meditation posters, wedding rings, and shampoos, and at the Whole Earth Provision Company you could get tent supplies and hiking equipment. On game days in the parking lot of Mother Earth, a club not far from campus, you could barter football tickets for weed. Saturday nights could be spent listening to Willie Nelson—for $3 in advance or $4 at the gate.

Tom Swinnea, who was a teenager from a deeply Baptist suburb of Dallas when he was admitted to UT in 1972, remembered his older brother telling him: "You will not understand Austin till you see a woman breastfeeding on the Drag." And sure enough, on virtually Swinnea's first day in town, walking along the sun-drenched commercial strip on Guadalupe Street long known as the Drag, on the university's western fringe, he saw, to his astonishment, just such a woman.

That summer of 1974 saw the fifth Austin Gay Pride Parade—needless to say, there weren't gay pride parades in Tyler. You could catch the psychedelic rocker Roky Erickson playing with the roots rocker Doug Sahm, or Townes Van Zandt, or the young bluesmen Jimmie and Stevie Ray Vaughan. Van Morrison and Bruce Springsteen played at the Armadillo World Headquarters, a former National Guard armory that had been converted into a live music cavern; the ladies' room had a mural painted by Royal's late daughter, Marian. If you missed Sahm at the Armadillo, you could catch him and Clifton Chenier at the Soap Creek Saloon. Just off campus, the Bread and Roses School held courses on socialism: "We need more emphasis on local issues," a school organizer announced in the *Rag*. "How banks control our city, who develops Austin and for what, utilities and how people can control them, what can be done about sexism and racism in our public schools, etc." Seminars included "Marxist Theories of Women's Oppression" and "Vietnamese Liberation Day Sing Out!" The Bertolt Brecht Memorial Guerrilla Theatre Troupe performed on the UT campus in January 1975—proceeds went to medical supplies for the Vietnamese. That year, university students helped elect one of the most liberal city councils in Austin's history: the first Latino member; an African American; three women, including one who campaigned on a "Think Trees" slogan; and a Jewish mayor in his thirties. Molly Ivins said it "looked like an affirmative action program gone berserk."

The Austin scene was a counterpoint to the sort of buttoned-down discipline that Royal required on the gridiron. Touring the Armadillo one night in 1970 with James Toback, the *Harper's* journalist, the writer Bud Shrake, an investor in the club and a friend of Royal's, explained, "The whole approach they're into now is antipodal to football: to its competitiveness, its strict regulations, and its violence. They're trying to be gentle, communal, passive. They're after a more *authentic* experience." Royal, in his way, tried to bridge countercultural and football values. Among his closest friends was Willie Nelson—he once described himself as a "kicked-in-the-head Willie Nelson fan." He liked to hang out with and host house parties for what he called "pickers"—country-and-western singer-songwriters, among them Johnny Rodriguez, Waylon Jennings, Kris Kristofferson, and Billy Joe Shaver. "They've experienced some of the same life I have," Royal once said.

> But my ambitions and goals are opposed to some of my picker friends . . . I envy them that they can have the attitude they do. Listen to the words in this song: "Movin' is the closest thing to bein' free." I can't move to the point where I can't take care of my responsibilities. How does that Kristofferson song go? "Freedom's just another word for nothing left to lose." What they are saying is that they aren't willing to sacrifice their freedom for material things. I'm opposed with some of their lifestyles . . . it's not offensive . . . I just can't live that way.

In the same vein, he had told Toback in 1970 that hippies would "like nothing better than to turn on my football players, get them to quit the game and go over to their side."

> You know why? Because football is the last bastion of traditional American values. It's the last institution where you have rules to obey—in bed at ten, lights out at eleven, breakfast at seven. Hell, it's no *fun* living a Spartan life, but if you want the rewards, the eighty thousand fans cheering for you, the glory, the money, the satisfaction of achievement, you've got to do the hard things first. You think I like everything I have to do? I'd say forty per cent of my job is a pain in the ass. But in order to get the sixty per cent, the joy, the sense of fulfillment, I've got to put myself through the mill. That's the kind of thinking the hippies are trying to pull us away from. They're promising one hundred per cent for nothing. But in the end the only thing nothing will get you is nothing.

In a sense, Royal, the colossus of the city, bestrode progressive Austin and official Austin. And despite his dig at hippies, he had the whole city—much of the black and Latino East Side, the pols at the Capitol, working-class grannies who had never foot on campus, and, yes, long-haired students—cheering for Longhorn football.

During this period, the Capitol and the university, the city's two touchstone institutions, were still slow-walking the implementation of US Supreme Court decisions that were one or two decades old. In 1964, the Court found the state was violating the one-person-one-vote principle—an electoral district in Dallas had a population of 951,527, while an adjacent rural one had 216,371 people—and ordered a redrawing of districts by the state. And so, two years later, in 1966, three African Americans, one of them the famously eloquent, deeply moral Barbara Jordan, became the first black members in the Texas Legislature since 1896. Further reforms ahead of the 1972 election led to changes en masse—at least 70 of the 150 Texas House members were women or people of color, the most diverse freshman class in the history of the legislative body. Mickey Leland, a brilliant, politically skilled antipoverty activist from Houston, shook up the Capitol with his shoulder bags and African garb; he was a "badass—he was the baddest son-of-bitch who ever set forth on the earth," said Ron Wilson, a classmate and friend of Campbell's at UT who went to work for Leland.

The University of Texas had changed in the wake of the *Brown* decision, but only reluctantly. As late as 1971, three years before Campbell arrived, UT's entering law school class was absolutely devoid of African Americans. "We have found continued lip-service to non-existent action on the part of the administration," John L. Warfield, chair of the university's newly established African and Afro-American Research Center, confided in October 1973 to state representative Senfronia Thompson, a Democrat from Houston: "The failure to aggressively recruit and admit Black students is the most visible failure; however, the micro-presence of Black faculty . . . is a criminal offense in itself. Likewise the university's failure to demonstrate any positive administrative intent regarding Black curriculum has made what might become an outstanding academic achievement in African and Afro-American affairs a mediocre referral agency of questionable tokenistic value." That year, 1973, out of 1,600 faculty members at the university, only 13 were African American—and they made, on average, less money than similarly ranked white counterparts.

When Earl Campbell arrived on campus in the fall of 1974, 12 percent of the state's population was black—but at the University of Texas there were only 600 black students out of 41,000 (1.5 percent of the total). Out of more than 1,500 students at UT's law school, only 10 were black. "Sometimes I get the feeling I could go all day without seeing another black face," one student told the *Daily Texan* in 1972. The previous year, Ernest White, a black freshman accounting major, told *Daily Texan* reporters for a story titled "Social Life Called Deficient; UT Blacks Afforded Little Mixing" that he frequently felt "out of place, like when you walk up to someone, and he acts like you're not there." "Sometimes you get the feeling you're naked," another student said. Gary Bledsoe, a law student who would later lead the Texas chapter of the NAACP, reported in 1975 that a bit of graffiti in one restroom was changed from "niggers don't graduate from UT law school in three years" to "niggers don't graduate from UT law school at all," and then to "we don't want niggers at UT law school."

The UT regents appeared to have little interest in the isolation of black students. In 1974, Allan Shivers, the former governor who had appointed the regents during their resistance to the *Brown* ruling and who now chaired the board, led his fellow regents to approve $400,000 over four years for scholarship funding, ostensibly to increase diversity at the university; by comparison, they also allotted $500,000 to resurface the freshman football field with synthetic turf. That fall, in a struggle over power at the university, the chancellor ousted the UT president, a botanist who had tried to promote the recruitment of minorities to the faculty, student body, and staff. The following year, in the spring of 1975, UT's new president, Lorene Rogers, who had been scolded in the school newspaper for pronouncing the word "Negro" as "Nig-rah," rebuked a group called United Students Against Racism at Texas over its demands regarding the treatment of minorities on campus. The group had asked for the elimination of standardized admissions tests; the creation of a division of minority affairs; departmental status for the Afro-American and Mexican-American Studies programs; funding for black and Chicano newspapers; and the establishment of a grievance committee to hear complaints of racist practices by the faculty and administration. "You convinced us so well to integrate," Rogers responded, "and now you want to separate." First they would ask for a department, she told the students, then they would want a school—and finally they would want the entire university.

Two decades after the *Brown* decision, the university was dragging its feet so much that some African Americans not even born in 1954 decided to go to UT specifically to hasten the integration of the university. "Coming to UT was a sort of pioneering thing," Stephanie Friggin, a sophomore from Wichita Falls, told a reporter in 1975. "You came and then other blacks followed. I'm getting the best education in the South and may as well get used to prejudice now and learn to cope and adapt quickly here." Michael Hurd, who entered UT as a twenty-seven-year-old US Air Force veteran in 1976—Earl Campbell's junior year—and who had bunked with whites while serving in Vietnam, said it "felt funky walking across campus" as an African American. Students who were friendly within the classroom wanted little to do with him outside it, he said. In a poignant essay, Erna Smith, then an undergraduate interning at the *Austin American-Statesman*, wrote that being black at UT meant "hoping the next class will have at least one other black person"; "trying to keep a straight face when the classroom discussion turns to American blacks and your white classmates automatically turn to you for expert testimony"; "feeling hollow inside after passing a crowd of whites and overhearing several off-hand racial slurs"; "trying to keep your temper when a well-meaning instructor sympathetically asks if you're a 'slow learner'"; "hoping your white roommate's parents won't object or create a scene if he or she rooms with a black"; "walking alone across the campus at night and trying not to look suspicious." "Peer counseling," she wrote sardonically, "is one black student telling another who are the 'redneck' professors."

More than four decades later, those four years are seared in Smith's mind. Now teaching courses in journalism and social justice at UT, she opted to meet me at a crowded café called Thunderbird on the East Side of town—a mile or so on the other side of the interstate from campus. Once the area was dominated by African Americans and Latinos, but today, at this café, at the epicenter of gentrification, she is the only black person around. She said that in the mid-1970s, at the time Earl Campbell was wearing UT's burnt orange jersey, students had to take a swimming test to show that they could tread water for five minutes. "It was my only class that was predominantly black," she said ruefully. "I'll never forget all the kids hanging by the side of the pool." A freshman-year roommate told Smith that university administrators had asked whether she was willing to room with a black woman—as late as 1972, UT kept dorms segregated by asking future residents to indicate their race on housing contracts. "One black senior spoke of being assigned to live with a black freshman," Goldstone reports in *Integrating the 40 Acres*. "'We have nothing in common,' the woman said, 'except our both being Negroes.'" The pressures of being on a predominantly white campus manifested themselves in other ways. Erna Smith's friend Thomas Collier, an African American student, was stopped several times by campus police because he had a fancy bike. And if more than three African Americans sat outside on the steps of Jester—the dorm that also housed Earl Campbell—the campus police would start swarming around until the students waved their IDs as they continued talking. "It took all my confidence," Smith said. "It was only getting out of there and getting away from it that I realized I could achieve. I thought I was a second-rate person."

She offered a story about a ceremony to celebrate the students who made the dean's list. Her parents came in from the country, and Norris Davis, the dean of the School of Communications, greeted them. "He didn't know what to say to my parents. He was trying to be friendly, but all he could say was: 'There are a lot of Smiths in the phone book.' I remember my father smiled and said, 'A lot of Davises, too.'" After Davis moved on to greet other guests, Smith's father, Junious, a retired military colonel, turned to Erna: "I don't want to hear your complaining again. You should feel sorry for them. They're scared." "He thought these people were so inferior—'Why are you bothering to be upset?'"

Earl Campbell had been an object of fascination ever since appearing on campus—especially to his fellow incoming UT recruits. They had read about him in *Dave Campbell's Texas Football* magazine or heard from cousins or friends who had squared off against him. "Anybody who played football knew of Earl Campbell," his former teammate Randy McEachern, an undersized quarterback from Houston, told me. McEachern said the hardest hit he ever took was from Earl Campbell. One day in practice, he handed off to him and failed to get out of the way. A defensive lineman on those Longhorn teams remembered that Campbell's body seemed "chiseled from stone." Another teammate recalled his relentless perfectionism, the way he ran into the end zone on every play in practice. Heading into Campbell's freshman year, Royal tried to tamp down expectations. "He's got a lot of tools to work with and when he gets pointed in the right direction, he's pointed with authority," Royal said. Later, he admitted that Campbell was the only player he had coached who might have gone straight to the pros from high school.

On the practice field, said McEachern, coaches had to work with Campbell and other players on certain timing issues. Royal ran the wishbone, a highly choreographed affair that he and his offensive coordinator had dreamt up in the late 1960s to take advantage of a backfield stacked with talent. The formation called for three runners to line up in a V in the backfield, thus giving the quarterback a number of handoff options and leaving defenses befuddled about which person to tackle. The story goes that over breakfast with his quarterbacks in August 1968 at the varsity cafeteria, Royal used salt shakers, ketchup bottles, a sugar bowl, and water glasses to explain how the wishbone would work—and the team soon rattled off thirty straight victories. The creation of the wishbone, Willie Morris observed, was "a discovery more pleasing to some Longhorns than the vaccine against cholera."

"When you get to college, there's a little more detail about reading defenses and a lot of footwork that was not practiced in high school," said McEachern. But, he added, "as far as teaching [Campbell] to run, they didn't have to do anything."

Earl Campbell might have remained isolated and, like many others before and after him, ended up as a highly touted recruit who flamed out amid the buffeting winds of the University of Texas campus. In Campbell's first months in Austin, dislocated geographically and isolated racially, he was decidedly homesick. Royal observed that Campbell, like a Muslim genuflecting toward Mecca, "would sit on the curb and face in the direction of Tyler." Only a few years earlier, Julius Whittier, the first UT black varsity player, had reported being ostracized on campus, and Gary Bledsoe, in his brief time on the team as a walk-on, had seen white teammates grow suddenly silent when he entered the locker room. Unbeknown to Campbell, Marty Akins, the starting quarterback during his freshman and sophomore years, was prone to writing verse with unironic titles such as "Our Lovely Dixie"—a copy of which is in the archive of the Darrell Royal Papers at UT:

> Put that ole gray suit on your smooth, Southern body,
> Then march out over your lovely Dixie to war.
> Now fight for the land that you've known from a child,
> Fight for the Confederate stars and stripes and your
> neighbors too.

The poem goes downhill from there.

But everyone loves a winner, and Campbell gained his footing, his identity, and wide admiration on the football field partly because of an unhappy injury suffered by one of the few African American forerunners on the squad. Coming into his freshman year, Campbell expected to defer to Roosevelt Leaks, the record-setting, widely-hailed senior. Teammate Lonnie Bennett said in 1973, "[Leaks] has provided an image of a black superstar for us. It may not help us in recruiting today, but kids are growing up who now idolize him. In five years it will make a big difference. That's what he's done for blacks here." Campbell, despite his reputation, was still just settling into campus that fall—subjected to standard freshman hazing, he had to sing in the dining hall and shine the shoes of upperclassmen. On a questionnaire distributed to the players in the fall of 1974 by the university's sports information department, Campbell answered a prompt about "Plans after college" with a single phrase: "Working on our farm." "He was very modest, very quiet, didn't make a big splash—he did all his work on the field," McEachern said.

Leaks was injured in spring drills when a player's helmet hit his knee, and he remained hobbled as the season got underway. Now he was drafted to help Campbell adapt to the college game. "During practice I was like a coach to him," Leaks once said. "I'd show him the little things. I wasn't quite ready to play again. Earl was better than me, no question about it. He was bigger and faster, and he had that natural instinct." Campbell ended up taking the lion's share of the carries that season—and lived up to the hype, averaging 5.7 yards per rush and becoming the first UT freshman to start his first six varsity games. He helped out on special teams, too, just as he had done in high school. Against Arkansas, introducing himself to a national television audience, he lined up against the noseguard and stormed through the middle of the line to block a punt for a score. "That shows how smart coaches are. The first time he tries to block a punt he got one, and we quit doing it," Royal said. "You can win a game with a blocked punt. We chose to win the easy way, by running Earl 30 times." Sure enough, Campbell also went for 109 yards on eight carries in that Arkansas game, including one sixty-eight-yarder through a hole on the right side that included the sort of stuff-your-face-in-the-turf stiff-arm that he had patented in high school.

In an upset of eighth-ranked Texas A&M that season—UT won 32-3—Campbell ran for 130 yards on twenty-eight carries, including hauling a piggybacking defender with him for much of a twenty-six-yard gain. Aggie linebacker Ed Simonini held such deep antipathy toward the University of Texas Longhorns and yet such reverence for their star running back that he shook hands only with Earl Campbell. "He's the only one I think is a man," he explained, "coaches included."

Campbell cut another figure in private, with his teammates. In the locker room of Memorial Stadium following the upset of A&M, as Royal finished a postgame talk, Earl asked whether he could say something. "He got up on a bench and asked for silence," Robert Butler, a defensive back, told a reporter in 1975. "I thought, 'Here comes a rah-rah, gung-ho speech.' He suddenly struck a silly pose and yelled, 'Ain't I cute? Ain't I cute?' It broke everyone up."

In Campbell's sophomore year, he bullied his way to 1,118 yards and 13 touchdowns. He was now a black folk hero, fast becoming beloved on a mostly white campus. An Austin band had put together a song in praise of Ann Campbell—"Lord Don't Let It Rain on Mrs. Campbell's Roses"—and limericks were written in Earl's honor:

There once was a Texan named Campbell,
The monster can certainly amble;
They point to the goal,
And open a hole,
And he's off on a 60-yard ramble.

In the team's season-ending 38-21 Astro-Bluebonnet Bowl win over Colorado, he was picked as the game's outstanding offensive player. Presented with the award, he said, in his genuine, golly-gee-willikers way: "I would like to put in a vote for Ann Campbell."

Black students had turned their backs on the Longhorns. At basketball games in the early 1970s, they chanted, "More black students, more black students" every time an African American made a free throw. And when an integrated UCLA football team visited in 1970, Gary Bledsoe remembered cheering for them over the Horns. But now, in the late period of Royal's reign, they voiced full-throated approval. "He was special," said Bledsoe. "We were rooting for Earl because he was a symbol." Erna Smith remembered that people back home would cut to the chase when welcoming her back from UT: "I'm so proud of you—but baby, have you met Earl?"

The experience of seeing Earl Campbell, an African American man, run roughshod over opponents in the recently desegregated Southwest Conference, was therapeutic. "Earl was like a buffalo out there. It was like thunder, the night train was coming—you could see it in their eyes," Erna Smith said. "He was running downhill for all of us—and it was lovely." The black sociology professor John Sibley Butler, who mentored Campbell, put it similarly: "Earl didn't come here to say, 'I'm a minority.' Earl came here to say, 'I'm going to put my foot in your damn face and run over you.'"

"Earl was an activist, but not that kind of activist," said Ron Wilson in a conversation at the Million Air Club, a high-end private hangar at Houston's Hobby Airport. He was wearing blue jeans and white sneakers and a navy University of Texas shirt, and picked at a small bag of pretzels. As a person, he remembered, his former classmate was quiet. "But when he got the football, he was a monster. I guess that's kind of an activism. Earl exhibited who he was by the way he entered the field, the way he carried the ball, the way he got up. Earl was Earl. He was a monster. Earl wasn't this"—he broke off here—"fuck you, man, fuck you." He directed this at no one in particular, more as emotional venting. And he started, suddenly, to cry as he recalled the catharsis he felt, as a black man, while watching Campbell run: "Shit, whew. They would take these films of Earl, they'd show him running, catching the ball. The way he'd run, run over people, man, just flatten them. And you'd go, 'Fuck you, motherfucker.' You hit those motherfuckers the way he does, run over the son of a bitch, and give the ball to the referee after he finishes. That to me was the ultimate—what's the right word?—the ultimate sacrifice for his people and for him."

White fans, too, were pleased to root for a winner, no matter his color. Only a few years earlier, many of the older white alums at Memorial Stadium hadn't been able to countenance the idea of a black Longhorn. But white fans, the sports sociologist Erin Tarver has observed, "are content to identify with black football players for as long as they are useful on the field, to imaginatively project themselves into the physical power and hypermasculinity that (fans imagine) they embody." Texans were not sending in the sort of hateful letters they had posted only a decade earlier, when the regents had mulled over integrating the football team. (They still were happy to indulge in racist cheers. Through at least the mid-1970s, a common cry from the stands during games against Rice went: "What came out of the Chinaman's ass? Rice, rice, rice." And Gary Bledsoe remembered that when UT finally played a black quarterback, in the late 1970s, and the player faltered, the team's rooting section jeered him with the taunt "Go back to Africa.")

For all the self-assuredness of these black athletes on the field, going to class at the University of Texas, especially at the beginning of their undergraduate years, could be frightening. "I don't think anyone convinced Earl or myself coming here to play that we were not going to face any type of discrimination and that that was not going to exist—including from other members of the team," Campbell's teammate and roommate Alfred Jackson said. "Sometimes, you can be shackled down without actual handcuffs on."

Still, Earl Campbell, beloved football player, had a very different UT experience from that of Ron Wilson or Michael Hurd—or probably from that of any other black student on campus, including other Longhorns. "You might hear things about white and black people down here, but I don't see it on this campus," Campbell told a reporter at the outset of his sophomore year. "The players play football like we're all one color, and we try to reach out to each other afterwards. I'm the kind of guy who says 'Come on, take a ride with me,' no matter who it is."

The boosters set him and his twin brothers up with jobs—working, of all places, at Don Weedon's Conoco station, the one that only eight years earlier had been the site of protests after Weedon had used the n-word and challenged a black undergraduate to a fight. But now, with the Longhorns integrated, Weedon's impulse to support the football team was apparently greater than his aversion to African Americans. "I worked on him till black athletes got free gas," Bill Lyons said with a Cheshire grin.

To explain how jarring it felt to enter a classroom for the first time at UT as a young black man from rural Texas, Jackson observed, "If you grew up black you had luggage."

> You had luggage that was real: you grew up poor, you grew up unexposed, you had certain feelings about being black and knowing you were black, and there were discriminatory views about you because of how you were treated in everyday life. That was real luggage. Then you had perceived luggage, too. We perceived and I perceived when I was going to be discriminated against . . . The reason most Anglos have no perception of that, of the internal strength it takes to deal with that, is they've never had to deal with it. My first class was a liberal arts class. Five hundred people in the class. I walked into that class and I was absolutely horrified. First of all, I had never been in a classroom that size, and to be in it with five hundred people that I thought disliked, hated me—I was there, but inside, the feeling was a scared, terrified feeling.

The Longhorns' "brain coach," Lan Hewlett, a former science teacher, once described the added burden athletes faced in the classroom: "If a guy works in a bookstore, he puts in his hours and that's it. But a player on scholarship is always full of anxiety. He is constantly preparing like an actor to perform before thousands of people."

Schoolwork didn't come naturally to Earl Campbell, and his decision to dedicate himself to passing courses at UT was tied up in his on-campus isolation.

I was sitting in front of Gregory Gym all mad, thinking, here I am at this big, old school going into my second year, and I'm kinda like the big hit, you know? But I have no money in my pocket except for 15 bucks a month from the NC-two-A. That was my laundry money. By the time I worked during the summer, tried to save some money, tried to send Mom some money, I didn't have any. I didn't have a car. The girls never really came around because I didn't have anything to offer them. So I tried to position myself to look toward Tyler—whenever I got lonesome I would think about what was going on at home. Out of the blue, this voice said, "Yes, you will get a degree from here." From that day I started working at it, and working at it.

To teachers and classmates, he made an impression as countrified and genuine. A young professor, Betty Fine, who taught Campbell in a 1975 class on speech and communication, remembers being "impressed with his gentleness and his sincerity." For an assignment on how to execute a task, he gave a talk, naturally, on running the football. He had been an indifferent student in high school, but now, recognizing his challenge, and determined not to return to the rose fields back in Tyler, he found himself thinking about college strategically. He began sitting in the front row so his professors would see he was in attendance. And he never missed a class, according to Butler, the sociology professor. "Not only did he never miss a class, he made all his teammates go," Butler said. (After Campbell declined, his senior year, to attend a television special to honor all-Americans, Bob Hope offered to send a jet for him. "I can't," Campbell said. "I have a test.")

In Earl's junior year, it fell to Gary Gallagher, an American history graduate student, to tutor him in a course from the colonial period to Reconstruction. He was a slight white guy who had left his native Colorado as a twenty-two-year-old in January 1973, the temperature thirty-seven below zero, only to drive into Austin and see people play tennis. "Lots of graduate students tutored jocks back then," said Gallagher—though not many were in one-on-one sessions with the university's greatest athlete and the city's most popular person. One evening a week, Gallagher met with Campbell in his undergraduate dorm room. Earl favored cutoffs, and four decades later, Gallagher, who would become a noted Civil War historian, still remembers Campbell's physique with some astonishment. "He told me he never lifted weights, but he was hard—just sculpted. You could have bounced a dime off his thighs."

Gallagher was equally impressed with Campbell's modesty and easy manner: "There was no artifice whatsoever about him. He seemed absolutely comfortable in his own skin." As a student, Campbell struggled with language and writing, Gallagher said. "He talked a lot about how—and he kind of resented it—once they figured out how great he was at John Tyler, all he had to do was show up Friday night and do nothing else, and that put him behind the curve. He knew that football was his way out, and he knew that football was the reason he was never held to account for anything."

The tutor and the pupil chatted about sports, about country music—Gallagher had never really listened to country music—and about recruiting. "I'd never understood the degree to which big-time college athletics was a job," he said. As the semester wound down, Gallagher invited Campbell to his apartment, in married student housing, for a dinner of enchiladas. He had no expectation that his famous pupil would accept.

But Earl said he would make it.

"It was amazing. When word got out Earl was coming, all these little boys from married student housing lined up and watched Earl come up. We had our enchiladas, Earl signed a football for Will, *Earl Campbell #20*"—Gallagher's son, Will, was eight years old. "It was an incredibly generous thing. He didn't rush in and rush out; he ate a bunch of enchiladas and greeted all the little kids."

That was the last time Gallagher saw Campbell off the field. In the end, Gallagher said, Campbell got a hard-won C in the course. "He wrote the essays and took all the exams. When he wrote, he wrote slowly. He did everything slowly. He'd think about stuff. He was a very deliberate, cautious guy."

Royal and Campbell were suddenly close. They had come together over, of all things, music. Under the tutelage of Darrell Royal, Campbell said he went from being a Marvin Gaye fan to a Tanya Tucker fan. At an intimate Willie Nelson concert organized by Royal, Campbell was the only black player who showed up. "It was kind of strange at first," Campbell once remembered. "Willie, he had this big old beard—and I know him well enough now that I can say this—he looked like a tramp. Darrell Royal was trying to tell us that as athletes we needed to be clean-shaven, we needed to do this and that. And we were thinking, 'Man, how in the hell can he tell anyone to be clean-shaven when he's got this hippie with him all the time?'"

For most of his players, Royal was both beloved and unknowable. "Despite its impersonal nature, the relationship between the players and Royal was tied in a multitude of powerful knots," Gary Shaw observed in his 1972 book. "For us, Daddy D was in part the authoritarian father of whom our fear, awe, and respect were ever-present." He continued: "This detachment of Royal's increased his power. He was more unknown, more untouchable, yet still had the final word. The other coaches did nearly all of the individual coaching so we could at least see them sweat a little, but Royal saved his role and words for selective moments which increased their significance." Chachie Owens, a Longhorn fullback in the mid-1960s, told Shaw that he "respected [Royal] as a coach and a judge of athletic ability, but he was totally impersonal. We were so many head of cattle and he was going to milk us for all he could. It was a business proposition and they ought to admit it." James Street, Royal's onetime star quarterback, put it this way: "We sure never went to him for fatherly advice."

Partly, undoubtedly, Campbell's relationship with Royal had to do with fatherlessness: "I lost my mom three years ago," Campbell wrote in a kind of eulogy for Royal in *Sports Illustrated* in 2012. "Now I've lost a father figure." Campbell himself observed the singularity of their relationship: "I'm one of the only players who really got close to him." Maybe that was because he was one of Royal's few black players, and their relationship was built on racial reconciliation. "I just remember people saying, 'Darrell Royal hates blacks. It's a prejudiced school. You're not going to make it,'" Campbell said. "I felt the one person I was going to have most of my dealings with was Darrell Royal. I made up my mind when I was 18 years old, that if he's prejudiced, he's going to have to respect me because I'm going to respect him."

Heading into his junior year, Campbell appeared poised to lead the Longhorns to another national championship for Darrell Royal. His first two years had been fabulous, and he acknowledged that he had come to Texas with a lot of publicity and that "it is a relief to have sort of lived up to it." But then something happened: Horsing around the first day of spring practice in 1975—a few months removed from the Astro-Bluebonnet Bowl—he challenged some teammates to a forty-yard dash. They hadn't yet warmed up and stretched, and halfway through the sprint, just as he got to top gear, he felt the back of his right thigh twinge. A hamstring pull. Normally, such an injury would be treated simply with rest and patience, as well as mild physical therapy. But this was Campbell's first real leg problem, and he was unready for the setback. The injury ended up dooming his season, and with it that of the Longhorns. Ultimately, it would spell the end of Royal's coaching career.

That summer in Tyler, loading trucks in a warehouse for $2.60 an hour, he exercised sparingly and ate poorly. He put on twenty-five pounds. Any time he tried working out his legs, he seemed to reaggravate the problem. Back at school in the fall, the whole thing left him befuddled and disaffected: "I kept reinjuring it. I'd never been hurt like that before, so I didn't know how it was supposed to feel. I'd go out and push myself too soon and hurt it again."

His junior season began inauspiciously. Against Boston College, an underdog, Campbell carried only five times for twenty-three yards. Boston College won in a 14–13 upset. Over the next five games he appeared uncomfortable. During a 208-yard performance against North Texas State, he broke loose for an eighty-three-yard run—but in trying to avoid stretching his ailing leg, he ran the distance with a hobble. Earl Campbell was rarely caught from behind; this time he was tackled on the four-yard line.

Royal tried to put a sunny face on it—"He was running under wraps but he was still outstanding"—but acknowledged that his star player had been hamstrung. "He wasn't the old slashing, quick Earl he's been," Royal said.

The next game, the annual Red River Shootout against Oklahoma, broadcast on national television, was one Royal wanted badly. He had owned the series against his alma mater until the impish, rapscallious Barry Switzer had shown up to coach the Sooners. In his first three seasons, Switzer lost only one game and won two national titles. And he dominated the Longhorns. Royal was often good-natured enough to make light of it. Once, after a loss to Oklahoma, Royal was pressed on his weekly television show about what went wrong. "Darrell, we brought you down here to Texas to beat Oklahoma. Now we have suffered yet another defeat by the Sooners. What do you have to say about that?" The camera zoomed in for a close-up of the coach's face. Softly and earnestly, he said: "I've done a lot of thinking about this situation. And I've turned to that famed scholar Oliver Wendell Holmes, who once said, 'As I look back on the days of my life I appreciated my defeats more than my victories, because I have learned more from my losses.' Well, I've been thinking about those words of that great man and I'd just like to say, 'Screw Oliver Wendell Holmes!'"

But for all the joking, Switzer had gotten under Royal's skin. In many ways, Switzer's success stemmed from his willingness to take risks on players that Royal wouldn't approach—including some black players. (Oklahoma was the first college team in the South or Southwest to integrate.) For his part, Switzer liked to crow about how Royal had become obsolete. In 1975, Switzer told a group of

Oklahoma alumni that the careers of some coaches faltered because they spent too much time hanging out with country-and-western musicians. "Some coaches don't want to coach anymore. They would rather sit home and listen to guitar pickers," he said, in a bit of Royal baiting. He boasted: "I know exactly why we had so much recruiting success. We outwork 'em. I'm young. My staff is young. Our hair is still growing. We can jive with the kids, dance with them." To some extent, this was true: Royal had trouble relating to kids, especially black kids, from Texas's big cities. And as the game integrated, football coaches in the Southwest Conference had to recruit those kids to remain competitive. But Royal found high schoolers increasingly brash and was uncomfortable courting them. How much of that was wrapped up in race in hard to say. He appeared more at ease when recruiting African Americans from small towns in rural areas—Campbell from Tyler, Leaks from Brenham, a place best known as the home of Blue Bell ice cream—than from urban areas.

"I don't care if a coach is on vacation in Greece, sometime every day he's thinking about some sophomore back home," Royal told Jan Reid in 1982.

> I've gone on vacation and spent two or three hours a day talking to recruits on the phone. Sure, we ruin 'em. Every year I read where the top prospects say, "I'll be glad when this is all over. This is some pressure. I can't even turn around." Well, Earl Campbell didn't suffer all that pressure. He didn't feel the need to yank all those old men around. They make appointments with you and not show up. So you think maybe he forgot, maybe he misunderstood. They keep you jangling at the end of their string. And then when it's all over, they say, "I never was interested in Texas in the first place." I just decided I didn't need that anymore.

There's a story that the final straw came when he tried to recruit Eric Dickerson. When Royal arrived at the Dickerson home, probably sometime in 1976, Eric was out, and so, as he had with many other relatives in many recruits' living rooms over the years, Royal sat down with the kid's grandmother and told her about the Texas program and about the education Eric would receive. Just then, Eric came home, walked into the living room, stared at Royal, and said to him: "You're sitting in my chair." Humiliated and angry, Royal stood up, said, simply, "Here you are, son," and wished the family good luck before walking out the door—never to return again.

In the lead-up to the game against OU, smarting from more pronouncements by Switzer that the UT coach was growing old and obsolete, Royal announced that his staff had collared an OU spy in Memorial Stadium during a closed Longhorn workout. The coach challenged Switzer, an OU assistant, and the supposed spy to take polygraph tests, offering them each $10,000 if they passed. The Oklahoma crew, Royal told an AP reporter, were a bunch of "sorry bastards." Switzer gleefully struck back. "This is Secret Agent Aught-aught-six," he told a *Dallas Times Herald* columnist. "Six, because we're fixing to strap it on them for the sixth straight year. If they ever catch an OU spy, (Royal) has got my permission to castrate and assassinate him," Switzer said. (Later, it turned out Oklahoma had indeed spied on UT practices, likely giving it an advantage in certain crucial situations—including the blocking of a UT punt. No one was castrated.) The night before the game, OU fans gathered outside Royal's Dallas hotel chanting, "Sorry bastard, sorry bastard."

Underlying the matchup was a mutual enmity between Texas and Oklahoma. The proving ground for their ongoing dispute about who was better was the territory both sides thought they knew best: the football field. In the early 1950s, OU's president had promised to "build a university the football team can be proud of." The night before the Red River Shootout each year, dozens—sometimes hundreds—of partisans from each side were arrested in downtown Dallas following the predictable drunken brawls. After someone started throwing desks and tables out of the windows of the Baker Hotel, one such eve went down in the annals as "The Night It Rained Furniture." "They are like tribes connected by a common hatred, two people who look on one another with the special loathing usually reserved for cannibalism," Gary Cartwright once wrote. "Oil and football prescribe the characters of the two universities, and to a degree the states. Longhorns see themselves as big, fast, wealthy, wily, capable, cultured and anointed by the Almighty. The good guys. They see Okies as poor, ignorant, Bible-thumping outlaws. Okies see Texans as loud, arrogant, smartass bullies. They see themselves as big, fast, wealthy, wily Bible-thumping outlaws."

The ensuing game, recalled Stephen Ross, who was then the sports director for the Austin ABC affiliate, was "easily the most bizarre, brutal and vicious athletic event I have ever witnessed." In the stroll out to midfield for the pregame coin toss, President Gerald Ford walked between Switzer and Royal—not a word, not even eye contact, was shared between the two men. With OU stacking the line of scrimmage with defenders, Campbell was ineffective, and UT clung to a 6–0 lead late in the game. After recovering a fumble, Oklahoma ended up scoring a last-minute touchdown. It was left to Uwe Von Schamann, the OU placekicker, who had nailed 140 consecutive extra points, to ice the game. But OU also had a walk-on deep snapper, one who had bounced at least one snap earlier in the day to the punter. Right before the snap, Ross reported, Longhorn linebacker Lionell Johnson leaned across the line of scrimmage to the walk-on and hissed, "I bet you snap this over his head." Von Schamann, his head down, remembered Ross, "never saw the ball as it sailed almost all the way to Waxahachie." The game ended in a 6–6 tie, and pretty much everyone afterward was angry. Royal could be found, in his misery, dry heaving in the tunnel leading to the locker rooms as an unhappy crowd of seventy thousand people made their way out of the Cotton Bowl. The coach, observed Ross, "looked like he had aged ten years in three hours."

Among the correspondence Royal received after the game was a handwritten note from Tyler, one that suggested how genuinely tight he had become with his star pupil's family—as well as the deep level of empathy felt by that pupil's mother: "Coach Royal, I want you to hold your head up . . . As long as the world stands there is going to be some body that's going (to) want to be out front without paying the price . . . You have friends and lots of them. One is Ann Campbell. . . . Every time I waked up last night after looking at Sun. paper with your head down, it (did) something to me. Always remember that you are not out there alone . . . Love, Ann Campbell."

With a 3–1–1 record, UT journeyed to Lubbock to play Texas Tech. Royal later confided that after the OU game, he had lost some of the fundamental urge to continue coaching. "We finally have Earl back in shape," he remembered. "He's ready to go, the team's ready to go, I feel like we're well prepared. We have a sell-out crowd, a national television audience: All the ingredients that should excite a coach. And I'm sitting in my hotel room thinking, 'Why am I continuing to do this?'" Earl was indeed back in shape, but only briefly: He went out for sixty-five yards on just seven carries, and then, just as it appeared UT had a favorable wind, he pulled the hamstring in his left leg. The Longhorns lost the game, and with Campbell watching from the sidelines, three of its next four as well, including a 30–0 thrashing at the hands of the University of Houston, Texas's first loss in its home stadium in forty-three games. It was a dreary time for a Texas football team accustomed to winning. "I wanted everything to go my way, and it didn't, and I got disgusted," Campbell said. "I felt sorry for myself. I got down on myself. There were mornings when I hated to see daylight." One reporter joked that Campbell "spent the entire frustrating season wondering whether he could just get from the vegetables to the desserts without pulling up lame with a nagging hamstring injury."

Previously, Campbell had appeared indestructible; now his commitment was questioned in barely disguised racial terms. Columnists wondered whether he was "dogging it"—a term Earl found insulting. Another columnist likened Campbell to Duane Thomas, the black Dallas Cowboy running back once nicknamed the "Sphinx" after refusing to talk to management or reporters following a contract dispute. Thomas had been quite clever—a sportswriter once recalled asking him, before Thomas's first Super Bowl, in 1970, how it felt to be playing as a rookie in the ultimate game. Thomas replied, "If this is the ultimate game, how come they play it every year?" But his new silence drove people batty, in a way that was wrapped up in words like "removed" and "sullen"—and that foreshadowed the criticism of Colin Kaepernick after he famously took a knee during the national anthem. "Everyone from the Black Muslims to the Fellowship of Christian Athletes—lawyers, agents, Lions Club program chairmen, women with indecent proposals—wanted a piece of him," Gary Cartwright wrote of Thomas in 1973. "Here was this handsome studhorse black kid fresh out of the ghetto, running like crazy, and now they wanted to *hear it* from his own lips. Hear *how grateful he was.* They wanted him to say it so they could hear."

To the extent Campbell did pick himself up slowly after a tackle, or take his time getting back to the huddle—that was not laziness, said Golden, the Austin sports columnist. "He picked that up from Jim Brown: He'd work you over, and get up slowly—that's how he got his rest. And then he'd give you the business again." Writing in the early 1980s about the black high school phenom Marcus Dupree, Willie Morris deflected a similar charge: "Even the criticisms of his 'laziness' had a certain logic for me; I perceived from this first game that whenever he got up slowly from a tackle, or moved indolently into a huddle or off the field, or dallied between plays, he was—in the words of the Gershwin brothers—merely biding his time, awaiting that instant flickering of time when he was free, open, and gone." The notion, now, that Campbell was slow coming back from injury was, like the charge of laziness, freighted with a kind of racist impatience.

With Campbell sidelined, Royal, so long approaching sainthood in Texas, was vulnerable. He had a falling-out with two key patrons. The first was Frank Erwin, who, during his second six-year term as the chair of board of regents, had amassed more power than anyone else on campus, and who, in 1975, after Texas's new governor declined to name him to a third term for fear of giving him even more, convinced the UT System to hire him as a special counsel for $1 a year. In a nod to his clout and his uncanny ability to loosen purse strings at the Capitol, the board wanted him handling its legislative program. Erwin had long considered the Forty Acres his fiefdom. "Whatever you say anywhere on the University of Texas, you are saying on my territory," he once said. "I've got your balls in the palm of my hand. If I don't like what you say, I'll squeeze. And if you don't shut up, I'll rip 'em off." The single thing that mattered most to him was a victorious football team. "For all his bluster and his cold-hearted politicking," Ronnie Dugger observed in his 1973 book *Our Invaded Universities*, "Erwin has never quite outgrown being the jock-sniffing undergraduate who wrote in his 1937 Texas yellbook: 'A university is a benevolent association for the preservation of football.'" But now he and Royal were on the outs. Once Royal's champion when the coach was crushing the opposition through the 1960s, Erwin had grown restless about his commitment to winning. He was upset, said Jenna Hays McEachern, a former Longhorn cheerleader who is married to Randy McEachern and is a sort of unofficial historian of the football team, that Royal was unwilling to participate in the sorts of unsavory recruiting practices that were becoming common in big-time college football. More darkly, and perhaps accurately, he suspected Royal, in the wake of his daughter's death, of having lost his competitive drive.

But the call on Royal's future would ultimately fall to another key patron, Allan Shivers, the former Texas governor who now chaired the board of regents. And with each loss—three weeks after the Houston game, UT again lost at home, 27–3, to hated Texas A&M—rumors that Royal could be squeezed out grew in volume. "You can go from great to average in a hurry," Ken Dabbs, the coach whom Royal brought on board in 1973 to recruit Earl Campbell, said. Shivers's differences with Royal were over style as much as anything else. The smooth-as-mink former segregationist governor—he served from 1949 through early 1957—had appointed many of the regents who once fought to keep the University of Texas from admitting African Americans and had delivered conservative Democrats to Eisenhower in the 1952 election, thereby warding off federal intervention in UT's foot-dragging on integration. He couldn't stand Royal's multitudinous guitar-picking friends, hangers-on, and retinue. The coach had invited Willie—a known pot smoker!— to watch games from the sidelines.

Royal favored eating at Cisco's, the unpretentious East Austin Mexican diner famous for its biscuits, and he lived in an upper-middle-class South Austin subdivision, not far from a golf course, in a house with a large central room decorated with pictures of a diverse group of people. There were photos of the musicians Willie Nelson and Charley Pride; his fellow Oklahoman James Garner; Pete Dominguez, a onetime Austin busboy who rose to fame as the proprietor of a Dallas Mexican restaurant; a black music teacher named Bill Caldwell, a graduate of the Tuskegee Institute whom the Royals had befriended and supported as he worked his way through graduate school in Austin; Luis Murillo, a handyman who long helped out around the football stadium; and Earl Campbell with his mother. The rank-and-file UT fans loved him. Years after he retired, people he had never before met would respectfully approach to confide a sad sort of secret: "You brought me more years of happiness than anyone I know." His friends, Royal once said, came from "all walks of life. Some of my blue-blood friends—and I've got some blue-blood friends—can't understand my other friends."

Shivers, who lived in an antebellum, plantation-style mansion in tony West Austin, had been one of those friends. Once upon a time, Royal and Shivers were close enough that the governor took the coach with him to golf at exclusive Augusta National—Shivers was the sort of guy to belong to a club that desegregated only in 1975 (membership to women was granted only in 2012). Royal, for his part, liked to golf with Willie and, later, Earl. But now the blurring of the two Austins—officialdom and mellowdom—was something that had worn thin for Shivers.

Weary of the demands of coaching, Royal visited Shivers to tell him he planned to retire and to inform him that Mike Campbell, his longtime defensive coordinator, was his choice as successor. "It wasn't his interest that waned," Mike Campbell said of his mentor's departure. "What waned was the damn personnel. We ran out of Earl Campbells." But determined to make a full break, Shivers not only told Royal that he would be barred from participating in the selection of the next football coach, but even threatened to fire him as athletic director.

Just before the final game of the season, against Arkansas, Royal, feeling slighted, found himself in final negotiations over his exit. He had enlisted Joe Jamail, a high-dollar trial attorney and running buddy of his, to represent him—this was not an amicable divorce. As members of the UT Athletic Council, a group composed of donors, faculty members, and administrators, hammered out the details, they had to periodically interrupt the meeting to call Shivers to make sure they met with his approval. The deliberations ran so long that Royal finished his twenty-four-year career as a college head coach by missing the prekickoff meeting with his team, the first and only time he had ever done so. He managed to hold on to the athletic director job—though within a couple of years, feeling like a perpetual lame duck, he opted to leave the department altogether to become a special assistant to the UT president.

Campbell, who had suffered through the most miserable stretch of his playing career, now deemed himself ready to play, eager to perform for the coach who had won his affection. He ended up taking the ball thirty-two times for 131 yards, leading the Longhorns to victory over Arkansas, thus ensuring that Royal would finish his career without a single losing season.

At a press conference after the game, with Royal's resignation public, players dropped in and out to grab snatches of their coach's valedictory. The only Longhorn to stay for the whole thing was Campbell. The coach who had for so long shunned black players, who had earned a reputation in some quarters as a racist, now looked up to see Campbell fixed there on one of the cheap folding chairs. Reflecting on that time, Bledsoe, the former UT undergraduate and law student who had practiced as a walk-on with the Longhorns and later headed the state NAACP office, said that "you can see there was a change in Royal." Earl Campbell "no doubt helped change Royal. And even as Royal was leaving coaching, Royal is such an institution here that changing his views on race had to be an asset on a lot of different fronts." As the postgame press conference wound down, the coach was asked the most difficult part of stepping away. "I'm leaving Earl Campbell," he said.

It was an abrupt end, and Campbell had an empty feeling. But leaning on his Baptist background, he declared afterward that "if it weren't for the dark days, we wouldn't know what it is to walk in the light." And sure enough, in the following 1977 football season, no player in the college game would burn brighter than Earl Campbell.

Every morning at precisely 6:30 during the sweltering Austin summer of 1977, the phone in Earl Campbell's off-campus apartment jangled on the hook. It was now unlisted. After his breakout sophomore season, he had gotten too many calls from well-wishers and hangers-on to keep it in the phone book; even gamblers, posing as journalists, were known to call Longhorns to get the inside scoop before games. Morning light streamed through Campbell's bedroom, decorated with pictures of Reuna, his girlfriend since ninth grade, and a plaque with the words "Keep Me Going, Lord" that he received from a little kid at the Mount Olive Baptist Church, the black East Austin congregation that Earl and his twin brothers attended every Sunday. The plaque was a gift as Earl struggled through his junior year, one in which he considered quitting football altogether. And yet here he was, on another early morning, answering the wake-up call from a mahout of men preparing to put Earl Campbell through another round of football-related misery. On the other end of the line, in a wide-awake voice so peppy that it was designed to rouse Campbell from sleep, came a single sentence—"I'm waiting on you." And then a click.

Frank Medina, all of four-ten, had served as a sports trainer for nearly his entire life, excelling in devising back-breaking exercises—character building, they called it back then—meant to transform young men into better versions of themselves. With a white towel over one shoulder, as if he were a bartender, he examined not pint glasses but biceps. Squat and bowlegged, with a chesty, muscled body, "his dark crusading face," in the words of former Longhorn Gary Shaw, was "always marooned by the pure white of his ever-present towel, and this combination gave him the look of an errant, stubby Don Quixote." By the time he was sixteen, in 1931, Medina, customarily described in old press releases as a "full-blooded Cherokee," had landed a job as a sports trainer at the Haskell Institute in Kansas, at the time a boarding school meant to assimilate American Indians into white culture. He was hired in 1945 as a strength and conditioning coach at UT. He was old-school. When, in the 1960s, a player appeared in the locker room in sandals, Medina accused him of looking like a hippie. He barred "smutty or foul talk." He famously could never remember players' names, so he called all of them "Mr. Man" or "Son." "It was like a little bitty man training elephants," said Ted Koy, who played halfback for the Longhorns in the late 1960s.

The father of fourteen adopted children, Medina was beloved by his university charges—to keep things entertaining, he divided players into their Christian denominations during running drills, called the "religious relays"—and was known to now and then dole out cookies. Run afoul of the rules, though, and you were subject to Medina's will. The 1960s star UT—and later NFL—linebacker Tommy Nobis once remembered that a missed class meant a dawn training session alone with Medina; the broad-shouldered, crew-cut Nobis was made to grab a blocking dummy and run up the stadium stands twenty times, seventy-nine steps each time. The all-American hurdler Ray Cunningham once said that part of Medina's reconditioning program after an injury was driving the athlete up to the suburb of Round Rock, ordering him out of the car, and telling him to walk the fifteen miles back to campus. "You didn't want to go see him," Tom Stolhandske, a defensive end in the early 1950s, said. "If you got under his control for some kind of treatment, it was absolute horror. I'd walk into the training room and see somebody in the steam bath—locked in, pounding on the door, trying to get out. If Frank put you in there for x minutes, you were going to stay in there for that amount of time, whether or not you passed out." Stolhandske remembers once injuring his ankle against Oklahoma. "We got back to Austin and he said, 'Come get some treatment.' I said, 'Frank, I didn't hurt my ankle, I just thought I did. Tape it up.' He wasn't about to get me in that training room." Defensive back Keith Moreland, who overlapped with Campbell on the Longhorns for one year, especially remembers the brutality of late-summer practices. "When you're in two-a-days and the AstroTurf gets to 115 to 120 degrees, you really get to know the courage that human beings have; to be able to put up with all that and go through what you have to go through," he once said. "In those days, Frank Medina gave no water breaks. The only thing you had was a frozen sliced orange. Boy, that orange looked pretty good most days."

Campbell first met Medina the summer before his freshman year, when he arrived on campus and visited the training room just as Medina was working to rehab Roosevelt Leaks's knee. "I heard him hollering and fussing at Rosie. And as Rosie emerged, I asked him who that was. 'Oh, that's Frank Medina, you'll have your chance to meet him.'" It was in that training room in the spring of 1977, with Medina by his side, that Fred Akers, the Longhorns' dapper, boyish new football coach, first explained to Campbell, soon to be a senior, that he would be the center of the offense in the coming season.

Akers, like Royal before him, grew up in straitened circumstances, one of nine siblings in a home in northeastern Arkansas with no electricity or plumbing. By the age of ten, he was picking cotton to pay for his school clothes. A clever kid—he was the only one in his family to graduate from high school—he won an essay contest with a piece titled "The Importance of the Automobile to Our Community." The prize, Akers could remember decades later, was a hundred-dollar bond. How did he arrive at that subject? "I figured since Ford was sponsoring it, it'd be a good idea to talk about cars," Akers once told a *Dallas Morning News* reporter. The punch line: the Akers clan didn't own a car.

Like Royal, he was a slight, overachieving athlete. As a 153-pound senior, he was recruited by a slew of universities—he had lost only four football games since fourth grade. He went to Arkansas, where his game-winning twenty-eight-yard field goal against TCU sealed a share of the 1959 Southwest conference title.

There, the similarities with Royal ended. Unlike Royal, who had riled Shivers and wearied Erwin with his penchant for being weirdly fancy-free and horsing around with Willie, Akers was deemed a dependable man. By his own count, Akers drank twenty-five cups of coffee a day, each generally accompanied by a cigarette; his sole hobby, he said, was football.

And whereas Darrell Royal was an earthy wit, Akers was polished and glossy. *Football News* had named him to its best-dressed list, and he appeared at his inaugural UT press conference in a three-piece off-white suit. Accustomed to Royal's folksy stylings, the press recorded its first impressions somewhat smirkingly. Akers wore his brown hair in a style one described as "little boy regular." He was "a fashion poster for what the successful young businessman is wearing these days." One said he looked like a bank chairman. Akers was hesitant before the press, and serious minded: "He makes Whistler's mother look like a swinger," wrote the sportswriter Kirk Bohls. Royal had been fond of the phrase "Dance with the one who brung ya"; Akers, wrote Mike Jones of the *Dallas Morning News* in an article headlined "Akers Has Cool Emotions," "dances with the one who *brought* him." The new coach, wrote Jones, "always looks as though he had just shaved and showered." Not that anyone really asked, but Akers's dressiness was an emblem of his up-from-nothing striving. He described his predilection for wearing ties this way: "It was a long time before I ever owned one, so I'm going to wear one every chance I get."

Despite having served as an assistant coach to Royal in the late 1960s and early 1970s, before leaving Austin to become head coach of Wyoming, Akers had few supporters among the Royal-loyal Orangebloods or among the rank and file at the athletics department on which he was foisted. After Royal's resignation, the sentimental choice for head coach was Mike Campbell, Royal's longtime rough-hewn lieutenant—a Mississippian who had run UT's defense and was Royal's choice as successor. But the hiring committee, at Shivers's behest, passed over Campbell for Akers. As word spread across the coaches' offices at Bellmont Hall, secretaries wept, and one assistant coach after another paid their respects to Campbell, as if attending a wake. The athletics department was suddenly engulfed in an atmosphere of anxiety and suspicion.

Royal, miffed at the snubbing of Mike Campbell, never gave Akers a real endorsement. "We haven't had a confrontation because you can't have a confrontation without communication," Royal told a reporter a couple of years after the hiring. And when Akers was forced out ten tumultuous years later, despite compiling an overall record of 86-31, there was little question whom Diane Akers, his wife, had in mind when she told a reporter, "When I come back in the next life—and I believe in reincarnation—I want to be a defensive tackle because I want to hit somebody."

As Akers headed into his first season as Longhorn head coach, nobody harbored high expectations of him. With the team having barely dodged a losing record, and its longtime, revered head coach deposed, morale at UT was low. Akers, in that introductory December 1976 meeting with the press, did nothing to contradict the conventional wisdom about the prospects for the coming season. "I don't think this can be viewed as anything but a rebuilding year," he said.

Football soothsayers picked the Longhorns to finish fourth or fifth in their conference. With their huge fan base and championship pedigree, the Longhorns generally earned at least a few nationally televised games each season—but heading into the fall of 1977, they were a scratch, uninvited to appear on the national airwaves. Politically, Akers faced skepticism from influential alumni devoted to Royal. And many of the television stations that had carried Royal's weekly show demurred when it came to picking up Akers's version. Royal's had appeared on fifteen stations; Akers's would be broadcast on only six—and none in the Dallas–Fort Worth area.

Akers had a series of football problems, too. Apart from Campbell and a few other mainstays, the 1977 Longhorn squad was full of freshmen and sophomores. "We're so young we hold hands going onto the field," joked the new defensive coordinator, Leon Fuller. Medina, in a letter dated May, 9, 1977, just before the Longhorns headed off for summer break, exhorted them to be mindful of their shallow depth: "It is evident by our limitation of personnel that we can ill afford the laggard or the well fed happy claudicants," he wrote in characteristically idiosyncratic language, wishing his players well that summer. (A claudicant is someone who limps.) "This is not a missle [sic] of distress but just a few words of caution. Our backs are not up against the wall neither are we too far removed from the open elevator shaft."

And Akers had inherited a roster of no-name quarterbacks— talented high school passers were unenthusiastic about playing in Royal's grind-it-out wishbone offense. "We didn't average three passes a game," Rick Ingraham, a square-headed offensive lineman who would serve as Earl's closest friend and most trusted downfield rusher, said. Other players, including the running backs, were growing weary of the scheme—although novel in the late 1960s, when it led to thirty consecutive victories for the Longhorns, lately it had left Campbell feeling like a battering ram. In the wishbone, the fullback stands only three steps behind the quarterback, giving him little opportunity to accelerate before reaching the entanglements of offensive and defensive linemen. "When you're a wishbone fullback like I was," Campbell said, "you only run straight into the line and you get the hell beat out of you."

Akers decided to reshape the Longhorns' base offense into an I formation, moving Campbell farther behind the quarterback to afford his running back a little more acceleration before attacking the defense. "Akers saw what kind of speed Earl had, and instead of starting behind the quarterback only three yards, he was seven yards out; when he hit the line of scrimmage, he hit with full speed said Randy McEachern, the quarterback who was in the same recruiting class as Campbell."

National expectations for Campbell entering his senior year

were modest. A promotional tour of likely Heisman candidates organized by the NCAA and ABC-TV included a half-dozen players, from schools such as UCLA and Pitt and Ohio State, but no Campbell. Heisman hype was especially acute that year. The award, first given in the 1930s, had become the premier individual trophy in all sports—and the December 1977 event was scheduled, for the first time, to be broadcast live, from New York City, in prime time. "It came down to Earl's not having a good season last year," David Cawood, the NCAA public relations director, explained that August as the tour got underway. The tour drew as many as seventy sportswriters to a handful of key locations around the country—important exposure to potential Heisman voters, especially important if your team wasn't going to be on national television.

"Earl's got a lot of obstacles," Akers said over the summer. "He's definitely a candidate. I'll push him but that doesn't mean I'll go out and hire a blimp. I'm not going to buy advertising space or send out flyers, but I think it's my obligation to help." And again, he played down expectations: "He may not have enough of a supporting cast, though." Still, Akers made no bones about how much the Longhorns would lean on Campbell.

The day the players met for pictures for the Longhorn media guide, each wearing suit and tie, the new head coach tested Campbell's commitment to the coming season. "I need to know, Mr. Campbell," Akers asked him, "Do you want to run the ball for this university?" "Yes, sir, I do—real bad," Campbell said. "Good, Mr. Campbell. You're going to have to prove it to me, and it's going to take an awful lot of hard work on your part." *Hard work* because Earl Campbell, the man Akers hoped to build an offense around, was overweight. Hobbled by injuries and increasingly sustained by greasy-spoon enchiladas, Earl Campbell's body had become bloated, it could be said, from benign neglect. Once all-muscle, his five-eleven frame now carried nearly 250 pounds. "What we're asking Earl to do requires more quickness," Akers told reporters.

Meeting again in the training room with Campbell and Medina, Akers issued an edict: lose twenty-three pounds. Earl turned to

Medina and wondered aloud where he was going to find the twenty-three pounds to lose. "I don't know," Medina said. "It might be in your butt but we are going to lose it." He hadn't been down to 220 pounds since his sophomore year in high school, and now he had a little over a month to peel off the weight.

And so, every morning at seven, thirty minutes after Medina's call, Campbell showed up at UT's Gregory Gym, a classy art deco building in the center of campus, to meet the little man. He would pound the heavy bag for an hour while wearing a rubber sweat suit, and then, wearing a weighted vest and ankle weights, he would run the track—sprints, to build up fast-twitch muscles, followed by a mile run. Then, back in the rubber suit for a twenty-five-minute stint in the steam room. Some of that training would today surely run afoul of university policy. "Sometimes," Campbell admitted, "I would get hot and tired and crawl along the floor to push the door open. Medina must have been a genius because he always knew when I was going to do that. He always pushed the door shut, saying, 'I told you not to be opening that door, boy.'" To finish it off, three hundred sit-ups. Campbell would shower and then eat a low-fat lunch. The afternoons were spent working construction and making deliveries for a tile company. Years later, Campbell remembered Medina with nostalgia: "I can remember the days he'd serve me milk and cookies in his back room and then I can recall those days of him hollering at me, 'What are you saving it for, son?'"

The workouts left Campbell feeling trim, even as he remained thick with musculature. "In church the other day," he once said, "I felt like a 100 pound man in a 220 pound man's suit." His teammates, dedicated as they were to Royal, appeared inspired by the new leadership. Practices shifted from the traditional two-a-days to three-a-days. Akers "told us we could keep doing the same things losers do and we could have another 5-5-1 season if we wanted," Rick Ingraham, an offensive lineman, explained. The Longhorns were especially roused by Campbell's dedication. "Watching Earl go through that rigorous routine elevated all of us in practice. When we saw how badly Earl wanted it, then all of us adopted the attitude that we would elevate ourselves to his level," Ingraham once told the writer Paddy Joe Miller. "Despite all he had been through with Frank Medina, Earl never once slacked off in practice. Watching him out there running over people made all of us want to try harder." For Campbell's part, after a frustrating junior season spent largely on the sidelines, the workouts built up his appetite to play. "I don't think I've ever been this hungry for football," Campbell told reporters as the season kicked off. "I was hurt all season and it was bad, but it taught me a lot, too. The main thing it taught me was that regardless of how high you get, you can always be brought down. Let's be real about it. I want to spend part of my life earning a living from football. I've worked for the chances I've had since the fourth grade. And I know I am working for my chances now." He added, "This year I'm not settling for one guy tackling me. And I really don't intend for two of them to get the job done."

The season began with a nice team effort, a 44–0 defeat of Boston College. Campbell ran for a respectable 87 yards. Against Virginia the next week, he gained 156 on nineteen carries and scored two touchdowns—although he played less than a half. Texas won 68–0. When Campbell got into the open field, Alfred Jackson, the Longhorn wide receiver, remembered going downfield to look for someone to block: "But the defensive backs would be clinging onto us. I mean, they were hanging onto us, saying, 'I don't want any part of this.'" Facing Rice, Texas rang up 72 points as Earl went for 132 yards on just thirteen rushes.

The early-October matchup with Oklahoma now loomed. The previous year's Red River Shootout, the one that ended in a 6–6 tie, had finally unraveled Royal. And less than ten months earlier, in the December 1976 Fiesta Bowl, Akers's Wyoming Cowboys were rolled by Barry Switzer's Oklahoma Sooners 41–7—Wyoming scored its only touchdown with twenty-four seconds remaining in the game. Now it was Akers's chance to get some measure of revenge.

The game is played each year at Dallas's Cotton Bowl, a handsome stadium built in 1930 on the grounds of the sprawling Texas State Fair, which operates beneath the watchful eye of Big Tex, the fifty-five-foot-tall cowboy-hatted mascot with a hinged jaw synchronized to the timing of welcome announcements. Along with its impressive livestock and chainsaw-carving contests, its demonstrations in cattle milking and peewee rodeo, the fair today is renowned for its deep-fried everything: Oreos, Twinkies, pecan pie, hot dogs (corny dogs), butter (really), and banana splits. The winner of the Big Tex Choice Award in the Best Tasting–Savory category in 2017 was the Funnel Cake Bacon Queso Burger. Game day is a social and sports event. Helicopters and blimps float overhead as roller coasters whirl outside the stadium walls. You can smell fried dough if the wind blows in the right direction. Willie Morris described the pregame scene at the Cotton Bowl before the matchup: "Beautiful women in the Neiman-Marcus fashions escorted by their men in expensive ten-gallon hats milled among the crowds shouting twangy salutations. All about me was the ebullient, mindless affluence of the Great American Southwest, the mementos of the incandescent parvenu rich. And from all sides now, as the marching bands came onto the field with their impeccable resounding brass, a deep, nearly erotic hum of anticipation rose from the assembled thousands."

Among the official merchandise you can buy at the fair today are T-shirts announcing that the fair was established in 1886. No African Americans were allowed onto the fairgrounds back then, even though the South Dallas neighborhood encircling it was—and remains—largely black. They were not admitted until three years later, and then only on a single day, called Colored People's Day. When, in 1923, the State Fair of Texas hosted Ku Klux Klan Day, more than thirty thousand people attended to witness the swearing in of new members. As part of the 1936 Texas Centennial bash, fair organizers devised, as a cynical, and successful, attempt to sell more tickets, the rebranding of Colored People's Day as Negro Achievement Day—even as African Americans were barred from eating at fairground restaurants and concession stands on other days during the fair's annual two-week run. The Hall of Negro Life, one of the buildings constructed as part of the events that year, was the only one demolished after the centennial celebration ended.

Not until 1967, three years after the passage of the federal Civil Rights Act, were all attractions and food concessions open to people of all races. But even then, the State Fair of Texas plotted ways to discourage African Americans from attending. In 1966, the State Fair Corporation commissioned a planning report that included a survey of white fairgoers. Economics Research Associates, a Los Angeles–based research firm, found "intense emotional discomfort in middle-class white residents of Dallas" concerning the area surrounding Fair Park. Many felt "embarrassment . . . that visitors to Dallas (had to) see the 'other side' of the city." Especially concerning to respondents was that "so many colored and white people" had to intermingle during the fair. "The solution for all of these conflicts, at least in terms of Fair Park's location, is simple," determined the research firm, which had long conducted research for the Walt Disney Company. "All that is required is to eliminate the problem from sight. If the poor Negroes in their shacks cannot be seen, all the guilt feeling revealed above will disappear, or at least be removed from primary consideration." The report concludes: "This question was posed: 'If all the land around Fair Park were bought up and turned into paved, lighted, fenced parking lot, would that solve the problem?' The citizens of Dallas answered with a resounding, 'Yes!'"

And so a decade later, when Earl Campbell and the Longhorns traveled up I-35 to meet the Sooners at the Cotton Bowl, a vast new parking lot, covering many tens of acres, swept out from the fairgrounds. The reconfigured Fair Park layout was charmless, a brutal buffer keeping African Americans at bay. Old streets lined with appealing, though dilapidated, single-family homes now dead-ended into a never-ending chain-link fence warning residents their cars would be towed if they parked against it. The city had offered white families whose homes they seized as much as ten times what they paid black families. The properties were, indeed, paved over, used as parking for only a tenth or so of the year. Ashley Walker, whose family has lived near Fair Park for at least three generations, told the

Foundation for Community Empowerment for a 2017 report on the future of the State Fair of Texas: "It makes you feel like they're robbing you from where you've been all your life, you and your family. Someone you know is gone and there's just concrete. They're taking it away and there's nothing you can do—to make more parking lots for their Texas-OU games."


Heading into the 1977 matchup, the undefeated Sooners were ranked second in the country and had already beaten fourth-ranked Ohio State. For all the Longhorns' talk of using Campbell as a blunt instrument, six seconds into the game Texas tried a trick play—a Campbell pass—and turned the ball over on an interception. It got bizarre from there. On the Longhorns' seventh play, the starting quarterback broke an ankle; fewer than ten plays later, the second-stringer was stretchered off, having wrecked his knee after trying to throw a lead block for Campbell. So unaccustomed was he to playing with the third-stringer that Campbell stood on the field wondering who would convene the next huddle. The next man up was Randy McEachern, a slight kid who the year before had suffered a knee injury and spent the season helping out with radio broadcasts and who, in this, his senior year, had quarterbacked the scout team—the guys used as tackling dummies for the defense in practice. Akers gave some brief encouragement to McEachern while searching for signs of nervousness—the coach was thinking about an almost unprecedented move. "I was prepared to use all our time-outs right there to talk to him if he was shaking or anything," Akers said. The announcers couldn't pronounce the young man's name; he was so far down the depth chart that his bio wasn't in the Longhorn media guide. On his first play, McEachern carried the ball into the right side of the line. "He lost one yard," wrote Douglas Looney in *Sports Illustrated*. "But he didn't fumble, and he got up. Given the way things were going for Texas, this was a good play."

Ingraham, the Longhorns veteran offensive lineman, grabbed McEachern in the huddle. His message was simple: give the ball to Earl. Ultimately, McEachern was just good enough, leading the team on an eighty-yard drive that finished with a twenty-four-yard run by Campbell for a touchdown. "It all happened so fast, I really didn't expect it," McEachern said. Russell Erxleben, the Longhorns' phenom of a kicker, booted field goals of sixty-four and fifty-eight yards, and UT's stout defense, led by Brad Shearer up front and Raymond Clayborn in the secondary, held Oklahoma to six points. UT won 13–6.

Was he nervous? McEachern was asked after the game. "Oh, no, not unless you would consider your heart stopping a sign of nervousness."

What part of the game was the biggest thrill? "The end."

Back in Austin, the team was greeted by students with hastily made "Randy is Dandy" T-shirts.

Suddenly, the Longhorns were 4–0, ranked second in the country and readying for a contest against number eight Arkansas. At a press gaggle, Campbell was asked about the cause of the team's improvement. "Without taking anything away from Coach Royal—he made us work hard," he said, "the big difference to me is the split backfield and the I-formation." In other words, the offense that gave him more room to operate and show his full potential. That was about the closest Campbell came to tooting his own horn.

That Saturday, he carried the ball thirty-four times for 188 yards as Texas downed Arkansas 13–6. On the flight back to Austin, Campbell got a stewardess to let him use the PA system to address his teammates: "I set a couple records today, but I want you guys to know that those records belong to you as much as they do to me." And then the joke: "I'd like thank [guard] Rick Ingraham for telling me which holes to run in."

On the football field, Campbell "never once blamed anyone for anything," Ingraham, a white kid from the Austin suburbs who became the godfather of Campbell's sons, said over a plate of fajitas at Austin's El Arroyo. He still had a building-block frame. Wearing sunglasses and a polo shirt, he looked like a ratcheted-up golfer. "The easiest job I ever had was blocking for Earl Campbell." He smiled.

"I screwed up, he'd run right over me."

Earl was becoming an object of fascination nationwide, and UT's press team played him up. "The pork chops and dressing and the fried chicken waited on the steam tables Sunday at the Longhorn dining hall, and while on other days guys would hustle to make lunch, closing time is dependent on services at Earl Campbell's church," announced an athletics department press release the day after the Arkansas victory. "'Whenever Earl and the twins get here,' said a supervisor when asked what time the dining hall closes, 'that's when we shut down the line.'"

With Campbell now a bona fide contender for the Heisman Trophy, reporters looking for an angle were drawn to the story of his modest beginnings, and began making calls to Tyler. Ann Campbell rearranged her schedule for all the media calls, working the rose fields in the morning and talking to reporters at 2:30 p.m., after her bath. "I've thoroughly enjoyed it," she said, "I really have." Reporters, in turn, took keenly to her: "One of her front teeth has a gold jacket, giving a certain unassailable value to just about everything she says," Bruce Newman wrote in *Sports Illustrated*. She made the trip to Austin to watch her son play in a late-October matchup against Texas Tech, and when she was recognized by the public-address announcer, the crowd of seventy-nine thousand gave her a standing ovation. After the game—the Longhorns shut out the Red Raiders—Earl, always the sweet son, said he thought she could never get enough applause. "I don't think she could ever be as famous as I'd like for her to be," he said.

There remained one last major hurdle: the late-November grudge match at College Station against Texas A&M—the game sometimes known as the Hate Bowl. Tie-dyed UT and military-minded A&M could not, culturally speaking, have been more different, and their student bodies were equally suspicious of each other. Nothing would have been more delicious for the Longhorns than to seal a regular season number one ranking with a defeat of the Aggies, and nothing would have tasted better to A&M than spoiling the

Longhorns' undefeated season. On the line was the Southwest Conference title and the right to play Notre Dame in the Cotton Bowl.

The Sunday night ahead of the game, more than ten thousand UT fans showed up at a pep rally, dancing, swaying, and chanting. "'All I wanted to do is see what Earl looked like without a uniform,' moaned one coed looking over thousands of fans tightly squeezing toward a small orange-draped stage of University of Texas cheerleaders and football players," recounted one contemporary write-up of the scene. "That was the greatest party I've ever been to," Tom Swinnea, then an undergraduate at the university, remembered four decades later. "Beat the hell out of A&M," bellowed fraternity brothers.

The pep rally was organized by a campus club called the Texas Cowboys, the chaps-wearing students charged with blasting a cannon every time UT scored a touchdown. Partway through the rally, someone noticed something horrifying: a sign painted on the side of a shack that the Texas Cowboys were using as headquarters said, in large orange letters, "If an Aggie and a nigger jumped off the [UT] Tower at the same time, which one would hit first? Who cares?" An assistant dean, David McClintock, immediately had the sign destroyed. "The sign was put there by someone other than the Texas Cowboys . . . The Cowboys have been embarrassed and are making apologies for the incident," he announced following an investigation.

The pep rally incident "was really a black eye to the Cowboys," Tim Alexander, who was chairman of the club at the time, said. He hails from Tyler and now heads a bank there. "To this day I can't tell you who painted that there. It was a very, very bad thing, and we were being pegged as a racist organization." It was Campbell, said Alexander, who "kind of saved us" from that label by going public with an exoneration of the Cowboys, giving them some cover. His response was typically down-to-earth. "I feel sorry for those kinds of people in this world," Campbell said about the perpetrators. "I respect people and people respect me. I wouldn't know how to fight someone. We're all the same people, just different colors. But some-day we're going to have to go to one another for what we want. We need to mix together and care for one another." In his optimistic way, when it came to racial tensions, his inclination was to extend the benefit of the doubt. "I'm not trying to tell you there are no black-and-white problems at Texas because I'd be telling you a lie. But mainly I think they are communication problems."

Before the game at College Station, two days after Thanks-giving, the Aggies' quarterback, David Walker, made a frank admission: "We do wonder if we're going to stop Campbell, and if so, how."

The *Sports Illustrated* reporter Douglas Looney was in the Long-horn locker room as fifty-seven thousand fans started making a ruckus overhead. He described the atmosphere: "After carrying on about what a good team A&M is, how emotional the game will be, how hard-hitting, how important, Akers concludes, 'But gentlemen, it does not have to be close.'" Brad Shearer, a strapping defensive lineman, chirped up, as if shouting "amen!": "Never a lazy step." The head coach had the last word: "Akers, talking about the Aggie pregame precision marching show says, 'They've already done what they do best—march, hut and holler. Now we're going out and do what we do best.'"

As the team rushed out of the locker room, Akers pulled aside Campbell and talked to him quietly. "Earl, I really expect 170 yards out of you today." Akers, said Campbell, was the first to demand such greatness of him. "Nobody ever walked up to me before and said, 'Earl, you ought to have 150 yards this afternoon.' I started thinking I wasn't supposed to have a bad game. Or a bad practice."

Early in the game, with three wide receivers to his right, McEachern bootlegged out that way and then turned and floated a ball down the left side to Campbell. Campbell's receiving hands were legendarily bad. "If you poured a cup of coffee in your hands and then tried to catch a football with them," Alfred Jackson said, "that's what Earl's hands were like." One pro quarterback he played with said that Campbell "couldn't catch a cold." Some teammates called him "Old Brickhands." "He never caught that pass in practice," said Jackson. "They could still be out there trying to complete that pass for 12, 13 years. We must have been laughing all week." But he managed to haul this one in and run sixty yards for a touchdown. A few minutes later, he finished off another drive with a leaping touchdown run.

Back in the locker room at halftime, with UT ahead 33–14, Campbell yelled, "How bad do we want it?"

Starting on their own twenty to begin the second half, the Longhorns set out on a five-play, eighty-yard scoring drive: Campbell for no yards, Campbell for ten, Campbell for five, Campbell for fifty-nine, Campbell for six. By day's end, Campbell had gone for 220 yards and three touchdowns. The Longhorns won 57–28. "If he doesn't win that Heisman, they ought to throw it away," said Texas A&M defensive end Phil Bennett. An utterly exhausted Aggie linebacker named Kevin Monk explained that there was only way to bring Campbell down: "Grab, hold on and hope for help."

The season had been peppered with key plays by Campbell: the twenty-four-yard run to score the only touchdown against Oklahoma; a twenty-eight-yard dash after catching a screen pass to set up the winning touchdown against Arkansas; a fifty-eight-yard rush against SMU to turn a close game into a rout. Texas was leading Houston by a single point in the third quarter when Campbell cracked a forty-three-yard touchdown run—and on his next carry, he went on another forty yard dash, to the Houston one-foot line. And he had back-to-back runs of forty-three and twenty-five yards on a sixty-eight-yard touchdown drive against Baylor. "Earl is the best running back I've had the privilege—or whatever—of coaching against," said Southern Methodist University Coach Ron Meyer. "I hope I never have a similar privilege."

The regular season over, the Heisman awaited. A 1977 press release from UT touting Campbell's accomplishments had a section titled "People Run Over." In his senior season, Campbell ran for 1,054 yards after initial contact, and 1,744 yards overall—averaging nearly 160 yards a game. He scored 114 points. All told, over four seasons—including his injury-riddled junior year—Earl Campbell ran for 4,443 yards, at the time the fifth-highest total in collegiate history.

About a week before the ceremony, Rick Ingraham, Earl's trusted offensive lineman, went to his parents to ask for money for a haircut. At first, he was met with skepticism: "Why do you need to get a haircut?" "Earl invited me to go with him to the Heisman." Immediately: "Oh, you're definitely going to get a haircut."

Out in Tyler, Ann Campbell's pastor, the Reverend John Williams, announced on Sunday that she was going to New York, and asked the congregation to pray for her. They pooled a collection for spending money for Ann. Henry Bell Jr., the president of Citizens First National Bank in Tyler—Ann had been his maid since she was pregnant with Earl—paid for the hotel and all her transportation and food. And Joe Jamail, the UT-trained trial lawyer known as the "King of Torts"—his famous Pennzoil case, for which he was awarded a fee of $345 million, was still several years away—flew her up to New York in his private jet. A group of two dozen Orangebloods stayed at the Waldorf, the Park Lane, the St. Regis, and the Hotel Americana—the group included John Holmes, a wealthy driller whose son had, less than two decades earlier, inveighed against integrating the UT football team because it would hurt the team's success.

The award had traditionally been announced at a noon luncheon on the Tuesday following the Army-Navy game. But CBS had paid $200,000 that year for the broadcast rights, and was determined to lend the event some glitz. The production would be handled not by CBS Sports but by the network's broadcast arm. And marking the dawn of a commercial approach, the network moved it to prime time.

Old-schoolers weren't happy about it. The Reverend Edmund P. Joyce, the vice president of the University of Notre Dame, had harrumphed that college football "was not a Madison Avenue creation.

Earl before his boyhood home on the outskirts of the East Texas town of Tyler, 1979. (Shelly Katz, *Sports Illustrated*/Getty Images)

**TOP LEFT:** Ann Campbell, the revered matriarch of the Campbell family, tending roses on her small family farm, October 1977. (Lynn Flocke, *Austin American-Statesman*) **BOTTOM LEFT:** Earl mock arm-wrestling an opponent ahead of a high school football all-star game, 1974. "I was raised not to have negative racial feelings," Campbell said. (Ray Covey_HP © *Houston Chronicle*. Used with permission) **ABOVE:** Campbell and Royal, in an undated photo, talking strategy on the sideline. (Courtesy of the *Austin American-Statesman*)

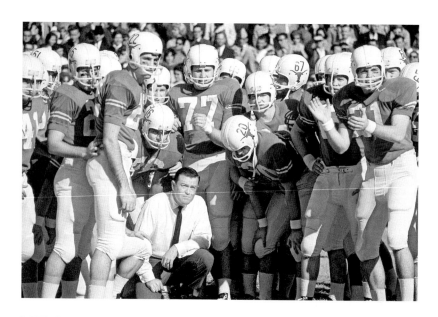

**TOP LEFT:** University of Texas coach Darrell Royal talking to his huddling Longhorns during their New Year's Day 1964 matchup against Navy at the Cotton Bowl in Dallas. Until 1970, there were no African Americans on Royal's varsity football teams. (Neil Leifer, *Sports Illustrated*/Getty Images) **BOTTOM LEFT:** When Campbell got into the open field, Longhorn wide receiver Alfred Jackson (not pictured) had no trouble finding someone to block: the defensive backs "were hanging onto us, saying 'I don't want any part of this.'" (By UT Texas Student Publications, Prints and Photographs Collection, di_02829, Dolph Briscoe Center for American History, University of Texas at Austin) **ABOVE:** As Earl won the Heisman Trophy in New York City in December 1977, his family, watching on television in Tyler, was jubilant. In the center and leading the celebration is Earl's nephew William Fields. (Photo courtesy of the *Tyler Morning Telegraph*)

**TOP:** Bum Phillips, Earl's lovable coach when he was with the Houston Oilers. (Larry Reese © *Houston Chronicle*. Used with permission)

**BOTTOM:** Campbell glancing back at Dolphin linebacker Steve Towle (56) as he outraces the Miami defense for a clinching touchdown on *Monday Night Football* during his rookie NFL campaign. Decades later, Towle said the moment still haunted him. (George Honeycutt © *Houston Chronicle*. Used with permission)

**TOP:** He meted out punishment . . . (RGD0006N-1981-2419-025G, Houston Post Photograph Collection, Houston Public Library, Houston Metropolitan Research Center) **BOTTOM:** . . . and received it. (George Honeycutt © *Houston Chronicle*. Used with permission)

Having endured a handful of knee and back surgeries and battled through an addiction to pain medication, Earl was working out again in 2012. (Reproduced with permission of Jeff Heimsath)

It was not designed as a vehicle selling soap or beer." In remarks that sound quaint today, Yale coach Carm Cozza said the Heisman "should not have any stigma of advertisement or show business . . . My concern is that when you put anything like advertising attached to it, you take away from the great achievement and pride of the young man who wins it."

The event was black-tie. On hand were O. J. Simpson, Reggie Jackson, Elliott Gould—in the winter of 1977, they were A-list sports and film celebrities. Only a day before, Ann Campbell had had her hands in the sand of her rose patch, and now here she was, on the forty-sixth floor of the Downtown Athletic Club, a view across the Battery to the Twin Towers spread before her. Henry Bell's mother, Nell Bell, who four years earlier had played a key role in steering Earl Campbell to the University of Texas, took a string of pearls from around her neck and placed them on Ann Campbell's. "I had no idea," Ann Campbell said quietly, "no idea, I had no idea that I would be able to enjoy the blessings I have behind that kid." And, being Ann Campbell, she revised herself: "I have enjoyed blessings behind all my kids."

Darrell Royal approached her, and she held his hand, swinging it gently.

Ahead of the award ceremony, some reporters, eager to get his feel for New York City—a small-town kid from Texas in a skyscraper made for a good story—cornered Campbell. A radio journalist asked him about race: he stood to be the first black player from a university south of the Mason-Dixon line to win the award. Only a decade earlier, or less, Earl Campbell, a talented African American kid in Texas, would have had to go to Michigan or Penn State to attend a major football program—or stay in the South and attend a historically black college. (In a sign of how much less exposure players at schools like Grambling or Jackson State receive, no player from a historically black university has ever won the Heisman.)

"I play football when I have my suit on," he said. "When I don't, I take care of my other business. I'm 22 years old and I don't know anyone in this world that I hate, and I don't know anyone that hates me. I don't see Earl Campbell as a black man. I see Earl Campbell as a man. I have too much other stuff going on to be drilling on the black and white issue."

*I don't see Earl Campbell as a black man.* If the answer reveals something about 1977—a black athlete in 1968, in the thick of raised fists, might not have demurred that way, nor would, for that matter, a black athlete in 2017, in the thick of lowered knees—it also says something about Earl Campbell and why, as Jenna Hays McEachern put it, he appeared to white fans as "unthreatening." Not four years earlier, Campbell had confronted Royal, telling the famed coach that Campbell men had been bought and sold for generations. And now, here, surrounded high up in Lower Manhattan by white Texas oilmen and bankers, people who normally would not associate with a twenty-two-year-old black man from Tyler, he was more politic. He was genuinely an open, generous, nonjudgmental country guy. Four years earlier, he had roomed with Lynn King, a white player at John Tyler High, and now the one teammate he invited along to the Heisman banquet was Ingraham, a white kid from suburban Austin. Or perhaps, with a professional contract floating before him, he was savvy enough not to say anything that might alienate potential employers. O. J., there in that room and already the golden TV pitchman for Hertz, had once ranked as his biggest accomplishment that "people look at me like a man first, not a black man."

Whatever the case, the answer echoed one he had given earlier that year to a student journalist for the *Daily Texan.* "I think my biggest thrill so far is being able to adjust to 41,000 people who go here, to be accepted as Earl Campbell the football player as well as Earl Campbell the man," he told Brad Buchholz. "Some people may be offended by this. I'm sorry, this is how I feel: I've learned how to deal with white people more. I learned how to respect them more as people—because I don't see myself as a black man. I see myself as a man. I've learned how to accept other men and other people as people."

The answers also suggest something about the varied topography of being black at a predominantly white university in 1977. Earl Campbell, star football player, was cosseted, praised, and befriended in ways that Erna Smith, a gay black journalist, also from rural Texas, surely was not.

That night in New York, though, Earl Campbell appeared to think of himself as just a guy playing football, one who was aware that his appeal was not world shaking. After all, his answer to the radio interviewer that night of the Heisman Trophy continued: "I am not a football player that brags. All I do is play. People that are interested will know what I do. Millions of Japanese won't know what I do no matter what. Football isn't the only thing. I enjoy making other people happy. Earl Campbell is happy all the time."

The radio interviewer apologized for asking him about race. "Look here," Campbell said, in a knowing joke about how his low drawl might come off to white people. "You didn't offend me. I just got a deep voice. You probably haven't heard me talk before."

The attendees were called to take their seats. Ann Campbell dabbed the perspiration from her brow. Earl was sporting an Afro above his bowtie, and a yellow rose was appended to his jacket. He and Rick Ingraham looked as if they were about to bust out of their tuxedos. In preparation for the broadcast, a TV director lectured guests about keeping their seats and talking quietly. When, shortly before live air, the director announced that "something is mechanically wrong," a smattering of cheers went up.

Despite the put-on glamour of the event, there was really no suspense to it. But after his name was called out for a warm-up award, for best offensive player of the year, Campbell suddenly got it in his head that he wasn't going to win the Heisman. He struggled to be gracious as he muttered through the remarks he had prepared—but he was shocked. "This isn't what I came to New York City for," he thought to himself.

Yet even as he was trying to sort out what had happened, Jay Berwanger, the first Heisman recipient, was announcing the main trophy of the evening, for the overall outstanding player. Ann Campbell crossed her fingers. Now Campbell's name was called again—he had received twice as many points in the voting as the runner-up—and he approached the lectern. But he had already said what it was he wanted to say, had already given the thanks he wanted to give, had already delivered his prepared remarks. "You know, when I was a kid and I'd get in trouble," he told the well-heeled crowd, "I'd always want to say, 'Hey, Momma, I'm in trouble.' So, 'Hey, Momma, I'm in trouble!'" The room burst into laughter.

Three weeks later, back at the Cotton Bowl in Dallas, Campbell took the field with the Longhorns in the national championship game against fifth-ranked Notre Dame. On a frigid afternoon, the Fighting Irish kept Campbell out of the end zone even as he picked up 118 yards on twenty-nine carries. McEachern's luck ran out, and he tossed three interceptions. On the opposite side of the ball, the Notre Dame running backs chewed up the Texas defense—and future Hall of Fame quarterback Joe Montana tossed a touchdown. The Longhorns lost 38–10.

For years after, Campbell's Heisman sat on a four-foot-tall pedestal, a chandelier above it, two wall-sized mirrors meeting in a corner beside it, in the home of his late mother, the home he built for her with money from his first contract, to play for the sweaty, rambunctious, growing, oil-rich metropolis of Houston.

# PART III
# HOUSTON

When Satan came to Houston,
He beat a quick retreat.
He loved its wicked people,
But he couldn't stand the heat.
  —*Houston Post*, July 1969

Heading into the late 1970s, Houston, Texas, a sprawling morass of a town, hot and mosquito-plagued, was the last place most professional football players wanted to end up. Its team was a mess, out of the playoffs for years. At its home games, at the famed Astrodome, half the seats were empty. Its owner was a fickle, uneasy man known for impulsively canning coaches and stonily waving off contract-renegotiation pleas from his most popular players. "When I was in Cleveland," center Fred Hoaglin once said, "if you had a bad game (the coach) would threaten to trade you to the Houston Oilers." Running back Vic Washington, dispatched to Houston in 1974 by the 49ers after three decent seasons in San Francisco, once said he considered the trade a form of punishment. During his single season in Houston, the team went 1–13; it was the second year in a row the team had posted that record. "We had no friends in the city," defensive end Elvin Bethea, who began playing with the team in 1968, once said. "Even my dog would bite me when I'd go home." Perhaps the plight of the Oilers was best summed up by a *Pittsburgh Post* columnist in the mid-1970s: the team is the "National Football League's garbage can; a disposal for the wretched refuse of 25 other, better football teams."

Once upon a time, in their early going, the Oilers had been a top-notch squad, winning, in 1960 and 1961, the first two American Football League championships. Team owner Bud Adams, fleshy faced, oleaginous, with layers of skin—he was once described as a hippopotamus of a man—had named the team after the family business. His father, Boots Adams, was chairman of Phillips Petroleum, and at age twenty-three, with a stake to his name, Bud had formed the Ada Oil Company. By 1959, when, in quixotic fancy, he formed the AFL with Lamar Hunt, another oilman's son, his was one of the largest gas distributors in the country. His office, modern in the way of a midcentury American executive, was cluttered with Native American artifacts and a Japanese rock garden.

There was something inscrutable about him. In the early 1960s, the franchise played its games outdoors, and no one could ever figure out why he wore a full-length leather coat in the muggy Houston heat. Eager to ingratiate himself with his players, he served lavish feasts with Black Forest stag and barbecued goat. "When we'd win," Dan Pastorini, his long-suffering quarterback told me, "he'd drag his rich political guys or rich rancher friends or rich oil friends, drag them down to the locker room and show us off like prize bulls—which is what we were." And yet he turned hard-hearted when top-notch, popular, homegrown players—players like Pastorini, who would get so beaten up behind a creaky offensive line that some Sunday evenings he couldn't lug himself to his second-floor bedroom—sought a contract renegotiation. After one of his best years, the outstanding Oilers receiver Ken Burrough approached the executive: "Mr. Adams, can we talk about me getting a raise right now?" "I think I pay you enough to do what you're doing," came the reply. "Let me know when you get married." A capricious man, he was free with his cash one day—he made a splash with his new team in 1959 by luring the Heisman winner Billy Cannon away from the NFL—miserly with it the next. During the salad days of the early 1960s, the team played at a high school football stadium, one so beaten up that the dirt had to be painted green on game day to make it look acceptable on television.

By the time of the 1970 NFL-AFL merger, the Oilers had spiraled into mediocrity, and then into something much worse. With its glory days seemingly in the past, the most notable thing about the team, apart from its perennial lousiness, was the stadium in which it now played. The Astrodome, which opened in 1965 and looked like something dropped from the cosmos, was a space-age temple to a peculiarly Houstonian vision of modernity. The world's first air-conditioned stadium, a feat of engineering known as the Eighth Wonder of the World, it stood as a testament to the singular capability of Texans to defy Mother Nature in favor of their own creature comforts. The stretched-out dome hovered over nine acres; a twenty-story building could have been built beneath its apex. Massive condensers moved two million cubic feet of air through the stadium every minute. Beyond wanting to cool what amounted to a giant solar oven plopped down among a cluster of highways, designers had worried particularly about the prospect of a cloud of tobacco smoke hanging in the air—not for health reasons as much as for the haze it might cast over the field.

Events hosted in the dome reflected something about the late-1960s, early-1970s moment: Muhammad Ali defended his heavyweight belt in 1967; the University of Houston snipped the UCLA Bruins' forty-seven-game winning streak in 1968 in basketball's Game of the Century; Sinatra emceed an event in 1969 to celebrate the return of the moon-landing Apollo 11 astronauts; Elvis performed in 1970; Evel Knievel jumped thirteen cars in 1971; and two years later Billie Jean King beat Bobby Riggs in tennis's Battle of the Sexes.

But by the late 1970s, what had seemed newfangled was cavernous, empty feeling, and pitiable. The dome, for example, was originally built with large glass windows to allow in sunlight for the natural grass. Yet baseball players found that the bright sun rays, in an otherwise artificially lit building, made it nearly impossible to locate a fly ball. Reflective panels to block out the sun were added, and in the place of the grass, the Monsanto Corporation created Astroturf. The problem, said Curley Culp, a former Houston Oiler defensive end, was that the turf was installed in fourteen-foot-wide ribbons, which was meant to make it easier to pick up and take down when the football field made way for a baseball field or a rodeo or a car show or any one of the thousands of events at the Astrodome. By the late 1970s, the decade-old seams between those ribbons of artificial turf had grown ragged, and players sometimes found themselves tripping over the carpet—and tearing knee and ankle ligaments. In a 1977 survey of players across the league, the Astrodome's playing surface was a nearly unanimous choice as the worst among the league's twenty-eight stadiums. Cincinnati's coach once threatened to pull the Bengals off the field if improvements weren't made. Compounding the problem was the lack of padding between the thin carpet and the concrete subfloor, making each hard collision with the ground feel bone crunching. "In the condition the field is in now," the beloved, Stetson-wearing Oiler coach Bum Phillips said in 1977, "a player could break his arm by simply falling on it."

If the Astrodome was space-age, the team's nearby practice facility was decidedly down-to-earth. A badly air-conditioned, drafty metal-frame building housed the weight equipment, dressing room, and training room. The floor was barely covered by a mangy, rotting carpet. Insulation hung out loosely from one wall. The coaching staff shared one shower stall. At least six players split lockers. And for more than fifty players there were three toilets and one whirlpool.

"To be real honest, when I first saw this place I couldn't believe it was where we really practiced," Tim Wilson, the team's fullback, said. "I'd say 50 percent of the high schools I've seen have better facilities than we do." The grass practice field was sometimes no better than packed dirt. "The Dolphins practiced here before the Super Bowl five years ago and I'm still taking abuse for it," another player, Carl Mauck, the center, said in 1979. "This place is a joke, the laughingstock of pro football."

In 1979, one month after Adams pledged to build a new practice facility that would be second to none, he backtracked with the unromantic argument that interest rates were too high. "I smelled a rat from the start," said the Oiler linebacker and resident motormouth Gregg Bingham. Upon hearing Adams's decision, Bethea, the team's longtime defensive end, turned to first-year Oiler Leon Gray, lying on the next table: "Leon, you're gonna be right there, on that same table, in 1984."

And to non-football-playing elites on the coasts, Houston itself, less than 150 years old, appeared to be a nouveau riche backwater—a hard-hat, roughneck town whose Stetson-wearing oilmen and their wives tried to acquire respect the fast way, with some of the best art, universities, and medical centers that crude could buy. At Cutter Bill, a western wear store frequented by the flush-of-cash crowd, browsing customers snacked on "Texas Crude," black-licorice-flavored jelly beans. Plied with cocktails by the staff—"It's 5 o'clock somewhere," they would murmur as they poured another drink—patrons might buy a fringed "Indian princess dress" with painted flowers and brass beads for $1,700. Or a "ceremonial warrior coat," laced with golden antelope fringe, with natural bone and beaded trim: "Just like Tonto!" trumpeted the catalogue.

Oil derricks were more than a red-and-blue decal on the team's helmets. They were like talismans, as popular as four-leaf-clover merchandise in Dublin. At Cutter Bill, named for the owner's champion cutting horse, you could buy, for $750, a fourteen-carat-gold ring ornamented by a derrick with three diamonds spurting from the top. There were oil-derrick-shaped table lamps and oil-derrick-embossed poker chips. They were a symbol of Texas industry and, perhaps, without too much imagination, manliness—the team's cheerleaders were known as the Derrick Dolls.

Houston in those go-go days couldn't elude the label of tacky. But in 1978, the year the Oilers, a team of sad sacks and misfits, managed to draft Earl Campbell, Houston found chic. Or, perhaps, chic found Houston. The oil derrick suddenly became cool. The very honky-tonks and down-market western wear emporiums, which Campbell, in his jock, authentically Texas way, patronized, suddenly zoomed to the forefront of the zeitgeist—cowboy became couture, country-and-western tunes reached the top of the charts. No one was more country than Earl Campbell, and at decade's end, the nation's tastemasters decided country was *it*.

The seeds of chic had been planted a couple of years earlier. The Johnny Appleseed was a twenty-nine-year-old from Itasca, Texas, south of Dallas–Fort Worth, who had moved to New York City to work in television and found herself striking out as a fashion photographer. On a visit to her hometown in 1975, Judi Buie asked her parents to buy her a pair of boots for Christmas. "Absolutely no one was wearing cowboy boots in New York back then. But I just felt they'd look great with my gypsy skirts," she said in 1982. Models, intrigued by the look, asked the photographer snapping their pictures to bring back boots from her next trip in Texas. By the following November, just about a year before Earl Campbell showed up in Manhattan to collect his Heisman Trophy, she threw a party at the newly opened Lone Star Café in New York City, a kind of Texas cultural embassy near Washington Square Park that sported a sculpture of a forty-foot iguana. The evening's motto was "Too Much Ain't Enough"; Andy Warhol and Halston showed up, and Texas chic was born. The café booked Willie Nelson and Asleep at the Wheel, and Buie started selling boots as fast as she could get her hands on them: Liza Minnelli, Barbra Streisand, Catherine Deneuve, and a young Brooke Shields were seen sporting her wares. Soon cowboy boots were selling for $2,000 a pop on Madison Avenue; Buie was pulling down $300,000 a year.

The man who managed to bring Earl Campbell from Austin to Houston was himself the quintessential urban cowboy. Bum Phillips's parents had saddled him with the first name Oail—"Can't anybody spell it or pronounce it or anything," he said—and his nickname was coined after his three-year-old sister Edrina, with her stabbing efforts at "brother," kept saying "Bumble," soon shortened to plain old "Bum." "As long as it's a name and not a description," he once quipped. In Beaumont, the site of Spindletop, the first great gusher in Texas, his father ran an auto repair business and kept some dairy cows on the side. At the outbreak of World War II, Bum joined the marine corps—and found, quickly, that he didn't care for that style of discipline and groupthink: "I never joined anything else the rest of my life. I went in as a private and 31 months later, I came out as a private. I thought they couldn't win that war without me. Then I got in there and they couldn't win because of me. The Marine Corps was real spit 'n polish. I wasn't." He continued: "I never have liked anything where a guy tried to make me do something. I don't mind somebody asking me to do something, but the Marines prided themselves on the fact that, 'By God, you're gonna do it because we told you to.' I just don't like for somebody to be bitchin' at me all the time."

Like many Beaumont boys during the postwar period of massive industrial expansion in that part of Texas, he found himself working at a refinery. That didn't last long either. He was told to contribute to a charity—one not of his choice, but of the company's. Chafing at the order, he told the foreman to have his check ready for him at the front gate and not to expect to see him back. That very day, driving home, newly unemployed, he passed Lamar College, saw players practicing football, and stuck around to watch. A coach came over, chatted him up, and suggested he try out. And so, even while riding in a rodeo on the side for spending money, he more or less majored in football.

A couple of decades later, having embarked on a nomadic, highly successful coaching career that included stops at no fewer than sixteen high schools and colleges, he won a big break when Sid Gillman hired him in the late 1960s as his defensive coordinator in San Diego. Gillman, who as a nerdy kid in Minneapolis working as a movie theater usher removed football segments from newsreels so he could play them backward and forward on a projector he had set up at home, was a cherished mentor to a whole cadre of coaches. And when Gillman took the job in Houston—the post came up frequently—Phillips went with him.

Gillman, who favored bow ties and smoked a pipe, stabilized the club, finishing with a 7-7 record in 1974, but that wasn't good enough for Bud Adams. Suddenly Phillips, who looked like an old rodeo clown—folksy, potbellied, and crew-cut, with an affinity for feather-banded cowboy hats, wide-collared western shirts, and thick-lensed, oversized eyeglasses—was the top man. Willie Nelson tapes cluttered the cab of his pickup. He could play a tune or two on the harmonica. Coors or Budweiser in hand, he convened his coaches for Thursday-night strategy sessions at tiny rural barbecue joint called The Swinging Door. On the sidelines on game day, he wore pressed jeans and spat tobacco.

His mama had told him never to wear his hat inside his own house, so he never wore his Stetson in the Astrodome. He favored hand-tooled boots, and in 1978 his boots of choice were a powder-blue pair made of anteater and ostrich skin. He got them from Sanders Bootmakers, a firm in El Paso that had its factory across the border in Juarez. His one piece of instruction: make the toes as pointy as possible. The toe had to be sharp enough, in cowboy parlance, to kill a cockroach in a corner.

"I'd like to get him into a more rounded toe, but he won't hear of it," the firm's owner, Reginald Sanders, said the summer before the 1978 season. And then he made a crack about Bud Adams's penchant for firing coaches: "I guess I don't blame him: You can't climb fences real fast with a rounded toe, and someday he's gonna be in a hell of a hurry to get out of the Astrodome."

During all those years as a high school football coach—in the East Texas town of Nederland, in neighboring Port Neches, and in the Panhandle city of Amarillo—he had refined a blunt, simple style of football, which made it easy to pack up your Xs and Os and teach them to the next group of youngsters. But would it translate to the pros? For eight seasons the Oilers had been shut out of the playoffs. Now, as the fall of 1977 came to a close with Phillips's team finishing 8–6—an improvement over the previous year's record of 5–9—and with his career hanging by a thread, the coach needed a vehicle for his style.

Earl Campbell, all power and speed, a physically candid runner, appeared to be the perfect match. But there was a problem: the Oilers were slated to pick seventeenth in the draft in the spring of 1978, and to be sure of getting Campbell, the newly minted Heisman winner, they had to have a much higher pick.

The Longhorns' big loss to Notre Dame in the national championship game worked in the Oilers' favor. Some in football thought perhaps Campbell wasn't as good as advertised. But Bum's son, Wade Phillips, who had studied the film, still thought the Oilers should go after Campbell. "Texas wasn't blocking well," said Wade Phillips, then a young assistant coach. "Campbell made some of the most impressive 3- or 4-yard runs I'd ever seen." Outmaneuvering the Los Angeles Rams, also keen to draft Campbell, Bum Phillips convinced Tampa Bay to trade its number one overall pick for the Oilers' tight end and four draft picks.

It was a steal, and the Oilers camp was giddy. "You know the old cliché about the kind of player who comes around only once every five or ten years?" one Oilers scout said. "Well Earl Campbell is the kind that comes around once every 25 years."

Seldom has an athlete been so closely associated with a particular moment in a particular state. In April 1978, less than two years after Buie started selling Texas boots in the Big Apple, a month before Earl Campbell was drafted by the Oilers, a soap opera about a wealthy feuding Texas family—the Ewings—premiered in prime time. That summer saw the Broadway opening of the musical *The Best Little Whorehouse in Texas*. (Commenting on the sudden national fascination with the Lone Star State, the journalist Gary Cartwright quipped: "Somehow, *The Best Little Whorehouse in New Jersey* just doesn't sound right.") Off-Broadway, Kathy Bates was starring in *Vanities*, a play about three former Texas cheerleaders who find their adult friendships dissolving—and at the Pussycat Theater in Times Square, you could catch the new movie *Debbie Does Dallas*. Ralph Lauren that year unveiled his western line—"It's not fashion, it's life," he announced, explaining that while traveling out west in search of cowboy clothes, he found none he liked and so decided to create his own. The cowboy, it seemed, was as much fantasy as reality.

Even in Texas: in Pasadena, on the industrial southeastern fringe of Houston, out on the concrete prairie, an area broken up by round, squat chemical silos lit up like gaudy Christmas trees at night, was a massive warehouse of a nightclub that catered to the marooned cowboy. The spot was Gilley's—named after the country-and-western star Mickey Gilley, a part owner of the club, a frequent performer there, and a cousin of Jerry Lee Lewis. It could hold at least 4,500 people for a Willie Nelson concert. It had a few dozen pool tables, shuffleboard tables, and booths selling ropes and saddles, T-shirts, and custom-made boots. It had a monthly magazine and a couple of recording studios. In this cathedral to country, cigarette smoke hung in the air and tobacco juice and used chewing gum soiled the asphalt floor.

More than anything, it had ways of geysering pent-up energy, of the physical or sexual nature. It was a place where steel-toe boots were traded for leather ones, where cheap Lone Star beer flowed fast, where aggressions were easily settled. A local Monopoly-like game had a card that said not "Go directly to jail" but "Go to Gilley's and get stomped." It had a whole bunch of punching bags, to keep the shitkickers from kicking the shit out of one another—and, famously, a mechanical bull. Mattresses, dozens of them, lay around the bull. Any time Gilley's customers saw a mattress put out on the curb, they would pull over and throw it in the bed of their pickup, for delivery to the club. Seven nights a week, country acts were on the live bill, the music loud enough to drown out the fists hitting the bags, the churning of the bull, and the sliding of the two-steppers.

When the house lights came up at 2:15 a.m. and the Mexican-American cleanup crews got to work, they found wooden chairs half flung about, great pools of liquid on the floor, broken bottles, glasses strewn everywhere, and huge pyramids of beer cans. The two trough-style urinals in one of the men's rooms were inevitably stopped up and nearly brimming.

The patrons were "country boys come to the stinking city to make some money and have a rambunctious time," the longtime Texas newspaperman Billy Porterfield once wrote. They (or their parents) had moved to urban areas from a rural South that had been left behind—poverty levels in those parts were about 6 percent higher than in any other region of the country as the 1980s approached. The combination of cheap land, a race to the bottom on tax breaks in the 1960s and 1970s, low wages, and an unorganized labor force contributed to what politicians and industrial recruiters called the South's "good business climate." But even as the standard of living increased for many southerners, a vast underclass was spawned in the rural areas bypassed by industrialization. The per capita income of rural black southerners barely reached 30 percent of the US average in 1980; early in that decade, over three-fourths of rural black children under eighteen years old living in a female-headed household—the situation in which Earl Campbell had lately found himself—were poor.

And so, if they could scrape together the money to afford the move, if they had skills to offer, a great tide of young men and women, the sons and daughters of farmers, fishermen, and ranchers, washed up on the fringes of Houston. Earl Campbell was one of those young people, and his skill, unusual as it was, was a prodigious talent for carrying a football. Another was Bum Phillips, a white man who had grown up in the petrochemical heartland as the area was transforming from rural ranches to oil and gas refineries. When he was a boy, his first cowboy hats, hand-me-downs from his grandfather, a ranch boss, were stuffed with tissue paper to make them fit.

They brought with them small relics of their old life: their Bibles, their photographs, and their recipes. East Texas African Americans migrated to Houston with their meat-smoking customs. In black barbecue joints, you could find smoked sausage links consisting of a heavily seasoned mixture of ground beef and suet stuffed into natural hog casings, also known as "grease balls," "juicy links," and "garlic bombs." Earl Campbell, who, after his pro football career, started a successful sausage company, had grown up with spicy hot links cooked on the grill; in Houston, a melting pot of flavors, he could indulge in a taste of home by visiting any number of barbecue spots run by black migrants.

More than 1.5 million people lived in Houston in 1978. Close to 100,000 people arrived in that year alone, and 142,000 new telephones were hooked up. All told, Houston added 670,000 jobs during the 1970s. Bank deposits jumped from about $6 billion to $24 billion; office space grew to 100 million square feet from 30 million. This was what an oil boom looked like.

"The unemployed pour into town in their hopeful thousands, clutching the want ads," the Welsh writer Jan Morris observed in a 1981 story for *Texas Monthly*. "Hour by hour the freeways get fuller, the downtown towers taller, the River Oaks residents richer; the suburbs gnaw their way deeper into the countryside; and what was just a blob on the map a couple of decades ago becomes more than just a city—an idea, a vision, the Future Here and Now!"

Pasadena, home to oil refineries and paper plants, was where many of those émigrés—especially the white ones—found jobs. Nicknamed "Stinkadena," the area was permeated by a stench that some cracked was the smell of money. The great mass of rural Texans and Louisianans flowing into Houston for work during the boom days of the 1970s got their evening kicks at honky-tonks like Gilley's. At their peak in the late 1970s, Armco Steel and the Baytown Works, two massive steel mills located along the Houston Ship Channel, employed more than 6,500 laborers who, in the heat and flash of liquid metal, cast untold tons of steel beams, giant plates, and drill pipes to feed the seemingly unending appetite for yet more oil and gas wells.

Who were these Gilley-goers? They were overwhelmingly white, working-class, and, often, members of their local unions. Soon enough, they would be labeled Reagan Democrats—and decades later, many of them were Trump supporters. The place was on the "redneck end of the hippie-redneck spectrum," according to the cultural historian Jason Mellard. Ninety-nine percent of the patrons were white or Hispanic, said Gilley's regular Gator Conley. About five miles from the club, the Ku Klux Klan operated a bookstore on the corner of a major Pasadena intersection—parked out front was a van emblazoned with the words "Nigger Go Home." Stop at a red light and you might get handed some literature from a man scurrying about under a sheet. A cell leader of the American Nazi Party, asked once why he had resettled from St. Louis as far south as Pasadena to lead a branch of the group, explained: "This was the whitest place I could find."

In short, Gilley's patrons put the honky in honky-tonk.

And nestled among them were members of the Houston Oilers: their fun-loving temperamental, libertine, the mop-headed and handsome and oft-cracked-ribbed quarterback, Dan Pastorini;

their stout six-four center, Carl Mauck, a blonde, boisterous crew-cut midwesterner who worked as a beer delivery man in the off-season; and as soon as he arrived in Houston, the black running back from deep East Texas, who took his turn on the mechanical bull and was always good for at least a couple of beers before heading home to his wife. Earl Campbell, catholic in his approach to the world, was perfectly comfortable scarfing down a garlic bomb at the all-black Kozy Kitchen before heading over to carouse at the all-white Gilley's.

The *Esquire* writer Aaron Latham, dispatched in the summer of 1978 to Gilley's to write about the sociology of the place, found it populated by "saloon cowboys" long divorced from the country, young men dislocated and unmoored, each trying to "escape from the overwhelming complexities of his petrochemical days into the simplicity of his honky-tonk nights."

Some of them had never set foot in rural, cowboying Texas. But they had parents born there, or grandparents, and Latham's piece is about how they channeled their dislocation into physical competition, a search for their inner Marlboro Man, at Gilley's. His article "The Ballad of the Urban Cowboy: America's Search for True Grit" appeared in *Esquire* in mid-September, just after the second game of Campbell's rookie season. It isn't hard to see how the Houston Oilers, a football team with a cowboy coach and a cowboy running back, migrants themselves to the big city, might have appealed to the Gilley's crowd.

"The story was obvious," Latham told *Texas Monthly* for a 2015 oral history about the movie *Urban Cowboy*, which was based on his *Esquire* piece. "These kids were coming in from the country to find themselves in a mechanized city, just another cog in the wheel."

Earl Campbell, descending on Houston in the summer of 1978, only a few years removed from Tyler, Texas, was one of those kids. He was black, yes, and Latham's version of the story was a white one—the country-and-western scene in Houston was dominated by Anglos, and virtually all the musicians they listened to were white—but Earl Campbell, in his ecumenical way, loved Gilley's.

During Campbell's senior year in Austin, his old coach, Darrell Royal, would call up his favorite running back after curfew and convince him to slip out of his dorm. "Come on over, there's goin' to be some pickin'," Royal would murmur, and soon they'd be holed up in a honky-tonk or at Royal's place, talking about—or with—Waylon Jennings and Charley Pride and Willie Nelson and Merle Haggard.

Now, unpretentious and very, very country—polite, handy, a smoker of meats, a rose farmer, more cowboy than urban—Campbell appeared a perfect fit for Houston, the great absorber of refugees from the rural hinterlands. He, in turn, embraced the city, freely quoting Merle Haggard: "Big city, turn me loose and set me free," he said once, about playing in Houston. When Willie showed up to play at Gilley's, Earl was often there, sitting with a pair of the Oiler faithful—an older couple named Whitworth who used to RV to the Oilers' summer training camp and all their games at the dome (Whit Whitworth worked in Baytown for Exxon)—just to the left of the dance floor, not far from the bandstand. When Willie sang "Mammas, Don't Let Your Babies Grow Up to Be Cowboys," Earl invariably joined him on stage. At one press conference, he announced that he would "walk halfway across hell and Texas to hear Willie Nelson sing a country song."

Perhaps it says something about Earl Campbell, about his easiness with the world, that he was comfortable in a club that was virtually all-white, listening to musicians who were nearly always white. "Earl was the whitest black man I ever covered," the longtime *Houston Post* Oilers beat reporter Dale Robertson told me. "His entire life philosophy was quoting country lyrics."

Ahead of contract negotiations with the Oilers, Campbell hired Mike Trope, a young agent in Los Angeles who had recently represented the running backs Ricky Bell and Tony Dorsett. "Earl made it a precondition that I visit his mother in Tyler," Trope said, and he retraced the pilgrimages that Darrell Royal and other college coaches had made to the old house. "It wasn't a business meeting;

it's more like you have to meet the father before asking her to marry you." Trope was charming, bright—and, perhaps, naïve. Following twenty hours of negotiations, Trope and Adams agreed to a contract worth roughly $1.3 million, including a $500,000 signing bonus. Cigars all around. But under Adams's terms, Campbell deferred all but $200,000; the rest would be parceled out $25,000 a year into the 1990s, ensuring that the bulk of the money remained in Adams's hands, where it would earn him interest or investment wealth for years. Either Adams snowed Trope, or the agent screwed over Campbell. "His grandmother could have done a better job for him," the agent Jerry Argovitz told reporters. "And she's been dead for 10 years." It probably hadn't helped that in the middle of contract negotiations, Campbell, interviewed by the *Tyler Morning Telegraph*, said he would play for $50.

His second agent, Witt Stewart, who originally joined Campbell halfway through his rookie season to work on endorsement deals, said Campbell didn't fully grasp the terms of the contract he had signed. "I mean, he didn't know what the word 'deferred' meant," Stewart said. "He told me he had trouble sleeping at night knowing that he was a millionaire. And I said, 'Earl, you can sleep real good.' And I explained to him the contract. And it was life-changing. He felt totally misled."

"Leverage was negligible," insisted Trope. Players at the time "didn't have freedom to select what team to play for." There was another problem: Campbell and other African American athletes were at a competitive disadvantage, Trope said, because some team officials took race unfairly into account. He said that during one negotiation, one general manager told him, "These black guys spend money as quickly as they get it, so what difference does it make?" Johnny Sample, a former professional cornerback, told *Jet* magazine in 1973 that during his time in the league in the 1960s, black players were usually offered $6,000 less than white players—in 1969, the average NFL salary was $25,000. And advertisers were generally less keen to hire black players to hawk their products, shutting them off from important endorsement money. In *North Dallas Forty*,

Peter Gent's thinly veiled novel about his time on the Dallas Cowboys, the narrator, Phil Elliott, a white wide receiver, calculates that he will have a favorable contract-negotiating position because several receiver or tight end slots have already been taken by African Americans: "They wouldn't give another black a shot unless he was awful good," he decides. "The color of my skin was the only point in my favor."

Indeed, a decade before he was drafted by Houston, Campbell—or at least a player not quite the star he was—might not have been offered a position on the Oilers at all. Through the mid-1960s, the Oilers had in place a "Negro quota system," a policy against having more than five black players at any time. Often, like most clubs, they would keep an even number (two or four) so that black ballplayers would always have a roommate and a white player would never be forced to share a room with one.

But in 1966, the Oilers hired Tom Williams, an African American former football and track coach at Grambling, to recruit black players. In an interview with *Jet* magazine, Williams said the Grambling athletic staff, disgusted by the cap on black players, used to turn off the television when Oiler games were broadcast. Claiming that the club's owner wasn't to blame, the Oilers' quota, Williams told *Jet*, "was the fault of the people who work for Adams." "I've been told to go after the best athletes, white or Negro," he said. The next year, with the quota dropped, the squad had fifteen African Americans.

Still, into the 1970s, the racial composition of southern teams—Colts (Baltimore), Cowboys (Dallas), Oilers (Houston), Saints (New Orleans), and Dolphins (Miami)—had a statistically significant smaller representation of African Americans than nonsouthern teams. "The management of southern teams may assume that their white fans"—for example, the urban cowboys and cowgirls who packed Gilley's, or the attorneys and bankers who lived in Houston's posh River Oaks neighborhood—"will be more predisposed to identify with the team if its black members are kept at a minimum," observed Jonathan Brower in his 1973 University of California at Santa Barbara dissertation, "The Black Side of Football: The Salience of Race." Explaining how the Oilers of the 1970s operated, former (black) Oilers defensive lineman Curley Culp, who overlapped with Campbell on the squad, told me the thinking was that "if your fans have a particular hue, you want that on the team." Brower interviewed NFL players, management personnel, and scouts. Among black players, he found, there was a "common belief that it is necessary for the black to be superior to the white in order to make the team." Even after quotas were wound down, NFL teams used a practice they called "stacking," which involved pitting black athletes against each other for openings informally reserved for black players. Here was how it worked on one team, as one scout explained it to Brower: "Two of the team's best offensive tackle candidates (both black) were competing against each other in drills on the practice field. One of the two outplayed the other, and this differential in playing ability between the two blacks justified cutting the less capable of the two even though he was better than most of the white offensive tackles retained by the team."

George Plimpton gets a similar explanation in *Paper Lion*, his story of training with the Detroit Lions in 1963: "Even in the strict business of football, despite what was said, if one probed it was easy enough to find the taint of prejudice. One of the coaches told me that as a matter of principle he would never want to have more than six Negro players on a team: cliques formed if you had that many—that was his idea—and the whole all-important concept of the team went awry." Into the 1970s, the Dallas Cowboys appeared to reserve one slot for a white running back and one for an African American. And owners were especially keen to snuff out political demonstrations. In a harbinger of the blacklisting of Colin Kaepernick, Brower found that black players in the 1970s who were deemed "troublemakers" because they complained about racism—being referred to as "boys," say, by a coach, while the white players were called "men"—risked being cut. Again, Phil Elliott, Gent's alter ego in *North Dallas Forty*, explains why more black players didn't speak out: "Fear. They all got too much to lose. To them being a second-class citizen on a football team is a hell of a lot better than being a first-class citizen in south Dallas. The ones that did speak up are gone."

By 1978, when Earl joined the squad, the Oilers had black players in key positions: Billy "White Shoes" Johnson, a speedster known for his Funky Chicken end zone celebration; Kenny Burrough, a wide receiver who had won high school state track titles in his native Florida—and who, despite being admitted to the University of Florida, he told me, opted to go to a historically black university in Houston after his family got threatening messages at home; linebacker Robert Brazile, known as Dr. Doom; the quick-as-a-cat cornerback Willie Alexander; and defensive linemen Bethea and Culp and offensive lineman Leon Gray.

Adams bet that Campbell, the Texas native son, would help sell tickets on Sundays—indeed, Oiler home games sold out after Earl was drafted. Phillips had predicted, rightly, the fan base would be grateful: "If there's one thing Texans hate more than losing their oil, it's losing their football players." The Oilers made a big show of the signing: Campbell was helicoptered from Houston Intercontinental Airport to the practice field to shake Adams's hand in front of the news media. In a demonstration of generosity, Adams bestowed on Campbell, then and there, on the field, a new Lincoln Continental Mark V. Columbia blue, with a white canopy—roughly the Oilers colors—and little porthole windows toward the rear; it was an impossibly long, bulky car, an impressive piece of machinery. It was apparently the second vehicle that Campbell had been given that year; in February, the people of Tyler had presented the twenty-two-year-old with a van as the culmination of Earl Campbell Day.

The automobiles marked a material and metaphorical manifestation of his journey out of Tyler. Earl had always had a special lust for cars, but his lifelong poverty had left him bereft of a vehicle of his own. Even during his first trip to Austin in the fall of 1974 in Henry Bell's Monte Carlo, he remembered "driving through Palestine and Corsicana . . . saying, 'I wish I had this car for myself.'" At the conclusion of an interview in his dorm room with a student reporter a couple of years later, Campbell reached for his UT letter jacket and a small-brimmed straw hat before asking for a ride. He and the student reporter, Brad Buchholz, walked to Buchholz's car, a blue 1956 T-Bird. "'I want it,' he says softly as we get in. What? 'I want it . . . the car.'" Mo Olian, a UT alum who volunteered as a mentor for black football students, remembered pulling up in his gray 1957 Rolls Royce Silver Cloud II and Earl Campbell's gobsmacked reaction—"so reticent to even touch it, asking if that was OK, in his always deeply reserved and so-humble way."

And as his senior year approached, Earl called Wally Scott, an Austin attorney and Longhorn booster who had helped steer him to Austin, and told him he "wanted to talk business." Scott said the two of them should meet at Don Weedon's filling station. Here is how Scott, who died in 2005, described the episode in an unpublished memoir:

> Earl said, "Mr. Scott, I need a car." I said, "Earl, you are poor, aren't you, and you have been poor all your life?" He said, "Yes, sir." I then said: Earl, if you had a car, you couldn't afford to buy gasoline. You room with Alfred Jackson, and he has a car. Borrow his car. You don't have to be poor but a few more months. But if you have to have a car, just go down to any bank in Austin and tell the receptionist, "I am Earl and I want to see the President." I can assure that she will put you in his office and if you tell him you want to borrow the money for a car to be paid back in two or three months when you sign your pro contract, he will loan you the money. However, you should also know that when you show up on the campus with a new car, all of our enemies will say, "I knew they bought him, and they are just now giving him his car."

That summer, he ended up buying a '67 Oldsmobile back in Tyler for a few hundred dollars—"Hop in my Rolls," he joked to passengers.

Now, after years of yearning for other people's luxury or classic cars, he finally had, it appeared, one of his own.

Shortly after the signing, however, Campbell drove the Lincoln back to Austin, where he got a call from the Lincoln dealership to arrange for the $289 monthly payments. Welcome to the Oilers: the car, it turned out, wasn't a gift after all. Campbell called his mother and asked her what to do. The following day, he got back in the Continental and drove it straight to Houston to return it to Adams.

(Suspicious, underhanded circumstances around Oiler contracts were not unusual: Culp, the defensive lineman, told me that Bud Adams would agree one day to terms and then the next present a contract with different ones. "Bottom Line Bud" was a behind-his-back nickname. Once, as a signing bonus, Elvin Bethea ended up getting a bunch of cattle and livestock from Adams. Later, said Pastorini, Bethea, came "to find out there was some kind of drought; all of his cows died and all of Bud's cows lived.")

Whatever the terms of Earl Campbell's contract—at each Pro Bowl and inside the Oilers' locker room, he heard that he was underpaid, until he renegotiated his deal in 1980—he finally had the money to get a quick start on what he described as his prime goal: "to build a house for my mother so that when she lays down at night she can't see the Big Dipper." He had grown up in poverty and subsisted on little in college, even as he made the University of Texas millions in alumni donations and national television exposure, and now, finally, he had cash of his own. Ever since people started telling him in high school that he could one day go pro, that had been his dream.

"It's going to be simple and it's going to be big," said Ann Campbell, who already had nine grandkids. "I want them to have plenty of room when they come see me. The main thing is to have a house that's full of love and a roof that doesn't leak."

The four-bedroom house—brick, low slung, insulated—was finished in May 1979. It was a middle-class sort of place, one that wouldn't be out of place in any number of 1970s suburban developments, but in the pines and farmland northwest of Tyler, it appeared grand and, especially, solid. The old ramshackle place remained, as a kind of house museum, just behind it. Ann Campbell opened the new house up to the public—visitors lined up outside her home to catch a glimpse of the Heisman Trophy, on a pedestal by the living room. She was asked what she made of her son's contract and how it felt to have a place of her own. "All this money don't make me nervous," she said. "I was always in fine places, beautiful homes. They may not have been mine, but I could enjoy them just the same."

To get away from the big city, the Oilers opened their 1978 training camp in the former frontier military outpost of San Angelo, a wide-streeted town of just under 75,000, a brushland, desertlike sort of place so dry that five years earlier one of the town's reservoirs had caught fire.

At the training camp were more than a few walk-ons hoping to catch the eye of a coach and be signed to the team. They included an operator of Houston cement trucks; an actor from a New York improv troupe; a grade-school teacher; a night guard at the state prison in Huntsville; an antiques refurbisher; the driver of an ice cream truck; and an industrial machinery salesman. But Earl Campbell, the reigning Heisman Trophy winner, didn't enter camp with any kind of swagger. The longtime Austin sports reporter Kirk Bohls, who had gotten to know Campbell when the running back was at the University of Texas, remembers an insecurity about him as he prepared for his rookie season: "I'll never forget one starry night at training camp in San Angelo in the summer of 1978 when a nervous Campbell and I sat on a curb outside his dormitory and he told me, 'I don't know if I'm good enough to play at this level.' I told him he was nuts because he was going to turn the league on its ear. I really went out on a limb there."

The rookie's need for reassurance also struck Tim Wilson, the second-year fullback who would act as Campbell's lead blocker. "I remember one time he asked me, 'Do you think I can really make this team?' And he was serious. I felt like telling him, 'Man, you probably *are* this team.'" Even players Campbell was displacing realized quickly they had little standing for complaint. "It was the second day of camp," recalled Rob Carpenter, who had led the team in rushing the previous year.

> Earl took a little off-tackle play to the right and accelerated into the line. At that point in camp, your linemen aren't going full speed, and it was one of those routine plays where the line is stalemated and the play is going to stack up. Most people would have turned it outside. Earl put his head down. Next thing anyone knew, he had his right shoulder pad on (offensive lineman) Ed Fisher and his left on (offensive lineman) Conway Hayman, and he knocked those guys about three yards forward. Then he pushed the whole pile into the defensive guys and knocked them back. It was only about a four-yard gain, but it's a no-gain for most backs. And I'm standing there, thinking, "Well, OK, he's proved his point to me."

In a sense, Campbell's was the kind of anxiety endemic among professional players, who constantly worry about playing time and compete for management's approbation. The fear is simple: if you don't outperform the guy next to you, you could be out of a job. Money was something the players and coaches talked about constantly.

What passed for glamour on the team belonged to the quarterback, the romantically named Dante Antonio Pastorini. A poor man's Joe Namath, Pastorini was a California heartthrob who had once counted as a wife the Playboy bunny June Wilkinson—known as "the Bosom." "She may be why Pastorini is continually having abdominal pulls," an Oiler PR man once told the writer Roy Blount. Pastorini had declined an invitation to appear naked as a centerfold—"It wouldn't have bothered me," said the then–Mrs. Pastorini, "I think his body is so gorgeous the whole world should see it"—but during that training camp he agreed to judge the weekly wet T-shirt contest at Danceland. Occasionally, the winner would show up with him at practice the next morning.

His spirit was emblematic of the team's. He drag-raced cars and starred in the B movies *Weed: The Florida Connection* and *Naked Sun* (aka *Killer Fish*), in which he played a skin-diving jewel thief who meets his demise courtesy of some hungry piranhas.

Pastorini was tough, too—early in his Oiler career, he was the first NFL quarterback to don a flak jacket so that he could continue playing with broken ribs. He spent most of his career behind a porous offensive line, and so despite a rocket of an arm—he was drafted by the Oilers with the third overall pick in 1971, after turning down an offer to play baseball with the New York Mets—he typically completed fewer than half his passes, tossing more interceptions than touchdowns in most seasons. But now, finally, he had a competent group of men playing ahead of him—and a premier power back behind him. "Every quarterback wants a running back like Earl," Pastorini said.

In training camp in San Angelo, Campbell, naturally, gained the most scrutiny. After he stumbled during a drill that involved sprinting backward, reporters asked Phillips for his thoughts. "If y'all think about it, we didn't draft him to go backward," he said. Another time, they asked about Earl Campbell's slow time in the mile run. Reporters observed that Campbell couldn't—or didn't—cover the distance without stopping. "That's all right," Phillips deflected, "We just won't give him the ball on third down and a mile to go." The coaches were actually thrilled about what they were seeing from Campbell: He "has two speeds—crawling and exploding," said running back coach Andy Bourgeois. "He's as far along as any rookie I've ever coached. We will get the ball to Earl enough times for him to set the world on fire."

Earl, for his part, remained resolutely country. "Easy Earl" he was nicknamed by one of his Oiler teammates for his laid-back way off the field. "You know what he reminds me of?" Bourgeois said. "A Sunday morning. Just an easy Sunday morning." In training camp in San Angelo, Campbell, like all rookies, was forced to sing a song.

He opted for "Mamma, Don't Let Your Babies Grow Up to Be Cowboys"—Willie and Waylon's version had topped the country charts that year. Here was a 220-pound, twenty-three-year-old man with a sizable Afro, standing in shoulder pads on a cafeteria table, belting: "Cowboys ain't easy to love and they're harder to hold."

In fact, just about the only notable matchup during that preseason was against the Oilers' cross-state rivals. The Cowboys had glamour, they had their famous cheerleaders, and they had victories—during the 1970s, the 'Boys won more games than any other NFL team. The Cowboys could arguably lay claim to having more fans in Houston than the Oilers. And the situation on Sundays in Tyler was indicative of that in much of the state: if both Dallas and Houston were playing at the same time, Tyler's sole broadcast television station wanted the Cowboys, native son be damned.

Compared with Houston, the Cowboys even had sophistication. "If you could count to three you could play for the Oilers," Thomas "Hollywood" Henderson, a linebacker who played for both teams, wrote in his memoir. "They were not a high-tech system. I never saw a playbook while I was there." The Cowboys, on the other hand, distributed notebooks three inches thick, "every page a defense and a diagram that I'd never seen," Henderson wrote. "Here was the 31 Safety Zone, the 41–46 Man, the 41–46 Zone, the 48 Banjo Flex Strong Tiger. There were inside defenses and outside defenses and (head coach) Tom Landry's famous flex weak and flex strong. And every defense had at least six variations." The linebacker coach, a longtime Landry assistant, gave each player a few colored pens. "'Your blue pen is for flow weak,' he told us. 'Your red pen is for 'fire' or flow strong. Your green pen is for passes—you draw the routes of the backs and receivers out of the backfield.'"

There was a kind of choreography to the way the Cowboys played. A beat after taking their stances, for example, the offensive linemen, in unison, would stand and reset—a maneuver intended to mask the pre-snap backfield motion known as the Landry Shift. The Oilers' style, as captured by Gray, the lineman who joined the team in 1979, was simpler: "Try to knock the other guy off the line of scrimmage. It's one-on-one, you against him. Nothing fancy. Either he whips you or you whip him. It's the lowest common denominator."

Chiefly, the teams were creatures of their coaches. Landry, who had won 116 pro games by the time Phillips was named Houston's head coach, was a stoic, a hard-ass, a brainiac; Phillips was folksy, emotional, a players' coach. "Dallas players are made to feel that Landry's system is what wins games and not the people involved," Steve Kiner, a linebacker on the Cowboys' 1970 Super Bowl team who also played for the Oilers, said. "It's sort of like the players themselves don't really matter, that the system would win anyway whoever you put in." Landry required that beards be shaven and moustaches trimmed at the corner of the mouth. He put his player through his notorious 110s: you had to run 110 yards and back in sixty seconds, ten times.

Phillips threw beer-and-pizza parties with his players and took them bowling. "Everybody makes fun of these little chickenbleep parties," he once said.

> But don't tell me they're unimportant. You gotta remember, friendship is nothin' you can take from a guy. He has to give it. That means sometimes you have to take the first step. It isn't that the whites don't like the blacks or that the blacks don't like the whites. They're just more comfortable staying by themselves. That's why I think you should have the parties. Force 'em to mix.

In this spirit, he would stop practice to surprise players with an ice cream truck. Thursdays were beer keg days at the training field. Saturdays, players could bring their wives, kids, and dogs.

> I don't want to say too much about this because I'm still trying to fool some of these guys, but the only secret I've found is to recognize that everyone's different and has to

be treated differently. There's not one right way to treat a player, just as there's not one right way to treat a coach. You deal with a player the way you want him to deal with you. You can't expect loyalty if you're not loyal. It doesn't work that way. Sure I'm close to my players, but I think you should be.

Race was not an issue in the Houston locker room, according to Campbell, Bingham, Burrough, Pastorini, Mauck, and Culp. Each of them, interviewed separately, said that Bum Phillips encouraged players to get to know one another—and their girlfriends, wives, and kids—so that the team would consider itself a family more than just a group of coworkers. "You won't fight for anyone like you will for your family," he was fond of saying. And so the white players would take the black players to a country-and-western bar—a place like Gilley's—and the black players would take their white teammates to one of their soul music hangouts. Years later, Phillips put his relationship with his players this way: "People said I was too easy on my players. We weren't too easy on them. I love my mama, and she loved me, but she whipped me when she needed to. That's how I felt about players."

That summer in San Angelo, Phillips's one major innovation was to add the I formation to the team's offense. It had served Campbell well at UT, he figured, giving him time to set up his run as each play developed. Now, against the Cowboys in a preseason game, the offense put it to good use. The previous January, Cliff Harris, the Dallas Cowboy free safety, had competed against Campbell in the Bahamas in *Superstars*, one of those off-season TV shows in which athletes challenged each other in feats of strength and skill: chin-ups, soccer shots, a sprint, rowing—that sort of thing. Campbell, at the time a month or so removed from winning the Heisman Trophy, struck Harris as retiring and mild. "I approached my first tackle thinking he was a nice, shy running back," Harris said. "That is, until I ran into him and he proceeded to knock me backwards and step on my chest." In all, Campbell went for 151 yards, including a fifty-five-yard scoring run. Harris, who is one of about a dozen players to have competed in five Super Bowls, said that he always scouted running backs to find what he called their "balance point"—the vulnerability that would leave them exposed to toppling. On Campbell, he decided, after viewing game film and playing against him, there was none: "There wasn't any place. Oh, there was one way. As he ran past, you grab him by the jersey, dig in your heels, and wait for others to pile on."

The Cowboys, wrote the Oilers beat reporter Dale Robertson, play "three-piece-suit football."

> Computer football. Orwellian football. I find that a little bit discomforting, but I'm not sure I like those talking cash registers in supermarkets, either. I guess it's all a sign of the times and the Oilers had no choice but to fall into line, or become a pair of brown shoes at the NFL's black-tie ball. Under Phillips, Houston had a very simple modus operandi: Campbell to the left and Campbell to the right, with everybody busting helmets straight ahead. No traps, no pulling guards, no misdirection. Just simple power football, may the better—and stronger—man win.

On the morning the Oilers were due to break camp in San Angelo in 1978, Gregg Bingham, the team's defensive captain, was asked by some black fans when the Oilers would take off for the roughly 365-mile drive back to Houston.

"One o'clock," he said.

About a half hour later, as if double-checking, one of the black fans again asked the same question.

"One o'clock," he said once more, wondering about all the interest.

Finally, at one the Oilers started to head out of their West Texas redoubt, ready for the long drive through remote and rural Texas.

"There was a caravan behind me of cars, and they're all black guys," says Bingham, who is white. "And I'm thinking, 'What the hell is going on?' And they told me: 'We're going through some towns that black people don't get caught dead in.'"

Perhaps they had in mind the story of Isaiah Hill. A black man from Austin, he had been arrested a year earlier in Brownwood, ninety miles east of San Angelo, for robbing a hotel. Hill told police he didn't do it—he said another person was to blame. But the Brown County district attorney reportedly told him, "This is a white folks' town and if you don't take this plea bargain I'm going to make an example out of you." Hill insisted he was not guilty, and in February 1978, an all-white jury convicted him and gave him a life sentence. (He was finally paroled a few years ago, after more than thirty-five years in prison.) Some of the other towns roughly between San Angelo and Houston—Boerne, Comanche, Hamilton, Goldthwaite—were so devoid of African Americans that the sociologist James Loewen, author of *Sundown Towns: A Hidden Dimension of Racist America*, has identified them as places where African Americans, through a combination of discriminatory local laws and intimidation, were not welcome after sunset. Census takers in these areas could find virtually no African Americans. Decades later, when the Texas Parks and Wildlife Department moved its training academy for game wardens to Hamilton, the few black wardens rebelled, calling the decision ignorant or intentionally racist. One of them, Melvin Fowler, said that as a child he learned that Hamilton County, a Klan stronghold, was a "drive-through" county—that is, a place where African Americans shouldn't stop for gas or chow. For his part, Bingham still remembers what he was told that August day by those black fans: "You'd be able to negotiate for us if anything happened, so we're following close on your ass."

Many Heisman winners flame out as professionals. They just aren't strong enough to compete against men much larger and faster, much more fearsome and desperate than the ones they faced in college. Any questions about how Earl Campbell would fare in the NFL were answered in that first month of his rookie year.

On his third professional carry, he took a pitchout and roared seventy-three yards for a touchdown against the Atlanta Falcons. In a game a couple of weeks later versus the Rams, Campbell took a handoff on second down at the Rams' twenty-two-yard line. Just as the all-pro 225-pound linebacker Isiah Robertson appeared to have him trapped for a one-yard loss, Campbell ducked his helmet and trampled him. "Earl flat ran over him," Pastorini said afterward, shaking his head. "He bleeping ran over him." The run kept going—he resembled a rodeo bull tossing its rider while surrounded by clowns. A Ram safety, foolhardy enough to think he could stop Campbell, approached at the twelve-yard line but got nothing more than a handful of Campbell's jersey. A couple of defenders managed to work together to pull him down at the six. Campbell, his jersey torn away, looked a little like the Incredible Hulk. (In 1979, following Campbell's rookie season, the NFL chose to ban tear-away jerseys altogether.) "I'm glad that cat's not in our division," defensive end Jack Youngblood, a future Hall of Famer, said after the game. "Once a year with him is enough." For weeks afterward, Youngblood and some Ram teammates nicknamed Robertson "Grauman's Chinese Theater" because of the footprints all over him. The play stuck with him. A few years later, shortly after his retirement, Robertson, reminiscing to a reporter, wondered whether he could still play in the league. "At times I've said, to myself, 'Could I play again? Should I?' Then I think about Campbell. That's when I go back to business."

Later that season in a game in Massachusetts, Patriot defensive back Rick Sanford lunged at Campbell in an effort to arm-tackle him. The follow morning found Sanford sitting by himself in the Patriots' training room, gently caressing his black and blue forearm. "I got Earled," he explained.

Then came the *Monday Night Football* game pitting the 7–4 Oilers against Don Shula's 8–3 Dolphins. Shula, Phillips had observed in a characteristic Bum-ism, "can take his'n and beat your'n or he can take your'n and beat his'n." A full fifth of American households were tuning in each week to watch Howard Cosell and Frank Gifford call the NFL's marquee matchup. Among the fans to see Campbell take over the game were Earl Christian Kinzie's daughter and son-in-law; Erna Smith; and Brad Buchholz. Earl carried the team to victory with his four touchdowns, and suddenly the Houston Oilers, long football's doormat, were considered contenders. Cosell said it was the greatest game he had ever broadcast. One Houston columnist wrote that Campbell "could run for mayor Tuesday and win."

That Tuesday in 1978, as it happened, the last Republican to serve as Houston's mayor was elected. He was chosen by a good-ol'-boy network of developers and business interests—he was a former head of the Houston homebuilders association—determined to keep Houston sprawling. Sixteen years earlier, in 1962, Houstonians had defeated, for the fourth time, an effort to adopt zoning restrictions, confirming it as the only major US city without a formal zoning code. The no-zoning argument has long rested on notions of vitality and openness, of a modern frontiersmanship, of architectural daring. It also opened the way to the development of vast suburbs—by 1980, Houston ranged over an area nearly half the size of Rhode Island. Thousands of Houstonians, seeking fresher air and more land—and, perhaps, more distance from minorities and integrated schools—moved out of the central part of the city.

Most of the new suburbanites were whites—but some were African Americans with newfound wealth. For those who could afford to participate, there was, at the time, a kind of migration out of Houston's traditionally black areas into middle-class neighborhoods. Less than a fifth of African Americans lived in the suburbs of most American cities in 1960; by 1980, more than a quarter did, the historian Andrew Wiese writes in *Places of Their Own: African American Suburbanization in the Twentieth Century*. It was to members of this class of newfound black wealth and stability that *The Cosby Show* had special appeal when it first aired, in 1984. In a sense, Earl Campbell would be one of those new suburbanites.

Though Reuna had remained in Tyler while Earl was in Austin with the Longhorns and then in Houston with the Oilers—it was not an infrequent occurrence for women in Austin or Houston to ask him whether they could feel his legs—she said they never broke up or gave serious thought to a future without each other. Still, she was surprised by Campbell's spur-of-the-moment return to Tyler on Valentine's Day 1980. He had hired a car to drive him from Houston, and he was carrying a ring in his pocket when he asked Reuna's father for his daughter's hand in marriage.

"My mother said, 'What are you doing home?'" Campbell once recounted. "And I said, 'I left something here years ago, and I came back to get it. I want to ask Reuna if she'll be my wife.'"

After they married in 1980 (because they thought "honor" was to be expected and "obey" was too subservient, he pledged to "love, cooperate with, and cherish" Reuna, and she promised to "love, support, and cherish" him), they bought a three-bedroom brick house in Fondren, an area of Southwest Houston, on what was then the city's fringe, named for the oilman whose ranchland had been converted into apartments in the 1960s and 1970s.

Earl used to practice cradling the ball by clutching his shoe as he walked around the house or watched television. It was the sort of place furnished with high-gloss woods and king-size beds. There was a game room with a pool table, and out back a Jacuzzi. It was a far cry from the old Tyler plank house in which Campbell grew up, the one in which he shared a bed in the front room with his brothers Herbert and Alfred Ray. In the old house in Tyler, insulation consisted of quilts nailed to the splintered wood; now he had a home lined with fiberglass foam, a place heated and cooled with the sort of thermostats that had seemed novel when he stepped foot on the UT campus just a few years earlier. In a place like Houston, a city built on oil, whose chamber of commerce promoted the advent of "manufactured weather" in the city's buildings and that branded itself as "the world's most air-conditioned city," the air conditioner was another demonstration of how Texans could domesticate nature. "One little thing, all by itself—AC—made the South go away overnight," one character observes in Nell Zink's 1960s-set comic novel *Mislaid*. An "unstoppable force" is "putting in central air everywhere until you don't know whether it's day or night."

The Campbells' life fell into a comfortable routine. With Earl asleep, Reuna rose at six to jog a mile or so with his teammate Tim Wilson's wife, Valanda. Earl drove a humble Corolla to workouts ("I always wanted the Rolls-Royce," he once said, "but my managers always talked me into a Toyota") and then returned home for a nap. He might answer some fan mail or mow the lawn. Thrifty by upbringing, he blanched when a landscaper quoted him a price of $150 a month to weed and trim his lawn; he thanked the man for his time and instead decided to mow the lawn himself. "Earl isn't going to waste any money," the Oilers' offensive backfield coach, Andy Bourgeois, once said. "He's a most frugal young man." As he did outdoor work, Campbell liked to wave hello to a neighbor and shout, "Que pasa?" He thought the man was Latino; the guy was Jewish, actually—apart from some athletes from the Rockets or the Oilers, it was a largely Jewish neighborhood, and neighbors brought chicken soup when Campbell was sick.

Afternoon practice lasted about two hours, and, according to a soft-touch profile in *People* in 1980, Earl was usually home for dinner by seven. "I've got a whole batch of cookbooks," Reuna told the magazine's reporter, "but Earl likes the same things at every meal—steak, broccoli, orange juice and a banana dessert." The young couple liked to unwind to *Dallas* on TV or watch rented videocassettes of westerns.

In these ways, Earl Campbell was more of a piece with white middle-class Houston than working-class black Houston. He was safely insulated from what the Houston sociologist Robert Bullard, who has long studied environmental justice issues, has described as the PIBBY policy of the all-white, all-male Houston government of the late 1970s: "In place of NIMBY (Not In My Back Yard) poli-

tics, Houston practiced a 'PIBBY' (Place in Blacks' Back Yard) policy," Bullard wrote in an article titled "The Mountains of Houston."
"Government and private industry targeted Houston's black neighborhoods for landfills, incinerators, garbage dumps, and garbage
transfer stations." In the late 1970s, Bullard found that although African Americans made up about a quarter of Houston's population,
all five city-owned landfills and six of the eight city-owned incinerators were built in black neighborhoods. Many of the industrial sites
that Bullard focused on were in northeastern Houston; Campbell
lived a half-hour drive away, in Southwest Houston, the diametri-
cally opposite part of town.

Even as Campbell, by nature reticent and inward-looking—
and with his newfound celebrity, increasingly wary—cherished his
privacy, Houston, an all-embracing city of sprawl, took to adoring
Campbell. He was the city's kind of Skoal brother: a pitchman for
the tobacco brand, he was a hardworking, soft-spoken athlete who
could wear jeans and a cowboy hat with a pinch between his cheek
and his gum. (In the ads' tagline, Campbell would urge, "Skoal,
brother," which ended up sounding like a play on "soul brother.") In
the late 1970s, the Bayou City was about half-white, a quarter black,
nearly a fifth Hispanic, and the rest Asian. The city suited him and
his upward trajectory. Campbell's remove—appearing politically
unengaged, geographically suburban—from the struggles of 1970s
black Houstonians was part of his appeal; even his style of football,
punishing as it was, drew white Houstonians to him.

"I think white Houston embraced him because, to generalize,
white Americans reserve values like hard work for white people,"
Joel Dinerstein, a Tulane historian who has written about the relationship between NFL running backs and black culture, said. "I
think Campbell transcended all the standard profiles of the great
black running back of that period. He was not a speedster with great
moves—Mercury Morris, OJ or Walter Payton—but he was the workhorse of that offense. Between that and his sheer physical power and
hard work, the embrace came, in a way, mediated by some sense of
what makes up a black-and-white set of skills. He was a great white

fullback, except he was black."

The line is a provocative one, getting at the changing perception among Americans of what—or who—constitutes a certain type of football player. In *Paper Lion*, Plimpton tells a story about an encounter following a Detroit victory out on the West Coast. Plimpton and some of his former training-camp teammates dropped into a bar and found the opposing quarterback wallowing in drink.

> He began criticizing the Negroes on his own team, and then he extended his criticism to the rest of the league. His idea was that the Negro backed away from contact, that he hadn't the nerves for the game. The people along the bar began shouting at him.
>
> "Look at this," he said, weaving. "*Listen!* Take the linebackers. The search-and-destroy guys are the linebackers. How many Negro linebackers you got in the N.F.L.? Maybe one or two. They haven't got it, I tell ya. They flinch. It's the same with the running backs. My guys do, they flinch, I tell ya, and I'd rather hand off to a gimpy fullback who's white druther than my guy, the guy they make me hand off to, who's got mush for guts. You know why I got to hand the ball to a colored back? Because the NAACP says so, that's why, and they're calling the tune these days, not the coaches."

Of course the observation is both racist and absurd—especially to twenty-first-century ears, when the prejudice has swung around in such a way that young African Americans are often slotted into the running back position—just as they're often still steered clear of playing quarterback. And in a funny way, to the extent black players by dint of their skin color are now deemed to make excellent running backs, Jim Brown and Earl Campbell are to be thanked. In their wake, the position was redefined as a black one. When, in 2017, the Carolina Panthers drafted the Stanford speedster Christian McCaffrey, he became the first white running back selected in the first round since 1974; during his rookie year, he was one of only four white running backs in the league. "When you read about white athletes these days and white skill possession receivers specifically, one word you'll always find is 'tough,'" McCaffrey told reporters during the 2017 season. "You'll rarely see 'explosive,' 'athletic,' stuff like that. People do the eye test and underestimate me."

In a period when many white Americans bridled at the new independence of black athletes, Campbell's modesty played in his favor. Dinerstein said the fact that Campbell was a "fairly quiet, hardworking, private guy—I have no memory of him being outspoken, or political, or racially engaged—helped his embrace by Houston." The longtime Austin sports reporter John Maher said, "Campbell was almost like a Joe Frazier, a contrast to the flashier athletes who were, in some cases, beginning to flaunt their new wealth and fame." In some sense, Campbell could perform quietly because the political struggles of the 1960s had removed some of the pressure on black athletes of the 1970s to speak out. As the broader civil rights movement subsided, the number of black athletic demonstrations on university campuses ebbed from 180 during the 1968–1969 school year to fewer than 30 in 1971–1972, the sociologist Douglas Hartmann observes in his book *Race, Culture, and the Revolt of the Black Athlete*.

As he had done in Tyler, in Earl Campbell's own telling, he and his teammates helped bring Houston together in a way that dissolved racial anxieties. That was one way to tell the story. "The thing about Earl," said Dale Robertson, the veteran *Houston Post* reporter on the Oiler beat, "was that performance-wise he never gave Houston fans anything other than to turn cartwheels over." Robertson called the comity between whites and African Americans over Houston Oiler football "a false brotherhood." The black quarterback Warren Moon, who went undrafted by the NFL out of college and was picked up by the Oilers in 1984 after a half-dozen successful years in the Canadian Football League, "wasn't even immune within the walls of the stadium. Things got nasty down there," Robertson told me, with Moon being called all sorts of racial slurs by the Houston Oiler faithful. "Earl was taken under this city's wing like no African American athlete then could have been. Was it the Texas connection? He clearly didn't have a 'yappy mouth.'"

His talking, as it were, was done on the field. Rob Carpenter, who became his backup, once marveled that "Earl could hit the wrong hole and still gain four yards." In Campbell's rookie season, each time he ran for 100 yards or more, a Houston butcher gave the offensive line beefsteaks—it happened eleven times. (The following year, eager to limit his meat exposure, he changed the rules, agreeing to pay up only when the Oilers scored twenty-four or more points; it happened just twice.) Campbell, who became the first rookie to lead the NFL in rushing since Jim Brown did it in 1957, got requests for about three hundred autographed pictures a week. He was self-effacing about it all, typically crediting his teammates for his success. Shy of reporters, he took a corner locker, one next to Tim Wilson, his lead-blocking fullback. When he was asked about this play or that, he would often say: "Why don't y'all talk to Tim? I'm nobody without Tim." "That wasn't bullshit," said Robertson. "Never for a moment did I think that was bullshit. That was just Earl."

The Oilers, perhaps because of Campbell's bulldozing style, perhaps because of Pastorini's long suffering, perhaps because their hardworking defense had long been the core of the team, perhaps because of those derricks on the sides of their helmets, perhaps, ultimately, because they were finally winning, were suddenly toasted in Houston beer halls. As the '78 season drew to a close, the six-four 250-pound Mauck—who once, half jokingly, warned Earl Campbell, "Be careful, all sportswriters are Communists"—penned a song he called "Oiler Cannonball." Naturally, he recorded it at Gilley's. Its chorus, which includes calling Pastorini, his roommate on the road, a "fancy passin' Dago," was set to a rousing country-and-western march.

The Oiler Cannonball:
Now listen to the blockin',
The ramblin' and the roar,

As he glides by along the sidelines,
By the hashmarks then the score.
From the fancy passin' Dago,
To the Tyler bowling ball.
Those Patriots can be taken,
By the Oiler Cannonball.

No one was going to mistake it for Merle Haggard, but despite Mauck's off-key delivery, the song got plenty of airtime on KILT, the country-music station followed by all those roughnecks who spent their nights at Gilley's and other honky-tonks. The Oilers were becoming the team of a certain kind of Texan: rough around the edges, blue collar, unpretentious. In a sign of the team's popularity, Mauck's single sold ten thousand copies.

In their enthusiasm, Astrodome fans started to resemble college football crowds: pep rallies before games, face painting, signs announcing: "Luv Ya Blue"—the new motto of the Oilers, coined by Campbell after the *Monday Night Football* game against Miami. "'Luv Ya Blue' was a chance for people of all races and backgrounds to come together as a city," he said, in true Campbell-speak, about the enthusiasm of the crowd that night. "It was a feeling that the players and fans shared without even talking."

The season ended on a miserable Sunday afternoon in Pittsburgh. An icy, slushy day, with freezing rain and sleet and a temperature of about 25 degrees. It was the AFC Championship Game—the winner would go on to the Super Bowl. This was far further along than anybody had thought the 1978 Houston Oilers would go. And this was where the road ended.

On the first play against Pittsburgh, Campbell took a handoff and was met head-on by linebacker Jack Hamm; the force of the collision cracked Hamm's helmet, and Campbell was stopped for a two-yard loss. Joe Greene, the Steelers' famous defensive lineman, told his teammates in the next huddle: "That's the way we're going to hit him all day."

"He can inflict more damage on a team than any back I know of," Greene later told a reporter. "O. J. did it with speed, Campbell does it with power. He's a punishing runner. He hurts you. There are very few tacklers in the league who will bring Earl Campbell down one-on-one. When we're preparing for the Oilers, we emphasize the importance of gang-tackling Campbell. We work on it."

In the second quarter, a nineteen-yard field goal by Oiler kicker Toni Fritsch cut the score to 14–3, but then the Steelers scored seventeen points during the last forty-eight seconds of the first half. First, Houston running back Ronnie Coleman lost a fumble, and moments later Pittsburgh wide receiver Lynn Swann caught a twenty-nine-yard touchdown pass. Then the Oilers' return man, having fielded the ensuing kickoff and sprinted into the clear, inexplicably coughed up the ball—leading to another quick Steeler touchdown. After the Oilers got the ball back, Coleman fumbled again, and the Steelers kicked a field goal to increase Pittsburgh's lead to 31–3.

"The ball didn't feel like a football," Coleman dolefully explained.

Houston never threatened the Steelers again during the game, turning over the ball four times in its six second-half possessions. All season long, Pastorini had benefited from having Campbell as his running back; fake handoffs to Campbell had halted onrushing linebackers, leaving the quarterback more time to pick out receivers. He passed for more touchdowns and yardage than he ever had before in his eight-year career. That day in Pittsburgh, Earl carried the ball twenty-two times, gaining only sixty-two yards and fumbling three times—that entire season, he had fumbled only seven times in more than 300 carries.

"For all his talent," observed a Houston sportswriter, Earl Campbell "cannot walk on water, much less run or cut or turn sharp corners on it."

Pastorini was no help, throwing five interceptions.

Bum, in his inimitable way, summed up the game thusly: "The behinder we got, the worser it got."

The whole scene was a bad one. Steeler fans pelted the Oilers with snowballs as they left the field, and then the team had to stew at the airport for five hours because of the weather.

What unfolded upon their arrival in Houston, however, said something about how beloved the team had become.

They landed in Texas at eleven that night, and a couple of buses whisked them to the Astrodome. Fifty thousand people punching white pom-poms in the air went absolutely bonkers upon their entrance. Earl got on a cop's motorcycle and did a kind of victory lap, waving his hand to hosannas. They sang, "Houston Oilers No. 1," one of the many fight songs they had adopted, like English soccer fans, and chanted a cascade of "Luv Ya Blue, Luv Ya Blue." You could see, for a moment, how Earl might have thought he had brought the entire city together.

During the summer of 1979, in a muddy, stenchy stretch by the banks of Brays Bayou, overgrown with weeds and high grass except for a tired running path squeezed behind an apartment complex and a small shopping center, Earl Campbell and a few of his teammates could be found doing sprints and calisthenics. Putting the players through their paces was Tom Williams, the team's former assistant general manager. He was a lean fifty-year-old with a closely shaven head. The players met there because Williams owned two shops in the little strip mall—a kolache and pastry shop and Touchdown Barbeque. When he first joined the group, receiver Mike Renfro said he thought Williams "was some guy who ran a doughnut shop and our guys had lost their minds."

One of the drills devised by Williams, who had previously coached at Grambling, was known as The Hill. On a steep fifteen-yard incline on the side of the bayou, Campbell and his teammates would charge up first forward, then backward, and then forward again. That was a single repetition; Williams might call for three sets of ten repetitions—an exercise meant to build up hamstrings, calves, and quadriceps—in short, explosiveness.

Campbell said the workouts trimmed four inches off his waistline in a month and increased his flexibility. "Look, used to be I couldn't even do this"—Campbell sat on the ground before a reporter, spread his enormous legs in front of him at a wide angle, and then bent forward, his forehead touching the ground. He claimed that he had added an inch to each thigh while cutting his ten-yard dash from 1.9 to 1.4 seconds.

Across town at Gilley's, John Travolta, only twenty-five and already a star, spent that summer shooting the movie *Urban Cowboy*. He had been jetting in and out on his private plane and was staying in Houston's tony Memorial neighborhood in a $10,000-a-week compound known as Fort Travolta. Each morning at six, a caravan of Angelenos would head out of West Houston to the grimy, oil-odored air of Pasadena to film at the club. Travolta would take locals in the cast out for lunch. "You ride in his limo, and he'd get on that car phone. 'What's your mama's number? Let's call your mama,'" Gator Conley said. "He'd get on the phone and say, 'Guess where your baby's at?'" Gator was a Gilley's regular who walked Travolta through country-and-western dance moves and more or less played himself in the movie, wearing his Gilley's getup of black jeans, black western shirt, and black cowboy boots. A small-brimmed hat, an alligator buckle, and a cigarillo completed the look.

That year, 1979, *GQ* devoted an issue to the style of the "New West." Hollywood, keen to jump on what was hot, green-lit a handful of country-and-western-themed movies: *The Night the Lights Went Out in Georgia, Honeysuckle Rose*, and *Coal Miner's Daughter*. In Houston, Travolta was an object of obsession. From the *Urban Cowboy* set, bottles of cloudy water collected from an on-set pothole that Travolta's character had fallen in were reportedly going for $25 apiece. The Bee Gees happened to play Houston that summer, and there, as a special guest, showing off moves from *Saturday Night Fever*, was Travolta. Women screamed, and cameras flashed like stars.

When the rookie Rich Ellender joined the team in the fall of 1979 to return kicks, he asked Bum what was expected of him. The coach replied, "I don't want you to fumble, and every yard you move the ball toward the goal line, that's one less yard Earl will have to get by himself."

Finally, after years of dire play, the Oilers were great. "Before Earl came along," Oiler defensive end Elvin Bethea said, "this was just a stopover for a lot of players. We'd show up on Sunday and give the other team a good fight, but we knew all along what the outcome was going to be. Earl put us at the watering hole; now we're going to drink with everybody else."

When the Oilers needed a play that season, they went to Earl. And even when the defense knew they would go to Earl—when everyone in the stadium knew they would go to Earl, even the little boys and girls cracking peanuts up in the nosebleed seats—he would deliver. In a game against the Chicago Bears, he racked up 206 yards, running nine consecutive times at the finish to kill the clock and preserve a four-point Oiler win. On fourth-and-goal in a game against the Colts, the Oilers handed the ball to Campbell. Touchdown. On fourth-and-three from their own thirty-eight in the same game, they handed the ball to him again. Move the chains. "I have never played against a back as strong as he is in short-yardage situations," Colt safety Bruce Laird said in the locker room after the game. "He gets what he needs every time. He is the key to their offense. We went into the game knowing we had to stop him to win and we couldn't do it." Cornerback Dwight Harrison sounded a note of awe when a reporter asked what he made of Campbell. "On film, it looks like guys just don't want to tackle him," he said. "But you get out there and try to hit him . . . my goodness. If you go low, he's a good enough athlete to jump over you and if you go high, well, that could be suicidal."

The high point of Campbell's second pro season was a game against Houston's in-state rival. The Oilers, led by Campbell, were carrying a 9–3 record, but the Cowboys, at 8–4, were favored by three points. Dallas since 1966 had compiled twelve winning seasons and three trips to the Super Bowl; Houston had four winning seasons and no Super Bowls.

"It may be the most noticed shootout on this state's hallowed soil since Sam Houston ambushed Santa Anna," Dale Robertson of the *Houston Post*, observed, with only a little irony. "We hate them and they hate us," said defensive back Willie Alexander. "You feel that the minute you step on the field. This is for the bragging rights."

Bum alternated between joking about how the matchup amounted to a Texas Super Bowl—"You think we're obnoxious now, you just wait and see"—and acting coy about the Cowboys, calling them "the team up north of here, I can't think of their name." In the locker room before the game, Phillips delivered this line to his players: "They're America's team—but we're Texas' team."

Roger Staubach, the upright former Navy man, nicknamed "Captain America," who later parlayed his fame and money into real estate and Republican politics—in other words, the anti-Pastorini—opened the game with a fifty-six-yard touchdown pass to Drew Pearson; Campbell answered with a sixty-one-yard touchdown run. It went back and forth like that until the Oilers finally made a stop late in the game.

In the end, Campbell went for 195 yards and two touchdowns as the Oilers won 30-24.

It was left to Cliff Harris, once more, to describe to reporters what it was like to face Campbell. "He's the greatest running back in football," he said. "All you can do is close your eyes and hope he doesn't break your helmet." After the win, Phillips told reporters: "Remember how I told you guys last week that was just another game? I lied."

The 1979 season, which saw the Oilers go 11–5, ended again in the AFC Championship—again in Pittsburgh. In the off-season, Bum had purchased special boots for games against the Steelers—eel and turkey skins in blue, and crocodile leather in gray. "Crocodiles like water," Phillips reasoned. "They'll swim out there and bite you. Hey, I need all the help I can get." Once more, the temperature at kick-off was below freezing. But this time, the game was tight. Facing a predictable Oiler offense, Pittsburgh stacked the line with seven or eight defenders to stop Campbell, especially whenever the Oilers' lone deep threat, Ken Burrough, headed out of the game. "We knew Earl would carry," Mean Joe Greene, the Steelers' defensive tackle, said later. Campbell, coming off a groin pull that had sidelined him the previous week, rushed for only seventeen yards on fifteen tries.

The game turned on a call that canceled an apparent Houston touchdown—officials called the pass incomplete, even as replays available to TV watchers showed that the Houston receiver clearly got his feet down in the corner of the end zone. The Steelers came out on top again, 27–13. Bethea, the twelve-year veteran who had played through Houston's most miserable seasons, cried in a corner of the locker room. "Last year was a nightmare, but this time we came to win," he managed to get out. "I knew we were going to win. I can't believe it." Pastorini, in what would turn out to be his last game as an Oiler, sat grim faced on a low stool as reporters circled. His upper leg was black and blue—he, too, was playing through a pulled muscle—and blood still dripped from an elbow. He had had a terrific game, but like everyone else was dwelling on the touchdown that wasn't counted: "I saw it," he said. "It was in."

Once more, the Oilers, beloved losers, got a hero's greeting upon touching down in Houston. All along the drive, people stopped their cars or went out on their front porches to cheer them on. Outside the stadium were about twenty thousand people who couldn't get in; the dome was again packed, with fans going berserk. Bum, wiping tears from his eyes, was asked to give a speech. "One year ago we knocked on the door." Pause. The man had a flair for delivery. "This year we beat on the door." Pause again. The crowd waited on his every word. "Next year we're going to kick the sumbitch in!" Everyone went bananas. Marching bands played a polka version of the Oilers' fight song. Even players were crying. The pledge inspired a new country song, as did everything Oiler: Tom Cantrell & the Newton Minus Dink sang "Bum's Promise," an entry in the trucker-outlaw genre of country:

Well, I was hanging out in Houston just before
    the season died
The thrill of victory left me so I hung my head
    and cried
Then a vision came to me and I lifted up my head
Stood a prophet in the Astrodome and this is
    what he said . . .

Later, Bum told reporters he wanted engraved on his tombstone the words "I'd live a lot longer if I didn't have to play against Pittsburgh three times a year."

"The only way the Oilers became who they became, and the last Houston team to reach a conference title game—and got there twice—was because of Earl Campbell," Dale Robertson says. "Without Earl Campbell, they were a perennial 7–9, 8–8 team. Earl single-handedly turned them into a team that could have got to the Super Bowl if they had caught a break. But that Steelers team had nine Hall of Famers. Just bad timing. Now he paid a horrible physical price for the role he played in those games. The Earl you see today is because of that."

Like most Oilers—or "Earlers," as they were now known—Campbell loved playing for Phillips, who was always easy with a wisecrack. He once updated reporters on Campbell's injury status this way: "Earl's walking better, but he's much more valuable to this team if he can run."

That joke got at a complicated truth about their relationship. On the one hand, Bum appeared to be another in a line of father figures to Earl. They had a deep loyalty to each other, and when Phillips was fired by the Oilers in the early 1980s and rehired by the New Orleans Saints, Earl followed him to Louisiana to finish out his career. On the other hand, you could say that Bum Phillips took advantage of Earl, running him ragged in a way that made Campbell appear both heroic and tragic.

As early as October 1979—when Campbell was merely twenty-four years old, a second-year pro—the daily newspaper in Austin, the *American-Statesman*, ran a story titled "Campbell's Style May Take Its Toll." "He runs with a lot of reckless abandon and exposes his body to some tremendously painful hits," Ron Johnson, a former New York Giant running back, said. "If Earl continues this way there's no question but that his career will be a lot shorter than if he adopts a style that brings a little more finesse to his running." And the Cowboys' star running back, Tony Dorsett, shuddered when asked about Campbell's methods: "If I ran that way, I'd get chopped in half. When you're dishing out the punishment like he does, you're taking a lot, too. I hope to get together with him this spring. I might tell him jokingly, 'Hey, man, why don't you let just one tackle bring you down sometimes?'"

Campbell has long been defiant—even defensive—when it came to questions about whether his running style was bad for him in the long term. "This perception of abuse on my running abilities is definitely wrong," Campbell said when he was still a player. "In fact, I want the ball thirty times a game. I'd be upset if it didn't turn out that way." He had a favorite phrase during those playing days, as if he had studied the physics of football: "It's the hitter versus the hittee. The hittee gets hurt worst."

Reporters asked Bum Phillips about leaning so heavily on Campbell, especially late in a game in which the result was no longer in doubt. "Many of y'all have questioned my use of Earl Campbell, since it's obvious that it takes him longer than most players to get up off the ground," Bum Phillips said about his charge. "That's true. But did y'all ever notice that it also takes a long time for Earl to go down on the ground?" It was the sort of line that endeared Bum to the press, to the fans, and to his players. "He's the kind of guy you've got to give the ball to lots of times—25 to 30 times a game—no matter what he's doing," the coach said. "He wears a team down. Eventually he's going to break one. You can feel it, like a time bomb ticking. He keeps rocking, rocking, and all of a sudden, he's gone." "Earl Campbell is the best running back who ever put on a pair of shoulder pads," he crowed about his star player. "He always got better from his twentieth carry to his thirty-fifth, 'cause by then he'd done hammered 'em way down."

The hammering went both ways. Years later, after Campbell got both knees replaced in his fifties, after he began undergoing nerve therapy to combat the effects of a neurological disorder called chronic inflammatory demyelinating polyneuropathy, which can lead to declining strength and sensitivity in the arms and legs—even after all this, Bum Phillips told an interviewer: "I never felt like he carried the ball too much, and he didn't either: He hurt people, he didn't get hurt."

The official last breath of cowboy chic came on the evening of June 5, 1980. On that sultry night, the sun still high in the sky, crowds with their Instamatics pressed in outside a shopping-center movie theater for the red-carpet premiere of *Urban Cowboy*. The Derrick Dolls performed. Travolta, wearing a black hat, green sport jacket, and two-tone satin western shirt, whooshed in to lots of clicking.

In *Texas Monthly*, the reporter Michael Ennis described the whole scene as "the day cowboy chic ended and cowboy schlock began." There were glitter, gold, silver, reptile skins, feathers, sequins, beads, fringe, satin, suede, and rhinestones. White mink boots and white mink coats. "As the procession thickened to include stars, producers, directors, and local plutocrats, cowboy schlock congealed on top of cowboy schlock like molten rock solidifying into a fearsome menacing lava dome," he continued. "It was entirely expectable. You take the greatest schlock dressers in the world—the Hollywood–Beverly Hills smart set—mix them with the second-greatest schlock dressers in the world—the coterie of wealthy Texans with show-biz fetishes—throw in the cowboy theme, and you get a sartorial hallucination."

The after-party, hosted by a Houston socialite whose husband was an oil tycoon, was held, naturally, at Gilley's. Buses laden with champagne and caviar shuttled out-of-towners from a movie the-

ater downtown to the club, where 3,500 fans waited breathless-
ly for Travolta, who wore all black, and his costar, Debra Winger,
who wore an old-fashioned lace dress, done up all the way to the
top of the neck. In the dirt parking lot, the pickup trucks had been
displaced by Mercedes and limos. Margaritas, Lone Star beer, Tex-
Mex food, and table dancing were on tap. With the Gilleyrats shar-
ing space with Houston doyennes, the whole thing was an "eerie
spectacle," Ennis wrote. "It was as if Gilley's had been removed to
another planet as a tourist attraction, and the extraterrestrial den-
izens had carefully studied garbled transmissions of *Hee Haw* and
*The Country Music Awards* in an effort to populate the display with
authentically costumed actors."

Lines were long to the bathroom, where in-towners and out-
of-towners were snorting bumps of coke. Partying, everybody
called it back then. Diane von Furstenberg, wearing leopard-skin
tights and rainbow suspenders over a white button-down shirt with
a sheriff's badge that said "Disco Sucks" and a black cowboy hat
and zebra-print boots, straddled the mechanical bull. "Good Time
Charlie" Wilson, the gun-running lush of a Texas congressman,
popped up wearing a Doc Holliday leather vest, accompanied by a
much younger-looking woman wearing an off-the-shoulder feath-
er-fringed number. Irving Azoff, a Pan-like Hollywood record pro-
ducer who had bought the rights to Aaron Latham's *Esquire* story
about Gilley's and conceived the movie as a vehicle to promote
his country-and-western talent, prowled about the bar. The de-
partment-store magnate Robert Sakowitz, wearing a silk scarf as a
bow tie on a velvet western jacket, had his arm around a Swedish-
looking babe with pigtails. The president of Cutter Bill, the ritzy
western-wear store, wore a massive white mink jacket despite the
summer heat. Arts patron Dominique de Menil and Louise Cooley,
wife of the famed heart surgeon Denton Cooley, were on hand.

And amid all this, rubbing shoulders with the riffraff, was Andy
Warhol. "You can make a career out of avoiding all the events and
occasions at which Andy is trying to sell something in Dallas or

Houston," Ennis snarkily observed. "So naturally he was here, in a pink tie, jeans, and black boots." Warhol and von Furstenburg traded pictures of each other atop the mechanical bull. The artist wrote about the scene inside the club in his diary, including a comic moment involving his friend Bob Colacello:

> And, well, once Travolta was at our table it became really impossible because the crowd pushed in on us, and this policeman was standing right behind trying to protect us, and he was drunk, the policeman, and I said, "Don't look now, Bob, but you have a big gun and a big cock one inch from your neck." And the policeman said, "Can I do anything for you?" and Bob laughed and said, "Just stay right here." And he did. And he had two guns in his holster, very good-looking, and he kept hugging us and bumping into us and rubbing cock against us and saying, "Is there anything you need, anything you want?" But he was great because he kept screaming to the waitress and got all this food for us. The whole table. And all these drinks, and beer. And he said, "You're not eating your pepper," to Bob, and Bob said, "Are you kidding? It's so hot. I only took one bite," and he said, "Well, I'll just show you how to eat a pepper," and he took the whole big thing and slipped it into his mouth and ate it and then winked at Bob.

It's hard to tell, now, whether it was all one big joke. The moment was purely Houstonian—both unpretentious and ostentatious, earthy and ritzy, a total mishmash of folks. Gator Conley brought along his seven older siblings and his mother and father—"To say we had a modest lifestyle, would almost be exaggeration: we were dirt poor," he told me. "That was a pretty big deal for me, that I got to share that with my family. A few years after the movie, I was down in Louisiana with my dad and he tells everyone: 'He has to keep the beard because he's under contract with the movies.'" The club moved from something gritty and ridiculous—"real" was the word that Tom Brokaw used when he visited for a report in the late 1970s—to a kind of amusement park. Soon you could buy Gilley's underwear and T-shirts saying: "I rode the bull at Gilley's."

The partying atmosphere had infiltrated the Oilers and just about every other NFL team. During the 1980 season, Thomas "Hollywood" Henderson, the outspoken former Cowboy linebacker now playing for the Oilers, was freebasing at all hours. At three in the morning he would head to the Astrodome parking lot to buy more drugs; in his nine weeks with the Oilers, he spent his entire $110,000 salary on coke. "I was madly stalking Houston full of freebase," he writes in his candid memoir *Out of Control: Confessions of an NFL Casualty*. He would show up at Gilley's "all screwed up," remembered Gator Conley. Henderson ran with the longtime bouncer, Killer, who later died from an overdose—he had gotten a settlement from a work injury and spent the first check on dope, said Conley. "Hollywood would joke about sending hookers with drugs to key players the night before a game to screw them up."

There is no suggestion that Earl Campbell did cocaine—in fact, his old teammates remember him as clean. "The peer pressure for me to snort cocaine got really strong in the late 1970s," he once said.

> I was in my early 20s, I had just moved to the big city, and I was making a decent living. Some of the pros I played with would say, "Hey, Earl, we believe that you do drugs." . . . But I never did. I was right in the middle of it, yet I still made my decision not to. . . . Once they knew I didn't mess around one bit, they left me alone. We stayed friends and I had a good time, yet I stayed by my decision not to do drugs.

But in a graphic June 1982 tell-all in *Sports Illustrated*, a defensive end named Don Reese wrote that cocaine "now controls and corrupts the game because so many players are on it." The Oilers hired a drug abuse consultant, but the NFL Players Association discouraged players from participating in management-sponsored rehab programs.

"I wouldn't think anybody would use (the consultant) because of the trust factor," Elvin Bethea, the Players Association rep on the Oilers, said at the time. "We just don't trust the owners in this area. You might wake up the next morning and see your name in the headlines or find out you're being indicted for something."

Like much of what went on in this period in the NFL, the use of drugs—and who was suspended for it—was wrapped up in race. The *Washington Post* reported in 1986 that 86 percent of the players whose drug use had become public since 1980 were black. The Dallas Cowboys' president, Tex Schramm, said that drug use "has been predominantly a black thing." But the former all-pro running back Calvin Hill, who had worked as a substance abuse counselor, told the paper, "Anybody who says it's a black problem doesn't know what he's talking about. Whether it's denial or racism, it's an erroneous statement. If you look hard enough [for drug use among NFL players], you'll find it across the board. I know there's a tremendous sense of anger over this among blacks in the league, that it's another example of how the system discriminates against us." The Reverend Jesse Jackson told the newspaper that the league had adopted a double standard to protect its white players.

If *Urban Cowboy*'s premiere night was halcyon Houston, a severe hangover was in the offing. The go-go days fell apart as the Oilers and an oil bust sent Houston, and Gilley's, and Earl Campbell, south in a hurry.


"There's two kinds of coaches," Bum Phillips once explained. "Them that's been fired, and them that's gonna be fired."

The 1980 Oilers ended the regular season 11–5, and appeared, finally, to have it all together. Twice that year they had won on *Mon-*

*day Night Football*, and Campbell, now in his third season as a pro, had logged four games with more than 200 yards apiece, leading the NFL in rushing for the third consecutive year. They were poised to make good on Bum's promise to "kick the sumbitch in!" But just about the worst feeling is to lose when you expect to win—like a school kid who thinks he has aced a test only to get it back with a C in a circle and a "Please See Me" at the top—and that was the sensation the Oilers and their fans carried with them after they lost to Oakland 27–7 in the first round of the playoffs. The Oilers handed the ball to Campbell twenty-seven times, but the Raiders held him to about three yards a carry—a mediocre day by his lights—and only twenty-nine yards in the second half. The Oilers' quarterback, Ken Stabler, who had been acquired from the Raiders in the off-season in exchange for Pastorini and was known to study his playbook by the light of the Gilley's jukebox, was sacked seven times and threw two interceptions against his former team.

The simplicity of the Oilers' offense worked against them. Tight end Dave Casper called Phillips's passing game "kindergarten level, like painting by numbers."

The Raiders derided Houston's "high school" offense. Lester Hayes, the Raider cornerback who picked off Stabler's passes and sacked him twice, characterized the Oiler offense as "something out of the 1940's—all brawn."

And then, three days later, on December 31, 1980, Bud fired Bum. The man who had turned the team around, the man to whom the fans were attached, was out of a job. The conventional wisdom was that Bud, a cipher unliked by his fellow Houstonians, couldn't handle the adoration showered on Bum. The papers called it the New Year's Eve Massacre.

"It's got to be a joke," Houston's all-pro linebacker, Robert Brazile, said. "All that Bum Phillips has done for this team. Maybe some players or someone else should get fired, but never him. He was a father, not only a coach, to most players. He treated us like men. When you lose, you put the blame on the players, not on Bum."

In a postmortem, Dale Robertson wrote that Bum's style was "football at the OK Corral." "Steel guitars, three-cord harmonies, feathered hat bands and shoot-'em-ups on Main Street," he wrote. "Finesse? That was for them sissies up in Dallas. Houston's game plan possessed all the sophistication of a barroom brawl. The truth hurt. But it was painfully obvious the Oilers would not be sophisticated enough to cope with the NFL of the 1980s. The Wild West show had played itself out. Even *Gunsmoke* didn't last forever."

That off-season, feeling underpaid and unhappy about Bud's treatment of Bum, Campbell asked for a raise. Only a year earlier, at the close of Campbell's second season, the normally tightfisted Oilers had agreed to restructure Campbell's contract, adding performance incentives that could boost his pay to $3 million over six years. But they were immovable on the deferments baked into the original contract, the ones that doled out Campbell's wages over a couple of decades.

The knowledge that he continued to be exploited rankled, in ways that made him rethink his relationship with the team's management. "Everything for Earl became about money," Stewart said. And so in January 1981, after another stellar year on the field and only a few days after Bum's firing, he and Stewart approached the Oilers and demanded that Campbell's salary be doubled, to $1 million a year—-about $3 million in today's dollars. Otherwise, Campbell threatened to sit out the coming season.

Trying to paint Campbell as greedy, the Oilers general manager alerted the press to Campbell's ultimatum—"We won't be blackmailed," he said—and suddenly Campbell, whose persona was humble and affable, was on the defensive.

The contract negotiation—especially the holdout threat— was big news in Houston. This was two months into the Iran hostage crisis, and surveying the crush of microphones that greeted them at one of their contract negotiation press conferences, Campbell leaned into Stewart's ear and whispered: "We're bigger than the Ayatollah."

"Campbell still doesn't have the security he needs," Stewart explained to reporters. "Earl really feels God chose him, not his brothers, to take care of the Campbell family." He said that Campbell had met with the financially troubled, scooter-confined former heavyweight fighter Joe Louis and had told Stewart, "I don't want to end up" like Joe Louis. And Stewart said that coming out of college, Campbell had "had as much chance as somebody who just landed on earth would have had against a slick real-estate salesman"—meaning Bud Adams. "He bought the land without knowing to check for problems with earthquakes or mud slides."

Campbell was a league superstar and was sacrificing his body weekly. But he was also being paid far more than the average NFL running back—-who made $95,000 in 1980—and for the first time in his career, Campbell felt the sting of public and press criticism for his attempt to renegotiate a contract that still had five years to run. "Heroes don't act that way, people said," Dale Robertson reported, with a heaping of wryness. "Davy Crockett wouldn't have asked for a raise at the Alamo. Shame, shame."

Some of the accusations of greed were tied up with race, and sometimes they veered darkly toward violence. One day, an FBI agent came by Stewart's office with a warning. The agency had infiltrated the Houston-area Ku Klux Klan and learned that Stewart had been put on a list to harass or injure if given the opportunity. "The whole point was that I was trying to help Earl, a black man, get more money." Stewart said the agent suggested he and Earl avoid Gilley's.

That January, in a comfortable house in Houston's Memorial neighborhood, a sixty-year-old osteopath and his twenty-nine-year-old son got into an argument over Bum's firing—and soon, they started shouting about Campbell's contract. Lon Tripp, the son, an oilfield worker, thought Campbell's demand was fair; his father, Franklin, thought the Oilers should trade anybody who asked for that much. Lon Tripp told his father he was like Bud Adams: "You want to make slaves out of people and have them work for you for nothing." A homicide detective wrote in a police affidavit that the "father got fed up with the argument, went into his room, got a gun, put it in his coat pocket and sat down in a lounge chair in the den." The detective said that the argument continued and that the son got up from the couch and walked toward the kitchen. The father then allegedly pulled out the weapon.

Young Tripp told his father, "either shoot that gun or I'll make you eat it," according to the detective. A .38-caliber slug hit the son in the chest, the detective said.

Franklin Tripp was charged with murder. At his trial that July, he said he had acted in self-defense, citing what he called his son's drug-fueled rages. He said that at one point he had picked up the phone to call the police, but his son grabbed it out of his hands. In the end, a Harris County jury acquitted him.

Ultimately the Oilers held fast—and Campbell, eager to maintain his reputation, reported to training camp. "Money's not the thing I'm after anymore," Campbell said. "I don't have a lot of it and I probably never will. That used to be one of my desires. But a man matures and learns a few things. If I had to say I deserved a little more, I'd say yes. But I don't ever want to get in a situation where I have to argue with management to get it. I'm too old to be arguing with people."

He was twenty-six years old.

"I think I love the game more now than I ever did," he continued. "Only thing I hate about it is I love my wife and I hate being away from her. I'm always worried if everything is all right when I'm gone, and Southwestern Bell won't give me no breaks. But, when I put on a jock strap, I get higher than train smoke."

Even if Earl was still in the fold, Bum's firing didn't exactly solve the Oilers' problems. Houston started the 1981 campaign 4–2, but fizzled out to finish 7–9. Campbell, though hobbled by injuries, compiled 1,376 yards—another monster year, but for the first time in four seasons, he didn't lead the league in rushing.

Decades later, Stewart ran into Bud Adams in Nashville, and conversation naturally turned to Earl Campbell and an upcoming get-together of former Oilers that Adams was organizing. "You taught him well," Adams, who died in 2013, told him. "He's the only player who ever demanded money to come to a reunion."

In November 1981, thirty-five-year-old Kathy Whitmire, a certified public accountant who had served as the Houston City controller, became the first woman to win the mayoralty, beating the incumbent Republican mayor and then, in a runoff, a sixty-three-year-old sheriff who had insisted on addressing her as "L'il Lady." Her pollster told the *New York Times* that Houston "can no longer be accorded the privilege of being called a Gilley's kind of town. That's not Houston anymore."

Less than 150 years earlier, in the summer of 1836, black slaves and Mexican prisoners of war had cleared the land for the original town site of Houston. At the outbreak of the Civil War, slaves made up a fifth of Houston's population and as much as half the people living in the plantation areas outside the city. At the time of Whitmire's election, more African Americans lived in Houston than in any Sunbelt city except Los Angeles. And they were growing more prosperous, though still trailing their white counterparts: in 1980, the median income for this rising African American middle class was still only 70 percent of that of whites. But the number of African Americans who counted themselves as professionals or managers had tripled since 1960, and the number of black college graduates in Houston almost doubled between 1970 and 1980. Court rulings and galvanized black and Latino political classes meant that minorities in Houston and other cities were finally enjoying representation at the Capitol in Austin. David Lopez, a Houston attorney who worked as a political organizer and school board member in the 1970s, said some amount of credit goes to Campbell. "To a certain extent, we were boosted by Earl Campbell and the success he had," he said. "This was a time of a real turning point politically, with more African Americans, more Hispanics getting elected. People see someone performing well—someone who is African American enjoy some success—and for a certain segment that really helps."

Houston's demographic and cultural shifts led to the forming of new bases of political power. In 1979, when a federal lawsuit over voting rights resulted in the creation of the city's first single-member districts, two men became the second- and third-ever black members of the Houston city council. With Montrose a thriving hub of gay life, the Gay Political Caucus became a major new force in city politics. Through the 1970s, city council members were dismissive of gays or explicitly homophobic. One member called them "oddwads," and the mayor whom Whitmire was trying to replace wondered publicly about the growing gay population, "What are we doing wrong?" (The year of Whitmire's run, 1981, eight men were diagnosed with a little understood autoimmune disease initially called GRID—gay-related immune deficiency. They were the first known cases in Houston; only two of the men survived through the end of 1981.) The decade also saw an influx of entrepreneurial immigrants from Southeast Asia. And Latinos, only about 10 percent of the population in 1970, were now close to 20 percent. (The trends have continued to this day, and according to Rice's Kinder Institute, the city is the most diverse in the United States.)

"There's room for diversity in this city, and I think that's good," Whitmire, a self-described progressive who cut her teeth in the women's rights movement but campaigned on a platform of fiscal conservatism, said just before the election. "Nobody has control. I think what my administration will represent is the idea that Houston can be managed like a business and that it doesn't have to be the captive of a few power brokers."

Gender politics inevitably shadowed the race. All of five feet tall and wearing neck bows and cheek-warming glasses, Whitmire was jeered by her opponents as "Tootsie." When the sheriff, in the run-up to the election, was wishy-washy about setting a date for a debate, Whitmire mischievously took out a full-page ad telling him to "come out and fight like a man." The national press was naturally keen to write about an election that upended conventional wisdom about Texas. That led to passages like this, from a (male) *New York Times* reporter trying to tie her political strategy to her appearance: "Until recently she wore her hair in a platinum, shoulder-length pageboy. She has changed it now to a curlier, shorter style in its natural honey color. It is less flamboyant, more in keeping with the tailored suits she wears and the moderate, sensible image she tries to project."

Whitmire ended up winning more than 90 percent of the black vote in the 1981 election, and about two-thirds of the voters who had moved to Houston since 1975 or were thirty-five or younger. This was the new Houston. These voters were drawn by her promises to run city services; they were unattached to the political network of good ol' boys that had long held sway, and undiscouraged by her gender.

"I'm a mayor who is also a woman, not a woman mayor," Whitmire announced.

But leave it to Bud Adams to harass a female mayor. In 1987, when Bud threatened to move the Oilers to Jacksonville if he didn't get $67 million worth of improvements to the Astrodome, Whitmire visited him at his basement office, known as the Bunker. The Astrodome was a county facility, not a city one, but she thought she might catch political blame if Adams made good on his threat.

At least four other people, including an Oiler general manager, Adams's son-in-law, a Whitmire aide, and a Houston city councilman were at the meeting, according to an account by Ed Fowler in his book *Loser Takes All: Bud Adams, Bad Football, and Big Business.*

"What can we do to keep the Oilers in Houston?" Whitmire asked Adams.

The Oilers' owner replied: "Mayor, I've got a little office in the back with a foldout couch if you'd like to discuss it further."

Four years later, in the fall of 1991, she was invited to participate in a halftime presentation at the Astrodome to celebrate the retirement of Campbell's jersey. It isn't hard to imagine why Whitmire opted to stick to a video tribute and not be there with Adams in person. The video was booed—not showing up live was deemed a political misstep. She was locked in a tough campaign in any case, and that November, after ten years as mayor of Houston, Whitmire lost her reelection bid.

The Oilers never had a great offensive line to open holes for Campbell—"He never got the best blocking," Mean Joe Greene once observed. "The line would shield, get in your way, and let him pick a spot." But as the 1982 season opened, it was weaker than ever. The team's only all-pro tackle had been traded to New Orleans for the quarterback Archie Manning—father of the future NFL quarterbacks Eli and Peyton; Carl Mauck retired after thirteen seasons in the league, his last six with the Oilers; and Tim Wilson, Campbell's trusty lead blocker, had been relegated to backup tight end. What was left was more a sieve than a cast-iron pot.

"Yeah, I'm frustrated," Campbell, rubbing salve over his battered body, told reporters in the locker room after a season-opening loss to Cincinnati. "I'm not trying to down the rest of the guys. What they do is their business. But I've spent half my life working out and the other half watching films. I stay at practice all day and when I get home my wife asks me why I'm so tired. I tell her I'm tired because I practice all day." He wiped the sweat from his face, sighed, and added: "Then we come up here and blow it." He broke into a smile: "It makes your wife wonder if you're really at practice."

Campbell was about to get a long unasked-for layoff. Up in New York, the NFL and the Players Association were embroiled in negotiations that were leading nowhere. The association's executive director, Ed Garvey, a lawyer and progressive firebrand from Wisconsin, was pushing for a revised pay scale, one that would fork over 55 percent of NFL revenues to the players—owners would have had to relinquish $1.6 billion from gate receipts and television and radio money over the next four years to the players. For the twenty-eight owners, that was a no-go. "They didn't like that," Garvey, who died in 2017, said, adding that Jack Kent Cooke, the Washington Redskins' owner, "thought it was communism and others thought it was socialism."

"It seemed like capitalism to me," Garvey said dryly.

After a Monday-night game in September, Garvey instructed union members to strike immediately. Owners responded with a lockout, declaring team fields, training rooms, weight rooms, and equipment off-limits to players.

Campbell, who never joined the Players Association, grew cranky as the strike wore on. (Stewart, his agent, said he instructed Campbell not to join because he did not want the Players Association to profit from Campbell's image.) The lockout was costing him $20,000 a week. In a newspaper interview, Campbell compared Ed Garvey to Jim Jones, the cult leader behind the mass suicides in Guyana in 1978: "I don't understand how Garvey, how only one guy, can control that many players. That's almost like Jim Jones, if you think about it. Garvey's speaking for a whole lot of people. He's messin' up a whole lot of stuff." Campbell said he felt "like an innocent bystander who gets caught robbing a bank. The man is sent to prison even though he's done nothing. That's me . . . I just hope Garvey knows that when he's messin' with me, he's messin' with 20 people. And that includes my mother, my brothers and sisters, my wife, my child who's due in November and my dog named Pam," a boxer. "Pam loves Alpo. But I haven't been able to afford too much Alpo lately."

He told all this to a reporter, Bill Brubaker of the *New York Daily News*, over lunch at a popular seafood place called Angelo's Fisherman's Wharf. Actually, Campbell didn't have lunch, exactly. He ordered a glass of water and then opened a can of tobacco and stuffed a chaw in his cheek. He sounded off about the union's demand for 50 percent of the owners' television revenues.

"It isn't fair," he said, rolling the chaw in his mouth. "Like, I have two people working for me in my store. If they came in one morning and said, 'Hey, Earl, we want 50 percent of your business,' I would sit down and tell them, 'Yes, I do agree you deserve more money. But I will not give somebody who works for me 50 percent of my business.'"

He took a quick glance around the restaurant and then spat a mouthful of tobacco juice into a napkin-lined plastic cup.

"I thought the strike was only going to last two or three days," he said. "I can't believe this is, what, the third week? I'm not siding with either the owners or the players. But I do feel the players deserve a raise. Like we say in Texas, if you take a mule to the field and work him hard, then you should feed him good. I think the owners should give every player a 35 per cent raise and a flat $100,000 to everyone who's been in the league two years or more."

Just then, reported Brubaker, the owner of Angelo's Fisherman's Wharf, Charlie Angelo, walked by.

"If the strike continues," Campbell said, "will you give me a job as a waiter?"

"No," Angelo said. "You belong on the cash register."

Campbell turned to his visitor and smiled. "Next time you see me, I might be workin' that cash register," he said. "That Alpo ain't gettin' any cheaper."

The strike exposed deep fissures within the Oilers. They had been a strong union team—but the renegade actions of a couple of players led the club to become a leader in the antiunion movement. Linebacker Gregg Bingham, a mile-a-minute talker eager to this day to expound on proper investment strategy in a free-market America, spearheaded a grassroots movement to push for acceptance of an agreement that union execs opposed. "Bingham," said Bethea, the long-serving defensive player who was the union's player representative on the Oilers, "is a company whore."

In the end, the owners agreed to provide severance packages to players on retirement, increase salaries and postseason pay, and award bonuses based on the number of years of experience in the league. But bolstered by the freelancing efforts of Bingham, they didn't accede to the Players Association's proposal of tying wages to 55 percent of league revenue.

"What really hurt was seeing those people taking credit or being given credit for settling the strike," Bethea said of Bingham and a few renegade negotiators. "I won't say a word. I'm still part of this team. I've got to play with them. I'll go out and perform to the best of my ability, but this thing is going to be with me a long time."

When the season finally resumed after the fifty-seven-day strike was settled, the Oilers played like a team that had lost faith in itself, one completely uninterested in winning. By the time the squad fell to 1–5, a return to the kind of pre-Campbell win-loss record the Oilers were famous for, the CBS affiliate in Houston began carrying the games of the New Orleans Saints—helmed, not coincidentally, by the still-popular Bum Phillips.

New Oiler head coach Ed Biles, determined to shift away from the run-heavy strategies of the Phillips period, scrapped the I formation in favor of a split-back formation, one that brought the halfback and fullback closer to the line of scrimmage to make it easier for them to slip into receiving routes. "In the I-formation," Biles told reporters, placing one fist over the other, "the backs are in tight like this, and they can't get outside fast enough into pass patterns to make the formation very effective on passing downs. There is no believable play action possible, and"—throwing in a possibly true but nonetheless unnecessary potshot at his backfield tandem—"Campbell and Wilson are not what you'd call great natural pass receivers."

The seemingly small tactical change was a big shift in philosophy and, as far as Earl Campbell was concerned, a vote of no confidence in running the offense through him. "Coming out of the I, even if Earl picked the wrong hole, he got 3, 4 yards every time," Rob Carpenter, his former teammate, said. "And being 8 yards behind the line of scrimmage instead of 5 was important to him . . . I think Earl needs that extra second of vision to make a cut. And after all those years of being a power runner out of the I at the University of Texas and with the Oilers, it's not easy to change."

Campbell appeared especially defeated, and opponents and journalists openly questioned whether all that ferocious running had finally tired him out. In an early-December date in the Meadowlands against the Giants, he was tackled four times for a loss. Twice, a 180-pound cornerback tackled Campbell, sixty pounds heavier, one-on-one in the open field.

Houston had a 14–3 lead in that game with just over eleven minutes remaining. Usually that was Campbell time. But Houston tried him twice, and he lost two yards. The offense went back to him only once the whole game. In the end, he went for only sixty-six yards on twenty-three tries. Houston, forced to rely on its weak passing game, ended up losing, 17–14.

One writer joked: "Earl set an NFL record today for most 2-yard runs in a single game."

In the Giants' locker room after the game, New York defensive end Harvey Martin was thinking about the performance in a more somber tone, the kind in which one athlete who spies the nearing end of another great athlete—and sees something distressing about his own future—might speak. "He isn't the same Earl Campbell who came into the league," Martin said. "That's obvious. You still have to respect him, even though you can hold him down. The years take a toll on running backs."

Campbell was only twenty-seven, had been in the NFL for just five years, but a career of powering through defenders was wearing him down. "I don't think it's the carries as much as the number of tacklers who hit him each play," Carpenter, the former teammate, now a member of the Giants, said. "It seemed like six or seven guys would get a shot at him every play. He'd get tired."

Campbell himself seemed befuddled by his performance, like a boxer whose hand speed has deserted him. "I really don't know why I didn't carry the ball more. I wish someone would tell me. I wish I knew the answer."

Even at that young age, he was groping with the sort of questions a man three times as old wonders about himself. "It gets harder all the time," said Campbell. "It's not the hitting as much as the losing that hurts so much. Maybe I am getting to be an old man. I'm just trying to be like the senior citizen who gets better when he gets older. I don't think my physical condition is a problem."

"People can say I'm slowing down, I don't care," he continued.

"Maybe I am. I'll play until they tell me to get out of there. I don't have to say anything on my behalf." It's the sort of thing a proud athlete might say, the sort of thing said by somebody who has always loved to compete and has always flourished at it, but it's also the sort of thing said by someone who grew up in tough circumstances and might make the same bargain again.

The following week, the Oilers were thumped at home by the Dallas Cowboys 37–7. Campbell, Dale Robertson wrote in the *Houston Post*, "is only a shoddy imitation of the No. 34 who hammered the NFL into whimpering submission his first three years in the league. Everybody seems to agree that he no longer runs with the same fearless determination of years past."

The city, too, was about to burn out. When the county judge who masterminded the creation of the Astrodome died in November 1982, his funeral cortege circled the Dome twice. The event might as well have marked the death of Houston's go-go days.

With the US economy in a recession, oil demand suddenly declined. The nation's drilling rig count fell from more than 4,500 in late 1981 to a low of 663 in 1986; oil prices slid over that period from about $40 a barrel to $10.

Traders were no longer wondering how much oil a drilling rig could pull up, but, eager to sell the metal as junk, how much it weighed. A Houston dentist reported an increase in teeth-grinding problems among the locals. And by 1983, the mills and petrochemical plants that employed many Gilley's locals were announcing major layoffs; the following year, Armco, a steel mill with several thousand workers, closed for good.

This came just as Gilley's overextended itself. In 1982, its reputation burnished by *Urban Cowboy*, Gilley's opened a 60,000-square-foot rodeo arena and a 10,000-seat concert and convention space. It was now a ridiculous kind of amusement park. A few years later, the club's owners had a falling-out, and by decade's end, mired in lawsuits and fending off creditors, Gilley's was shuttered. Other touchstones of the urban-cowboy moment also soon found themselves discarded. Federal agents raided Cutter Bill Western Wear, connecting the owner of the high-end outfitter to a drug-running operation; the goods were auctioned off, including a gold-leaf sculpture of the namesake equine.

In the fall of 1982, in a deep funk, Campbell decided to head to Austin to see Royal. His old coach now spent much of his time hanging out with Willie and puttering around the golf course. He offered a simple pep talk: "Earl, you didn't get where you are by quitting." Recounting the conversation to reporters, Campbell announced: "So I'm not going to quit. Things have to get better. They can't get any worse."

They did get better, in a manner of speaking. He ran for a touch over 1,300 yards in 1983—averaging four yards a carry. But the team was terrible. The nadir occurred when 1-11 Houston headed to Florida to play the 1-11 Tampa Bay squad—and lost. The Oilers finished the season 2-14, and Earl, forced for the first time to undergo knee surgery, suggested that he wouldn't oppose a trade.

The franchise's management and coaches, for their part, had come to consider Campbell nettlesome—a ball-demanding veteran who was no longer the player he had been. Midway through the following season, Houston, deciding to rebuild as it hemorrhaged fans—attendance had plummeted to forty thousand a game, down from more than fifty thousand in 1980, the team's last playoff year—managed to deal Campbell to New Orleans. He found out in his truck, on the radio—country station KIKK, naturally—after taking his son to get a haircut. He had said once, with some grandiosity, that when he thought about "the things I want to achieve—I want to accomplish those things in America." That was in the summer of 1981, while he was signing autographs at an Austin auto dealership. He elaborated: "And if God's willing, I'd like to spend the rest of my life in Texas. I've been to places like California, New York, New Orleans. And I don't want to say anything against those places, but Texas is the only place where I can wear my jeans, put on my boots and dip a little snuff." Now, three years later, New Orleans it was. That was it for a Texas hero, shipped out of the state without a wisp of notice.

The good news was that he would be reunited with Bum Phillips. It was a classic Bum move—trading a coveted first-round pick out of loyalty to a veteran player—one that spoke to how much affection they had for each other. "He had to have known Earl was done," Dale Robertson told me. "He thought because of the magic they might be able to do something great again. There was nothing Bum could have done to make it right."

Campbell played behind George Rogers, the Saints' young Heisman winner, and never got into a real rhythm with the team. The 1984 team finished 7–9. The Saints kept losing into the next season, and Bum's acquisition of Earl looked like a real blunder. As Bum left the field from home games at the Superdome, a Saints' regular leaning over the tunnel made a point of pouring beer on his head. "Lady," he told her after she showered him a third time during the 1985 season, "you're never gonna have a chance to do that again." He knew he was about to be fired. In the final game of the season, against the Atlanta Falcons in a half-empty Louisiana Superdome, Campbell broke into the open and surged forward. About twenty yards from the end zone, something popped in his leg and he grabbed his hamstring. He was caught from behind by a Falcon defensive back short of the goal line. It was the last run of his career.

Campbell was now bereft of his pro ball mentor, and no longer playing in the state that meant so much to him. He reported trim and fit for the 1986 training camp, but a carry in a preseason game against the Patriots in Boston in mid-August made his mind up for him: "Everything seemed right," he said about that moment, after he had gotten a clean handoff and a huge hole opened up before him. "I made my cut, I followed my blockers, but I only gained six yards." His old burst of speed, the one that would have gained him clusters of yards, as if biting luxuriantly into a bunch of little grapes, seemed no longer to be there. In its place, a strange sensation: he wanted to get off the field without getting hurt.

The feeling followed him back down to the Saints' camp in southeastern Louisiana. And there, in his dorm room in the small town of Hammond, his body so bruised that he had to practically crawl to the bathroom, he told his thirty-one-year-old self that he was finished. "Son," he has said he told himself, "you gave them a good fight. Earl, that's enough." He had played in twenty-four games with the Saints and scored exactly one touchdown.

He called his mother and Darrell Royal to tell them the news, spoke to Reuna, and then, after a brief press conference that saw him quoting a Merle Haggard song—"Everything changes except what you choose to recall"—he was out the door on a Southwestern Airlines flight to Houston, making sure to order a few beers from a flight attendant.

He was just shy of 10,000 yards rushing as a pro—but as he noted, "10,000 yards weren't going to do any more for me than 9,000."

A year later, the Oilers announced they would retire Campbell's no. 34 jersey. "If I had it to do all over again," he said, before a series of medical maladies took hold, "I'd run the ball that same way. I'd probably even do it harder on certain plays. And I want Bum to give me the ball 30 more times. I believe the more a guy runs as a running back, the better he gets. I loved every minute of it. I loved looking that guy in the eye who was across from me because I know deep down in my heart I'm telling him, 'I'm the best. I've got something to prove on third down.'"

# EPILOGUE

One afternoon in the spring of 1990, four years after retiring from football, Earl Campbell and a couple of young assistants, both white, were driving from Tyler to Austin. He had traveled back to his hometown to promote his sports camp and to make commercials for the US Census Bureau. Back on the road, stomachs rumbling, they stopped at a roadside restaurant for a late lunch.

Having been hired as special assistant to the president of the University of Texas, Earl now lived with Reuna in a 3,500-square-foot two-story house in Westlake, a suburb just to the west of Austin. With kindergarten on the horizon for Christian, their older boy, the family was ensconced in the Eanes Independent School District, an upscale, suburban, virtually all-white district in the Hill Country. On the night he won the Heisman Trophy in 1977, he said he didn't think of himself as a black man. At first blush, looking at his situation, he appeared to have escaped the fate of poor African Americans in Texas. But sheared of his celebrity, the world apparently still thought of him that way.

A waitress came to check on them, and Campbell started asking a few questions about whether the place sold chicken breasts. He was starting a hot-link business, the Earl Campbell Meat Co., one that would soon grow to $10 million in sales annually. This was his custom now, to do informal business research as he roamed Texas's byways. He was, arguably, the most famous black man in Texas, widely beloved, but perhaps she didn't recognize him behind his sunglasses. She grew agitated by his questions, he could tell, and suddenly she threw a salad bowl at him.

"I never felt so bad, so much like crying," he told the reporter David Maraniss not long after the incident.

> If I hadn't had the sunshades on, that salad bowl probably wouldn't have come flying across the table. If she had known I was Earl Campbell and not just some black guy. That's the only way I can look at it. Until three or four months ago, I thought things were getting a lot better. Now it just looks to me like all the things that people our age and before us worked for, what the great Dr. Martin Luther King and other people worked for, is being forgotten. People are forgetting how to treat other human beings with respect.

Though Earl Campbell tried, through carrying the football, to transcend race, race, exhaustingly, remained the prism through which Texans, and Americans generally, saw one another. After facing off against Campbell's John Tyler team in the 1973, the coach of Conroe, which had gamely stacked the line to try to stop him, talked about Superman being black and wearing number 20. Now, in his post-football journey, his cape retired, Earl Campbell observed what could be called a series of disappointments. His narrative was one of reconciliation and success through hard work; he had, in his religious-minded, Ann Campbell–oriented way, been open-minded regarding the world and had expected the same back. But he found the world didn't possess that ecumenical quality.

The late journalist Robert Heard, one of the two Associated Press reporters who penned the series in the early 1970s on racism on the UT football team, said of the university in the early 1990s, "Earl has done far more for them than they have done for him. Some members of the athletic hierarchy consider him just another dumb jock. There is some deep-seated and, in some cases, unconscious racism over there."

At the time, of the dozens of coaches, administrators, and secretaries who occupied the athletic department's corridors on the second floor of Bellmont Hall, Earl Campbell was one of only two black staffers—the other was a wide receiver coach.

"I think at this point UT has to start hiring some assistant athletic directors who are black or Hispanic," he said in 1990. "It's time to start saying, 'Hey, we've got to change it over for a while.' Even all the secretaries are white."

There had been several racist incidents involving fraternities on the Texas campus around that time. Some frat boys tattooed a black student's car with racial slurs; another fraternity printed T-shirts with the face of Little Black Sambo superimposed on Michael Jordan's body. Campbell found himself backing minority students who organized protests against the administration—including against his boss, university president William Cunningham. Campbell told Maraniss that he thought Cunningham had not responded quickly or forcefully enough to the fraternities' actions. "To be very honest, I'm very embarrassed by the situation," Campbell said.

> It may cost me my job, but Dr. Cunningham, being president of a major university, in a key position like that, I was surprised by the way he handled things. I think if he had gone on stage immediately after the incident and said (to the fraternity), "Don't come around this university anymore." Just kick them off. Take a tough stand. I'm the president and I will not stand for this. That's what I would have done. Instead, he gave a speech like he was talking at a commencement exercise.

It was not the last time he found himself ambivalently defending the university. A few years later, Lino Graglia, a sixty-seven-year-old constitutional law scholar at the university, told students that African Americans and Hispanics were "not academically competitive with whites" and that they had "a culture that seems not to encourage achievement. Failure is not looked upon with disgrace."

Campbell, a shy person who had suffered from panic attacks in the late 1980s and early 1990s, found his voice to speak up against Graglia. "I think that the University of Texas is a first-class university, and to have a person on our campus with the stupidity to do and say as he pleases—I don't think that is fair for any student," Campbell said. "We need to get together and prove him wrong."

Recalling the hard truth that Royal had learned, and making perhaps the most practical argument against the comments on a football-obsessed campus, he said Graglia's words would hurt recruiting. Speaking of his own children, he said: "If they were going to come to the University of Texas as minority students, it would be a big problem for me to let my kids come here."

And yet, back in Westlake, the Campbell kids were in one of the whitest districts in Texas. When Christian was in elementary school, issues of racism swirled around the high school. Ahead of a 1989 home game against largely black LBJ High School, located on Austin's East Side, someone had painted a racial slur on the visitors' seats. A black effigy was hanged. During the game, Westlake fans reportedly shouted a racial epithet at the LBJ band, and one supporter supposedly held a go-home sign repeating the slur. Westlake's principal at the time said he did not see it as a racial issue, and the Eanes superintendent called the episode a "minor thing." (Eventually three students were suspended for the graffiti, and the Westlake football team was reprimanded by the University Interscholastic League, placed on probation for the next school year, and ordered to come up with a racial-sensitivity plan.) Even into the late 1990s, well after Campbell had complained about the homogeneity of the UT athletic department, Westlake High had only one black teacher and one black assistant principal out of 235 staff members.

It was at about this time, as he approached his midforties, that Campbell's body and career began faltering, in a dizzying downward spiral signposted by one diagnosis after another. His knees grew balky and his back shaky—the discs in his spine were worn out like dusty mortar in an old brick wall. In the late 1990s, doctors discovered three large bone spurs on his spinal column and installed screws in his back. Then, when that didn't work out, he had the screws removed. One doctor announced that he had been born with an abnormally narrow spinal canal, one that could put pressure on the spinal cord—and had been lucky to get out of football without paralyzing himself. Another physician later told him it wasn't a congenital defect; the doctor told him there was "a Pittsburgh helmet on your back."

After a few successful years, the meat business became overextended. A restaurant he opened in 1999 closed quickly, and Earl Campbell Meat Products went bankrupt. His arthritis was soon bad enough that he could not make a fist or wear any of his trophy rings or even his wedding band. Nerve damage in his legs meant he could not raise the front of his feet to take a step. Doctors called it drop foot, a clumsy-sounding diagnosis for one of the world's great athletes. He began retreating, making fewer outings among an ever-adoring public. "Sometimes it gets to the point that I can't stand the pain, like when I've got to walk a lot," he once told a reporter. "Thank God I'm with people who understand me: 'Take all the time you need.' It's embarrassing when I've got to hop onto the back of a pickup and I need help." To use a bathroom upstairs from his office, Campbell, unable to grip with his hands or bend his knees, had to lean his forearms on the railings to drag himself up. By 2001, when he was forty-six years old, doctors told him he needed a knee replaced. He told a reporter he didn't want anyone feeling sorry for him. "It's like Merle Haggard said: 'I don't pull off the road long enough to bog down in the mud; anybody say I give a damn, they damn sure told you wrong.'"

He had played professionally only seven years, about average for an NFL running back, but by the age of fifty, beaten up by the wear and tear of a brutal football career, broken by knee and back surgeries, he could no longer get himself into bed, instead resigning himself to sleeping in his wheelchair. He found himself, at times, medicating his pain away—taking up to ten Oxycontin pills a day, washed down with cans of Budweiser. In 2007, at a thirtieth-anniversary celebration of his Heisman Trophy victory, held at an

Austin golf resort, Campbell stumbled over names and dates, even after being gently corrected, and he asked a reporter to help him get a car deal with a BWM dealership.

A group of Heisman winners, gathered to celebrate Earl, were shaken. "I stay focused and prayerful that I won't have to deal with the situation of Earl Campbell one day," said former Tennessee Titans running back Eddie George, who had won the Heisman at Ohio State in 1995. Tony Dorsett, the great Cowboy running back, said that Earl, his former rival, was the "biggest, baddest player in the game. He was my Skoal brother"—they both had endorsements with Skoal tobacco—"but no matter how big or strong you are, the game ultimately wins."

"It reached the point that I began slurring my speech, pushing my family away, struggling to remember things and allowing important business opportunities to slip away," Campbell wrote in a 2013 essay for Yahoo! that encouraged athletes to head to rehab. A few years earlier he had called the orthopedist who had performed his fifth back surgery. "I need to have more medicine," he told Stan Jones, the director of spine care at the Houston Orthopedic and Spine Hospital. "He wasn't communicating clearly," said Jones, who called Campbell's family. "We need to help your dad," he told them.

There was a you-tell-him, no you-tell-him moment between Earl's two sons before Christian sat down the family patriarch and said: "Do whatever you want to this day, tomorrow you're going to get help." "The thing that got me," Campbell said, "was when they said, 'Dad, did you see what happened to Michael Jackson? You keep doing this, that's going to happen to you.'"

Instead of the usual twenty-eight days at a rehab center, Campbell voluntarily pulled forty-four—he was a hard worker even at overcoming addiction.

His reformation lent him time to rethink the bargain he had struck to play the game that had given him so much. He once said that most black men growing up in his circumstances would have never made it past the Tyler city limits. Thanks largely to his prowess at football, he and Reuna had made it; from poverty, his siblings had climbed into a working-class, even middle-class life; and his mother had lived out her last thirty years in a comfortable house. But now, he wondered, whether the style of play that had given him such success was worth it.

For so many years, he had dismissed talk that football was somehow to blame for his ailments. "The most serious injury I got from football was a broken finger and broken ribs," Campbell had insisted. It started to sound like a kind of a cognitive dissonance. Loyal to the sport and proud of his reputation, he had long luxuriated in stories of his toughness, like his 1979 goal-line run against the Oakland Raiders and their all-pro defensive back Jack Tatum, nicknamed the Assassin for his brutal tackling. Tatum, making like a human torpedo, launched all his weight and power into a helmet-first tackle. Pastorini said the noise of their collision sounded like a train wreck. "He put a hit on me I will never forget," Campbell told a *Sports Illustrated* reporter. "He knocked the hell out of me. My neck popped out. My sternum shot back. But, you know, he forgot to wrap up, so I spun out of there and backed into the end zone." Tatum had fallen on his backside, dazed. He said he thought to himself: "How did I get here? Where is this?" "Jack came up to me after that game," Campbell liked to recall, "and said, 'I gave you the best I got.' I told him, 'That's the best I got too.'" Listeners used to grin as he told the Tatum story; now it seemed sad.

A constellation of players whom Earl played with and against have also limped into middle age. Telling a reporter in 2014, "I guarantee I have CTE," former NFL defensive back Doug Beaudoin especially remembered trying to stop Earl Campbell: "It's you and him, and you just go like a heat-seeking missile and hit whatever's moving and you take a knee. As his knee's coming up, to the crown of your head, it knocks you silly." An examination of the brain tissue of the late Frank Gifford, the former player and velvet-voiced partner of Howard Cosell who was in the broadcast booth for that 1978 *Monday Night Football* game between Houston and Miami, revealed the telltale neuronal degeneration of chronic traumatic encephalopathy. Postmortem tests on the brain of Ken Stabler, the quarterback who handed Campbell the ball during the back half of his Oiler career, showed that he, too, had suffered from the disease. The running back with whom Campbell was most often compared, the lightning-quick Dorsett, has had the sort of memory loss associated with CTE. At the time of his death, in 2018, Julius Whittier, the first black football letterman at the University of Texas, who had become a longtime criminal prosecutor before being forced to retire from early-onset Alzheimer's, was suing the NCAA over brain injuries he had sustained. Even the footnote players who bookended Earl Campbell's professional career—the player for whom he was traded on draft day and the backfield mate with whom he finished his career—have suffered CTE-associated symptoms.

"I will 100 percent tell you that Earl Campbell was the target," Gregg Bingham, his former Oiler teammate, said. "He was constantly beaten to death. All his issues come directly from football. No doubt in my mind. Earl would get hit ten times in one play. He just took an ass-whoopin'. And there was a price for that. You give up your life for something. You want to look at it and say, 'I did it damn well.' And Earl can. But he paid a price for it."

As someone who was widely regarded as one of the toughest guys in a tough-guy sport, Earl Campbell can still fall back on the tritely macho terms common to older athletes. "I can't play because I've got a hangnail on my toe. I can't play because I didn't get a pedicure this week. I don't play because my head hurt," he said as recently as 2017, waving away what he says are excuses from present-day players. "That wouldn't have got the job done back in my day." And yet today a copy of *League of Denial: The NFL, Concussions, and the Battle for Truth*, by Mark Fainaru-Wada and Steve Fainaru, a book about traumatic brain injury in professional football, sits on the mantelpiece in Campbell's office. A decade on from his stint in rehab, he remains sober.

"Sometimes I tell my wife, 'Shoot, if I knew it was going to hurt like this, I don't know if I'd have (played football),'" Campbell said. "It's a hell of a price to pay."

When Ann Campbell died, age eighty-five, she left behind nine children, thirty-three grandchildren, and thirty-six great-grandchildren. The obituary her family placed in the paper was modest as ever. It described her as "a housewife and rose grower" and a member of the Hopewell Valley Baptist Church and the Senior Ladies Sunday School Class. It made no mention that she had raised a Heisman Trophy winner in that old broken-down, immaculately kept house of hers. She was buried in the old Hopewell Community Cemetery in Swan.

The land that her father, Reuben Collins, had once worked and hoped to buy, land that was repossessed after his premature death of a heart attack, was now in Campbell family hands: Earl bought the 250 acres with his NFL money and christened it the 7 Cs Ranch, after the seven Campbell brothers. He runs a handful of cows on it, and some chickens and pigs. When he bought the place, while still a player, he talked about the purchase with a sort of poetry. "Everybody in the world has some place he wants to go home to some day," Campbell said. "Some people are lucky. They go back walking. Some go home lyin' down, dead and gone. When I finish football the ranch is where I want to be. I don't see anything wrong with making plans for the future. Some day, number 34 will play out. But Earl Campbell will still live."

If you go there now, it's likely you will find Herbert and Willie, his older brothers, and one of the twins, hunched in plastic chairs around a metal-framed fire pit, the metal branded with #34—Campbell's jersey number with the Oilers. On a cool autumn evening, with the sun setting, as you drive through a gate in the wrought-iron fence, a few dogs are running around the wiry grasses. The meadow reaches down to a faraway pond.

There's no sign of habitation beyond the small circle around the fire, a couple of massive pickups, and a rough corrugated barn in the middle distance. The three aging black men shooting the breeze seem totally at home, though, teasing one another, laughing and carousing, digging into some cookies, dreaming up the next smoked-meat cookout. The scene has something of the relaxed feel of a pre-football-game tailgate party, only instead of athletic grandstanding, the brothers are recalling with wry chuckles stories of the deeply segregated Tyler of their youth. How in the valley behind them, a small plane had gone down, and their grandfather's heart had given out from the rescue effort, right there, near that live oak, on land he had worked all his life to earn a piece of. Alternately graciously polite and benevolently sarcastic, their deep Piney Woods drawl can be difficult to make out. Around the brothers, the meadow recedes softly into the dusk. It is impossible, watching them, to imagine a more quintessentially Texan scene.

In town, in North Tyler, where Confederate Avenue crosses Martin Luther King Jr. Boulevard, an empty field sits behind a chain-link fence. Once there was a grand three-story building there—the old all-black Emmett Scott High School, which was closed in 1970 as part of the desegregation order.

Earl Campbell would have gone to Emmett Scott, like Herbert and Willie, if not for William Wayne Justice's desegregation order. The black kids who went to Emmett Scott still hold it, and their long-dead teachers, in high regard. They organize annual reunions—2020 will mark the last of the Emmett Scott fiftieth reunions.

As for the fiftieth reunion of the Robert E. Lee Red Raiders, Class of 1974, Bettye Mitchell, who is Campbell's age and was one of the black pioneers at John Tyler High's crosstown rival, won't be attending. She tells a story about running into a white classmate in the early 1990s, ahead of their twentieth reunion.

"In high school we were a nonentity, but he was one of a handful of whites that showed any kind of kindness to me in high school," she said. He asked whether she was going to the upcoming reunion, and she told him she wouldn't pay to go to an event for a group in which she felt second-class. She still remembered that at the senior prom, the organizers had refused to play any music that the black kids liked. But after much coaxing—and his offer to buy her ticket— she said she would go, just to see whether it would be any different.

At the reunion, he insisted on buying a raffle ticket for her. "I said, 'No, no,' and he said 'It's yours, it's yours.'" Sure enough, when they called the tickets out, she had won a prize.

> They had talked about the prize before the number was called, and I was sitting back, and the lights were dim, and I couldn't really tell what it was. When they called my name, I raised my arm, "I've won, I've won, I've won." The crowd was speechless. You could hear a pin drop, and I was thinking, "What is that about?" What I had won was a picture, as large as this fireplace, of General Robert E. Lee carrying a Rebel flag and a black slave carrying his things behind him. A hush went over the audience. I thought, "The more things change, the more they re- main the same." So they start offering to buy it off me. I thought, "This is what I won, I'll take it, I'll throw darts at it." I mean, it was the prize possession of the night. After the offers got up to $800, I let them have it. That was the last class reunion I went to.

When Bettye Mitchell and Earl Campbell went to their newly in- tegrated high schools in the early 1970s, the district served a student population that was 67 percent white and 32 percent black. Today, Tyler ISD's student population is 46 percent Hispanic, 30 percent African American, and 22 percent white. Robert E. Lee, virtually all-white when Bettye Mitchell attended, has a minority population of more than 60 percent. Citing the enrollment statistics, a feder- al judge in 2016 lifted Justice's desegregation order, saying it had achieved the desegregation goal. "We'll forever say this, that the dual system that was being operated prior to 1970 was sinful," Marty

Crawford, the district's superintendent said, "and that was certainly an error of our country that we should not be proud of."

The following year, on a muggy August evening, nearly three hundred Tylerites showed up to a school district meeting as the board took up the question of changing the name of Robert E. Lee High School. The notorious Unite the Right rally had just taken place in Charlottesville, Virginia, and now Tyler, like many communities, was reconsidering its attachment to Confederate names and symbols. The meeting came against the backdrop of a persistent, yawning economic gap between whites and people of color in Tyler. About 65 percent of Tyler's African Americans and Latinos lived in homes valued at less than $100,000; less than 30 percent of whites live in such modest homes. Some African Americans addressing the board wondered who had stood up for their history when Emmett Scott High School was closed down. A white father of three said that his children, who had graduated from Robert E. Lee, "might as well use their diplomas as toilet paper" if the school's name was changed. The school board tabled a decision for nearly twelve months before shying away altogether from a name change.

Every January, the Tyler Chamber of Commerce, along with the Visitors Bureau, hosts an annual Earl Campbell banquet. The event honors an outstanding offensive college football player with ties to Texas. Henry Bell, the president of the chamber, sweetly commissions little chocolate figurines depicting Earl in full football regalia to give out to guests.

The event is at the Willow Brook Country Club, on the west side of town, only a mile or so from the Tyler Rose Garden and Museum. Founded in 1922, the club long barred African Americans from membership. Sam Biscoe, who grew up black in Tyler—he and his mother, a maid like Ann Campbell, made extra money on Rose Festival day by selling cool drinks to onlookers—caddied in the summer at Willow Brook in the 1960s. It was, he said, "unthinkable for a black person to be a member. You could have won the lottery and shown up there, and they'd call the police on you if you weren't there to cook or caddy."

Today, on the course and in the dark-wood-paneled, leather-sofaed clubhouse, virtually all the patrons are, still, white; membership is by invitation only, requiring three letters by current members to "vouch for the eligibility and acceptability of the candidate." If your daughter was Rose Festival queen, there's a good chance you'll host her wedding reception poolside at Willow Brook.

Earl always invites some athletes in his circle to make the annual trip to Tyler for the event. In January 2017, one of them was former NFL player and star University of Texas running back Ricky Williams. Nearly two decades earlier, in 1998, Williams had become the only other Longhorn to win the Heisman Trophy. Williams had gotten a ride that morning from Christian, Earl's son, into Tyler, and with a few hours to kill before the banquet, he decided to take a long walk in a residential neighborhood behind his South Tyler hotel. As he strolled back, a couple of cop cars pulled up. A dash-cam video shows Williams being asked to put his hands behind his back. Things are taken from his pockets and put on the hood of the police car. He is frisked. When he asks evenly why he is being detained, he is told to calm down.

It's a maddening video—partly because the cops are so patronizing as they obviously profile him, and partly because what they are doing seems like such a humiliating violation of a person's dignity. The cops are white. As Williams, his hands spread on the dash, again questions why they are searching him, one policeman moves into a kind of defensive position behind him. It isn't hard to imagine that if Williams were less calm, an officer might have drawn a gun. Williams's Zen-like poise, admirable in its way, also makes the whole thing sad. "Do you know how many times I've been messed with by cops just for being black?" Williams asks. "I'm not saying that's what you're doing, I'm just sensitive to it."

"As long as everything is cool, go back to your hotel, we'll get out of your face," a cop says. But they continue to encircle him, and when Williams protests again that he hasn't done anything, another cop says: "You're acting really defensive."

Though they have found nothing, the police ask for his social security number and phone number.

Almost six minutes into the interrogation, Williams reveals that he is in town for the Earl Campbell Tyler Rose awards.

"Football coach?" a cop asks. Finally seeming to put two and two together, the cop asks, "You play football?"

"I'm retired," Williams says, still not using the Heisman card.

The officer asks him where he played; the University of Texas, he tells him.

The cops explain they were duty-bound to question him. One of the officers tells him: "If you're staying at the hotel, makes sense what you're talking about. But if you're coming from North Tyler"—that is, the black part of town—"you're not supposed to be here."

The cop slaps Williams congenially on the shoulder, as if to say, "We're all on the same team here," and they leave.

The mayor of Tyler, Martin Heines, later said he phoned Williams. "We both reached out to the other, and it was a very positive conversation," Heines said, according to the Tyler newspaper. "We visited about the incident, and we came to the positive conclusion that he's very welcome in Tyler, Texas. And I hope I can spend some time with him when he does return. I even invited him to stay with my family when he's here; we have a guest room he's welcome to."

But a Tyler police spokesman, Don Martin, stuck to the story that Williams had brought the incident on himself. "Bottom line, if this person had not gone back into an area and acted in a suspicious manner the way he did then this never would have happened," he said.

Williams, interviewed on KLBJ radio about the episode when he got back to Austin, said that while he ended up putting it behind him and having a good time in Tyler, he still feels disrespected.

"A black guy walking during daytime in South Tyler is like spotting Bigfoot," cracked one of the radio hosts, Dale Dudley, who grew up in Tyler. The radio guys played something that sounded like a police radio: "Calling all cars, black man walking in Tyler."

Williams said he was relieved that he had had his driver's license on him. "If I wasn't myself, I would have been in trouble," Williams said. "If I couldn't prove beyond a reasonable doubt who I was ..."

Back at the hotel that afternoon, he said, he started writing an angry tweet. But then he thought: "Earl invited me here. This is Earl's town. I didn't want to make a to-do."

Dudley, who is white and went to Robert E. Lee High, chimed in:

That's the hypocrisy that's always been in that town. There's nothing at all about the lynchings all around there. There's no history the kids are taught. You're taught that the rose queen is gorgeous—even though she's paid for by her father.

And it was this thing where, if you run a football well, we love you, and we'll put you all over the city, and you're the king—which Earl is, and God bless Earl, and I've got nothing but positive [things to say] about Earl.

But the people who championed Earl, that was because he did that [on the football field] and he got that kind of attention. My father was so afraid for me to go to Stewart Junior High, which was predominantly black, that we lied about where we lived so I could go to Hubbard Junior High.

And that stuff has lingered. I did a high school reunion, and I'm always trying to prove [to] people I did well. So the reunion was on a Saturday night, and I decided to host a party on Friday night. And I get a call from someone I don't even know—a friend of one of the people I invited— and he says, "Hey, man, you don't want to do it at that bar—that's where all the 'N's go." I'm looking at the cell phone going, "Did I just hear that in a normal conversation? I'm not even talking to a friend." It's a long history of the way that goes, and it sounds like it's in [the] police department also: "Hey, you see a black guy in South Tyler, stop him and see what he's up to."

Williams came back in at that point. "I hope that after this situation, they realize that black lives do matter," he told the radio hosts. "I've never wanted to say that, but this was a time where it fits. It fits in Tyler in that moment."

Sociologists talk about the distinction between the speaking black athlete and the smiling black athlete—the athlete who stepped out and the one who got along. Jim Brown and O. J. Simpson: Brown once proudly embodied the defiant black athlete, whereas O. J. listed not being viewed as black as a great accomplishment. Earl Campbell was a kind of amalgam. Campbell didn't preach revolt. He saw himself as a catalyst for racial conciliation. "I was raised not to have negative racial feelings towards the white people of Tyler," he told me. The line puts you in mind of what Donald Hamilton, Earl's sandbox playmate, adopted as his motto: you catch more flies with honey than with vinegar.

And as Earl Campbell grew famous, he shouldered the burden of many athletes, especially black athletes, especially now, again, in the age of Trump, of being picked apart over how they did—or did not—react to the political and social struggles of their time. In many ways, his public persona was that of a smiling athlete. Ben Carrington, a sociologist of race and sports, told me that Campbell always struck him as a "Disneyfied version of a black athlete, someone round and cuddly and smiley." Jenna Hays McEachern, the unofficial historian of UT football, pinned Campbell's appeal on his appearing "unthreatening." From the outset of his professional career, he was made mute by advertisers whose products he endorsed. (It was partly because he got flustered. Appearing in a 1979 Seven-Up ad with a couple of other football players, his sole line was scratched after he kept botching it on camera. "He would get really flabbergasted," said Verlin Callahan, whose family feed store in Austin employed Campbell as a pitchman, one time paying him with the use of a John Deere tractor for a year. "He could sit down and talk with you about anything. But he was a one-to-one communicator; he wasn't a camera communicator.") In recent television advertisements for his smoked meats—he now licenses his name and image to a sausage factory in a little Central Texas town—Campbell is rendered almost Jemima-like: poised over a grill, wearing an apron, always smiling but never speaking.

But in his own quiet, private way, he relayed his allegiances. In 1997, Ron Wilson, Campbell's old classmate at the University of Texas, introduced a bill in the Texas Legislature to eliminate athletic scholarships at state universities unless student-athletes met the same academic requirements as nonathletes. This move came in the wake of the *Hopwood* decision, in which a federal court struck down the University of Texas's affirmative action policy. (It was named for Cheryl Hopwood, one of four white students who sued the university's law school, claiming she had been discriminated against because the school gave preferential treatment to people of color.) Wilson's proposal—which threatened to undercut the competitiveness of big-time college football in Texas—was meant to startle opponents of affirmative action by essentially calling them on their logic. If affirmative action is a bad idea for nonathletes, it's bad for athletes, too. "Obviously, *Hopwood* means that a lot of average and above-average minority students won't be admitted through the front door of the University of Texas or Texas A&M," he told reporters after filing his bill. "If they don't want us through the front door, then they shouldn't be allowed to bring us through the back door." Admitting only athletically talented African Americans because of their "entertainment value" would create a "plantation education system," he said.

UT coaches stormed the Capitol in opposition to the bill. "It would be a disaster if it passed," basketball coach Tom Penders told the Senate Education Committee. "You might as well blow up the football field and the basketball courts and make parking lots out of them." He was joined by Darrell Royal, long retired, who had asked Earl Campbell to come down to testify against the bill. He even signed Campbell's name to a witness list. That day, as the committee heard from a stream of people, the question was whether Earl would show up. "You had a bunch of white coaches who needed him to legitimize their position," said Alberta Phillips, who was a reporter covering the bill for the *Austin American-Statesman*. Phillips, who is African American, was sure that Campbell would appear: "I was of the thinking that Earl was an Uncle Tom," she said. "But Ron kept saying, 'He's not going to come, he's not going to come,'" she remembered.

And he never did.

"My feeling about him changed that day," Phillips said. "Earl did have a social consciousness to him. Maybe he wasn't vocal, maybe it wasn't visible, but it was there." Given the amount of pressure the university must have exerted on Campbell—he remained an employee—the black lawmakers "were so proud" of him for his decision, she said.

"He left Darrell Royal hanging," she laughed.

In the end, assembling a coalition of lawmakers that included minorities, conservatives, and just enough egghead types who wanted to deemphasize athletics, Wilson managed to get the bill passed—but with amended language that excluded UT and Texas A&M.

After *Hopwood*, Campbell helped organize scholarships for students of color. And more recently, in 2016, Campbell presided over a celebration on campus of the first African Americans to attend UT, a revered group known as the Precursors. Their steadfastness in the late 1950s in an often-inhospitable atmosphere laid the groundwork for the African American students and athletes who would follow them, and in a sense, Campbell's appointment as the honorary chair of the event recognized his link to their persistence. The event came amid a newfound reckoning at the university. A few years earlier, in 2013, UT had hired its first black head football coach—"I was more surprised that UT hired a black coach than that the US elected a black president," the sports columnist Cedric Golden told me. In 2015, following months-long deliberations by a panel appointed by the university president, UT forklifted a statue of Jefferson Davis from its pedestal, which sat along an iconic promenade in the south part of the campus; in 2017, shortly after the Charlottesville rally, the president ordered the remaining Confederate statues in the same area pulled down in the dead of night; and in 2018 the law school unveiled, in its atrium, a portrait of Heman Sweatt.

How, in the final analysis, should Earl Campbell be regarded with respect to the fight for civil rights? "The way I would judge someone would be in terms of whether they did things within the realm of what they're capable of to help or advance things," said Gary Bledsoe, who was a law student at the University of Texas when Earl was playing football there. A lanky African American from Odessa, at the opposite end of the state from Tyler, he can remember his friends in the late 1960s discouraging him from attending UT as an undergraduate because, they said, "those folks don't want you down there; they're going to flunk you out." He went anyway, walked on to the football team after Julius Whittier broke the color barrier, and went on to graduate from the UT Law School before heading up the state chapter of the NAACP. He is now the dean of the Thurgood Marshall School of Law at Texas Southern, in Houston. He summed up his view of Campbell's role in the area of civil rights: "Being the activist, the vocal thing, that wasn't Earl's style. But Earl was a real asset to the advancement of civil rights in this state. There are different ways to do things and accomplish things. We can't judge everybody by the standard of Martin Luther King. He [Earl] did things in his way. We're wrong to try to prejudge that he should have done this or should have done that. Did he do things to hurt? No. Did he do things to help? Yes."

In the scars that mark Campbell's surgeries, a map of brutality, you can see what Wilson, the former lawmaker, called "the ultimate sacrifice for his people."

In 2012, the University of Texas invited Earl Campbell to flip the coin at the opening of its home football game against the Lobos of the University of New Mexico. It was an early-season game against a cupcake opponent. UT's football coach, the folksy Mack Brown—wide face, soft river-bottom voice—had asked Campbell to do the coin toss. The football team had had a disappointing campaign the year before, and what better way to start the new season than an appearance from a beloved star of yesteryear?

And yet: while nothing could be more trivial than a pregame coin flip, the invitation posed a flesh-and-blood problem for Campbell. Decades earlier, getting to midfield as a crowd of nearly 80,000 people cheered him on was something that Campbell could do while dragging defenders along like a father with his child wrapped around his trouser leg. But at only fifty-three, his legs beaten from a career of football, his back in terrible pain from a series of spinal surgeries, Campbell couldn't even stand in the shower. Walking the thirty-odd yards from the sideline to midfield—a distance likely not much farther than the one from your front door to your backdoor—might as well have been a hot-asphalt stroll across the entire state of Texas.

Campbell, naturally, was nostalgic about the prospect of appearing once more before the Longhorn faithful. On this field, on sweltering Saturday nights before throngs of fans making the "Hook 'Em" sign as if signaling devotion to some football divinity, Earl Campbell regularly accomplished heroics—sprinting past chaps-wearing Texas cheerleaders and the lined-up cannons ready to be lit on his way to the end zone. The brassy sound of the Longhorn Band—young men and women in short-brimmed white Stetsons and sequined burnt orange trousers, white leather fringe flying about their shoulders as they played—sang in his ears. Here, in this stadium, now named for the coach who recruited Earl Campbell from that modest home in East Texas, he once had such momentum following a long touchdown run that he ran into—and knocked down—Bevo, the 2,000-pound cud-chewing longhorn and team mascot. In videos, you can see him hit Bevo in the left flank, taking down a cameraman at the same time; the mascot, which had been mindlessly staring into space and was now half rolled over and clearly startled, yanked his head around toward Campbell. "Before I knew it, I was all up on Bevo," he later told the reporter Jan Reid. "I didn't mean to; I couldn't stop." He paused before laughing at the end of the story: "He said, 'Moooo.'"

But those days were gone. "For a long time everything was still attached pretty good," he once said. "But all those years of knocking and banging—there are some things you ain't supposed to do to that body. And when you get older, it comes back and says, 'Hey, remember me? How you did all that to me?' That's flesh and bone, man."

Any sentimentality triggered by Mack Brown's invitation was tempered with trepidation. The coach—a keen reader of athletes, and mindful of the once-rugged running back's ailments—gently suggested many months before the New Mexico game that Earl could simply take a golf cart to midfield. But Earl Campbell, whose vulnerability was matched only by his pride, did not want the fans, a whirlpool of burnt orange, to see him golf-carted anywhere.

But his friend and Longhorn lead blocker Rick Ingraham counseled him to participate: "This state wants to see you out on the field doing the Hook 'Em." And so, that March, six months before the New Mexico game, Earl Campbell showed up at the UT athletic facility to undertake private, early-morning workouts. He was forcing himself, effectively, to lace up his cleats once more. It fell to Caesar Martinez, a bright-faced onetime third-string college running back, to retrain Campbell, the human cyclone, to do the elementary work of walking.

Martinez and his team wondered what sort of discipline, what sort of consistency, to expect from their newest trainee. The answer came quickly: "I really want it bad," Campbell told them, and it was as if he had invited them back into a huddle in 1977, a time when, in his country way, his polite way, he would demand the ball. His athlete's perfectionism began to reassert itself. After finishing a ten-rep set of an exercise—stepping up and down from a little platform, for instance—he would turn to Martinez and say, "I'm going to do a couple of those again; I didn't like one of those reps."

Soon, in an empty stadium, he and Martinez began walking

those thirty yards. No cheerleaders, no band, no fans. Had they seen him just then, they might have wondered what had happened to Earl Campbell. At first, in the baking heat of the early Austin summer, he walked that modest distance haltingly. But as September approached, he gained something of his old footing, his thick-legged gait coming back. He appeared no longer diminished, but formidable.

Come game day, Martinez was nervous with pregame jitters. Campbell, though, was ready for his big entrance. The public-address announcer welcomed the Heisman winner to midfield, and suddenly the crowd, whose members had been busy with the usual pregame rituals, snapped to attention. Like an orange flag unfurling, they rose. Their old god had once more alighted.

# ACKNOWLEDGMENTS

From the very first time he and I chatted about my ideas for this book, Casey Kittrell, my editor at the University of Texas Press, lent a bright-eyed, infectious enthusiasm to the project. Casey was a true collaborator, joining me, at a variety of coffee shops around Austin, to hash out the shape and framing of the book. And once the drafts rolled in, his shrewd line edits improved the manuscript that much more. I am lucky to count the Press—and especially Casey—as a partner.

David Halpern, my funny and elegant agent, planted the seed for the whole thing—it was his idea that I embark on a biography. Shrewd and personable, he is everything you could want in an advocate.

My editors at the *Austin American-Statesman*—Debbie Hiott, John Bridges, Andy Alford, and Bob Gee—had enough faith in the project to give me an extended leave to work on the book. Thanks to them and to all my colleagues who picked up the slack while I was gone.

I am grateful to the dozens of people in Tyler, Austin, and Houston who were kind enough to welcome me into their homes and offices and sit for interviews, chief among them Earl Campbell and members of his family—including three of his brothers, two sisters, and his aunt.

The librarians at the University of Texas, especially Cindy Slater at the Lutcher Stark Center for Physical Culture and Sports and archivists at the Dolph Briscoe Center for American History, were generous with their time—and strong of limb, lifting, as they did, heavy boxes of clippings and memos for me to examine. In Tyler, Tiffany Wright at the Smith County Historical Society was enormously helpful, thoughtful about further avenues of inquiry, and tolerant of all my questions. Scott Fitzgerald of the East Texas Genealogical Society hunted down some background material about the Campbell family. John Anderson, in Tyler, and Michael Gillette at Humanities Texas also offered handy guidance. Nell Carroll, *Austin American-Statesman* photo editor, patiently walked me through the process of scanning old images. Phil Hicks in Tyler and Joel Draut in Houston were nice enough to burrow through photo morgues and send me some choice images. Mark O'English at Washington State University kindly e-mailed me copies of letters from the 1950s from that university's president to his counterpart at UT regarding African American football players. My former *Statesman* colleague Bruce Hight dug up from his garage a 1970 *Atlantic* piece about Darrell Royal that proved very useful. Speaking of garages: in August 2017, Dale Robertson kindly lent me a half-dozen bulging spiral notebooks filled with clips from his time covering the Houston Oilers. They turned out to be extremely useful for re-creating life in the Oiler locker room. I was lucky: a week later Hurricane Harvey struck, and his entire garage was flooded.

John Maher, Vicki Betts, Michael Hurd, David Barron, Cedric Golden, Leslie Blair, and Brian Sweany, as well as Aimée Brown Price, Monroe Price, Josh Price, and Gabe Price, read all or parts of drafts and gave crucial feedback. A very special thanks goes to copy editor extraordinaire Kip Keller for the enormous care with which he reviewed the manuscript. He and UT Press managing editor Robert Kimzey read the work with eyes of which eagles would be envious.

My friend and consigliore Jim Phillips, a contemporary of Earl Campbell's who grew up in Huntsville and attended UT, served as an invaluable guide through the landscape of 1970s East Texas. Over regular lunches at our favorite strip-mall Chinese restaurant, ones that inevitably spilled over to slurping tapioca at the bubble tea spot next door, Jim, elucidating the indecipherable scrawls he had left on my manuscript, set me straight on the particulars of that faraway time and place.

This book is dedicated to my parents and my brothers—Aimée and Monroe, Josh and Gabe—my earliest teachers and deepest influences. Having a little kid now myself makes me appreciate all they did to raise me. To whatever extent I have a sense of humor about the world, with whatever thoughtfulness I might examine it, I have the four of them to thank for the early example they set. I continue to learn from them, and while I feel keenly the geographic distance that separates us, I am grateful for the resiliency and intimacy of our relationships.

But my deepest gratitude is reserved for Rebecca Markovits. She drove with me to Tyler and helped me sort through old archives. She helped me bake linzer torte cookies for an initial interview with Earl Campbell's brothers—and every time I got in touch with them thereafter, they asked whether I was going to bring along some more. The writing of this book came as she conceived, nourished, and delivered (and nourished some more) our child—and yet even as she returned to her own work, editing a literary magazine, she patiently read over and advised me on one draft after another. It is she who cuts my hair (and, now, our daughter's hair), and like an experienced barber, she neatened my prose as if clip-clipping away with a pair of expert shears. In football terms, I'm not sure whether to describe Rebecca as the ever-dependable quarterback or the all-protecting left guard or the eyes-in-the-sky offensive coordinator. In any case, she gets my vote for MVP.

# NOTES

Most of the material in this book comes from interviews I conducted or from contemporaneous accounts: memos, letters, newspaper clippings, and the like.

Further research was conducted at five institutional archives: the Austin History Center (AHC); the Dolph Briscoe Center for American History at the University of Texas (DBCAH); the Houston Public Library's African American Library at the Gregory School (Gregory); the Smith County Historical Society (SCHS); and the H. J. Lutcher Stark Center for Physical Culture and Sports at the University of Texas (Stark Center). I also called on the clipping files belonging to the Houston reporter Dale Robertson (DRCF) and the *Austin American-Statesman*.

## INTRODUCTION

Interviews for this section were conducted with Tim Alexander (Mar. 2018), Earl Campbell (Feb. 2016), Herbert Campbell (Dec. 2015), Willie Campbell (Dec. 2015), Donald Hamilton (Apr. 2017), Alfred Jackson (July 2017), Carl Mauck (Aug. 2016), Dan Pastorini (Aug. 2017), Wally Scott (March 2018), Mike Trope (Oct. 2016), and Ron Wilson (Aug. 2017). Quoted material from these interviews is generally not documented further in the notes.

1    *Crunching power*: for Cosell's comments throughout the second half of the game between Houston and Miami, Nov. 20, 1978, see the recording of the game on YouTube, youtube.com/watch?v=HKYJcH4GjpU.
1    *Earl Campbell had some head-on collisions*: Kevin Cook, *The Last Head-bangers: NFL Football in the Rowdy, Reckless '70s—The Era That Created Modern Sports* (New York: Norton, 2013), 183.
1    *Big fellow, you got*: John P. Lopez, "Tyler Rose's Run on 'MNF' Set Standard," *Houston Chronicle*, Dec. 27, 2005, Sports, 1; see also Barry Lorge, "The Earl of Campbell," *Washington Post*, Dec. 27, 1978, D1, and Bruce Newman, "The Roots of Greatness," *Sports Illustrated*, Sept. 3, 1979.

2     *I swear, his eyes were closed*: Bill Sullivan, "Former Teammates Remain in Awe," *Houston Chronicle*, July 29, 1991, 1C.

3     *We make four sizes of thigh pads*: Brian Hewitt, "Earl's Thigh Pads Legal 'Weapons,'" *Chicago Sun-Times*, Nov. 16, 1980, quoting the equipment maker Byron Donzis.

3     *When that ball got in my hands*: Brad Buchholz, "Rock of Ages," *Austin American-Statesman*, Dec. 9, 2007, A1.

3     *the quality of potentiality*: Willie Morris, *The Courting of Marcus Dupree* (Garden City, NY: Doubleday, 1983), 80.

3     *You could always tell*: Kirk Bohls, "Campbell Was Unstoppable at Texas," *Austin American-Statesman*, July 28, 1991; Earl Campbell player file, Stark Center.

4     *Then I saw pure sideline*: Newman, "Roots of Greatness," 106.

4     *Don't you just love him?*: Dale Robertson, "Never a Rookie like Earl," *Dave Campbell's Arkansas Football*, Winter 1979, 62.

4     *My career with the Dolphins*: Harvey Greene, "Where Are They Now: Steve Towle," Miami Dolphins website, June 30, 2016, miamidolphins.com/news/article-1/Where-Are-They-Now-Steve-Towle/a21f4fdf-ac5a-4ebf8f76-a4e103528e61.

5     *We trained in southern California*: Peter Gent, *North Dallas Forty*, New York: Open Road, 2003, unpaginated foreword.

6     *One Orangeblood, as diehard fans*: Author interview with Wally Scott, Mar. 2018.

6     *only one African American had ever*: Al Reinert, "Closing Down La Grange," *Texas Monthly*, Oct. 1973, texasmonthly.com/the-culture/closing-down-la-grange.

7     *all ass and thighs*: Lee Jenkins, "Life's Roses (and Sausages)," *Sports Illustrated*, July 9, 2012, 70.

7     *Campbell's running style*: Lou Maysel, "Clayborn Talent Noted by Some," *Austin American-Statesman*, Dec. 23, 1976, E1. Assistant coach Mike Campbell made the observation.

7     *Every time Earl carried the football*: Mickey Herskowitz, "Campbell Earned Respect of All," *Houston Post*, July 28, 1991.

7     *played offense like he was playing defense*: Ta-Nehisi Coates, "Tony Dorsett has CTE," *Atlantic*, Nov. 8, 2013, theatlantic.com/entertainment/archive/2013/11/tony-dorsett-has-cte/281279.

7     *didn't hit tacklers*: Kirk Bohls, "God Made Only One Earl," *Austin American-Statesman*, Aug. 9, 1987, D8.

7     *Put a gun on him*: Jim Murray, "Campbell Breaks Free Again," *Los Angeles Times*, Aug. 15, 1991, C1.

7  *It's me first, Earl second*: Kirk Bohls, "Earl to Open Up on TV Monday," *Austin American-Statesman*, June 24, 2013, C1.

8  *I always thought Superman was white*: Clifford Broyles, "Clifford Broyles," *Bryan–College Station Eagle*, Jan. 27, 1974, 3B; see also Eddie Perkins, "Memories of Campbell Last for Coach," *Dallas Times Herald*, Aug. 2, 1986, Earl Campbell file, Stark Center, and Newman, "Roots of Greatness," 100.

8  *Earl Campbell is the greatest player*: Newman, "Roots of Greatness."

8  *Earl found a phone booth*: Dale Robertson, "We Just Want to Hold Him under a Mile," *Houston Post*, Dec. 20, 1980, DRCF.

8  *I was watching basketball*: Patrick Reusse, "Sobriety Saved Hall of Famer," *Minneapolis Star Tribune*, Feb. 3, 2018, 6C.

8  *His father, Bert*: Author interviews with Campbell's brothers (Dec. 2015) and Donald Hamilton (Apr. 2017).

9  *If they gave out a Heisman*: Earl Campbell, "Ann Campbell Wins 'Heisman for Moms,'" *Austin Weekly*, May 10, 1989.

9  *I always thought if I*: Buchholz, "Rock of Ages."

9  *Every time you hit him*: Bruce Lowitt, "Campbell's Style May Take Its Toll," *Austin American-Statesman*, Oct. 19, 1979, G1.

10  *Campbell told a friend in shop class*: Author interview with Tim Alexander, Mar. 2018.

10  *he played with a 101-degree fever*: Earl Campbell, thetylerrose.com/the-college-years.

10  *I hit him square*: Jenkins, "Life's Roses (and Sausages)," 70.

10  *You want to know what*: Author interview with Carl Mauck, Aug. 2016.

11  *I truly believed*: Author interview with Earl Campbell, Feb. 2016.

11  *To appreciate Campbell*: Ron Reid, "This Oiler's a Gusher of a Rusher," *Sports Illustrated*, Sept. 18, 1978, 24.

11  *it seems like something*: "Earl Campbell Press Availability Transcript," Sept. 9, 2012, Texas Sports, texassports.com/news/2012/9/9/090912aaa_732.aspx.

12  *My people were bought and sold*: Randy Harvey, "He Was Never Promised a Rose Garden: JT Superstar, Campbell," *Austin American-Statesman*, Jan. 13, 1974, C3.

12  *a kind of Horatio Alger*: "Campbell Receives Texas Hero Award," Cox News Service, May 8, 1981.

## PART I: TYLER

Conducting research about Tyler involved interviews with Tim Alexander (Mar.

2018), John Anderson (Dec. 2015), Lincoln Ashford (Jan. 2017), David Barron (Sept. 2017), Henry Bell III (Apr. 2017), Sam Biscoe (summer 2017), Gary Bledsoe (July 2017), Earl Campbell (Dec. 2015, Feb. 2016), Herbert Campbell (Dec. 2015), Linda Campbell (Apr. 2017), Margaret Campbell (Apr. 2017), Martha Campbell (Apr. 2017), Willie Campbell (Dec. 2015, Apr. 2017), Charles Clark (summer 2017), A. C. Flynn (Sept. 2017), Michael Gillette (Oct. 2017), Cedric Golden (May 2017), Donald Hamilton (Apr. 2017), Phil Hicks (Apr. 2017), Michael Hurd (Nov. 2017), Sam Kidd (Dec. 2016), Lynn King (Apr. 2017), Bill Kinzie (Dec. 2016), Joe Richard Lansdale (winter 2016), Thorndyke Lewis (Apr. 2017), Laura McGregor (Apr. 2017), Andrew Melontree (Apr. 2017), Clyde Nelson IV (Apr. 2017), Robert Peters (Oct. 2017), Erna Smith (July 2017), J. B. Smith (Oct. 2017), Mike Trope (Oct. 2016), Leon Van Alstine (Apr. 2017), and Tiffany Wright (Dec. 2015, Apr. 2017). Quoted material from these interviews is generally not documented further in the notes.

14    The story of Earl Campbell's birth and naming comes from a range of sources: interviews with members of the Campbell and Kinzie families, an oral history of medicine in Smith County, and scores of articles about Campbell's early years.

14    *born in the same bed*: Bruce Newman, "The Roots of Greatness," *Sports Illustrated*, Sept. 3, 1979, 98.

14    *Ann Campbell had wanted to name* and *They wanted to charge me*: Earl Campbell, *The Earl Campbell Story: A Football Great's Battle with Panic Disorder*, with John Ruane (Toronto: ECW, 1999), 2.

14    *The story of Kinzie*: An author interview with Bill Kinzie (Dec. 2016) filled in a lot of Earl Christian Kinzie's biographical details, as did a February 1984 interview with Kinzie as part of the Texas College of Osteopathic Medicine's Oral History Collection; see also Sam Blair, "Dr. Kinzie Delivered the Goods," *Dallas Morning News*, Dec. 11, 1977, 4B.000

15    *At Tyler's East Texas Tuberculosis Sanatorium*: Sue Low, "Kerrville State Hospital," *Handbook of Texas Online*, tshaonline.org/handbook/online /articles/sbk01.

15    *the meanest part of the state*: Michael L. Gillette, "The NAACP in Texas, 1937–1957" (PhD diss., University of Texas at Austin, 1984), 219.

16    *the family was wondering*: University of North Texas Health Science Center at Fort Worth, "Kinzie, Earl C., D.O." (1984), 12, Texas College of Osteopathic Medicine, Oral History Collection.

17    *The (white) family retained*: Chris Tomlinson, *Tomlinson Hill: The Remarkable Story of Two Families who Share the Same Name—One White, One Black* (New York: Macmillan), 2014, 79.

18   *the margin was about 25–1* and *they sent envoys*: Archie P. McDonald, *Historic Smith County* (San Antonio: Historical Publishing Network, 2006), 12; see also Joe T. Timmons, "The Referendum in Texas on the Ordinance of Secession, February 23, 1861: The Vote," *East Texas Historical Journal* 11, no. 2 (1973), available from Scholar Works, scholarworks.sfasu.edu/ethj/vol11/iss2/6. While Texas voted to secede by a margin of 46,129 to 14,697, Smith County went by a margin of 1,149 to 50.

18   *Tyler at least as long ago*: *Genealogy Roadshow*, season 1, episode 2, PBS LearningMedia, pbslearningmedia.org/collection/watch-full-episodes/2/#.Wobden4nZp8. This episode is no longer available on the website.

18   *a third of households*: Vicki Betts, retired archivist at University of Texas at Tyler, to the author, June 2018.

19   *not to take the testimony* and *reign of terror*: Barry Crouch, "The Freedmen's Bureau and the 30th Sub-District in Texas: Smith County and Its Environs during Reconstruction," *Chronicles of Smith County, Texas* 11, no. 1 (Spring 1972): 15–30.

19   *Sundays found the Reverend Albert*: Robert E. Reed, Jr. *Tyler: Images of America* (Charleston, SC: Arcadia, 2008), 67.

21   *The home of Mayfield*: Memorylaneinn.com.

21   *A little bit of Texas*: Dayna Worchel, "Many Politicians Make Tyler a Spot to Visit," *Tyler Morning Telegraph*, Feb. 17, 2013.

21   *you were in a different world*: Frank Kemerer, *William Wayne Justice: A Judicial Biography* (Austin: University of Texas Press, 2008), 89.

21   *The only things redder*: David Maraniss, "Justice, Texas Style," *Washington Post*, Feb. 28, 1987, G1.

21   *Tyler Rose Festival queen*: Newspaper clippings and videos on display at the Tyler Rose Museum, including "Rose Queen Aids in Old South's Rebirth," no byline, date, or publication title visible.

23   *grander than everyday life* and *It's like fairy dust*: Introductory video to a permanent exhibit at Tyler Rose Museum.

23   *They didn't want the history*: Rodney Lamar Atkins, *Remembering When We Were Colored in Tyler, Texas* (Tyler: self-published, 2007), 1:53.

23   *same as last year*: Lee Hancock, "Robert E. Lee High School, Race, and Segregation in Tyler: A 130-Year Timeline," *The Tyler Loop*, Sept. 1, 2017, thetylerloop.com/robert-e-lee-high-school-race-and-segregation-in-tyler-a-130-year-timeline.

23   *As a boy, if Earl Campbell*: Vicki Betts, "'For the Citizens of East Texas': The Desegregation of Tyler State Park" (2015), University of Texas at Tyler, Robert R. Muntz Library, *Presentations and Publications*, Paper 39, hdl

.handle.net/10950/487; Gillette, "NAACP in Texas"; Allan Shivers Papers, Box 86-107A, folder "Campaign: Negroes," DBCAH.

24 *fomented, encouraged, aided*: Plaintiff's Original Petition, *State of Texas v. The National Association for the Advancement of Colored People, et al.*, Smith County District Court, Allan Shivers Papers, Box 86-107A, folder "Campaign: Negroes," DBCAH.

25 *seeking to register students*: Order, Oct. 23, 1956, *Texas v. NAACP*, ibid.

25 *more $100,000 houses*: Paul Burka, "Real Governor of Texas," *Texas Monthly*, June 1978, 114.

25 *The Campbells were so hard up*: Martha and Margaret Campbell.

26 *We could never understand*: Campbell, *Earl Campbell Story*, 9.

26 *The annual East Texas Fair*: Bud Finlayson, *Mustang Country* (self-published), chap. 4, elitesoft.com/web/mustang/chap4.html; corroborated in interviews. From Finlayson:

> They (the Blacks) all lived way over on the north side of town, and were hardly ever seen on our side of town, except for the Black maids, yard men, and garbage men, who came south for work. Their houses were small, unpainted, and dilapidated, with weed filled, mainly dirt yards, compared to our large, brick, air-conditioned homes with lush grassy lawns. They had always attended separate schools. That year, however, integration began taking place in Tyler public schools. It was gradual at first, with only one out of every fifty, or so, being black; enough for my Dad to react with a threat to move us to Mississippi to keep our education White. They stayed on the north side and went to different stores, and different restaurants. At the East Texas Fair, there were different restrooms, "Colored" and "White." And everybody knew not to go to the fair on Thursday night cause it was "Nigger Night."

27 *"super-patriots" bombed a parked school bus*: Dianna Wray, "Tension Lit Fuse to Bombing," *Longview News-Journal*, Sept. 13, 2009, 3G.

27 *It was a sad day*: Lee Hancock, "Robert E. Lee High School, Race, and Segregation in Tyler: A 130-Year Timeline," *The Tyler Loop*, Sept. 1, 2017, thetylerloop.com/robert-e-lee-high-school-race-and-segregation-in-tyler-a-130-year-timeline.

28 *You will find some*: School desegregation file, SCHS.

28 *"bad Earl" phase*: Newman, "Roots of Greatness," 100.

29 *I was on the path*: Betty Lou Phillips, *Earl Campbell: Houston Oiler Superstar* (New York: McKay, 1979), 8.

29    *who didn't make trouble*: Michele Burgen, "A Very Proud Mom," *Ebony*, March 1978, 56; see also Newman, "Roots of Greatness."

30    *Earl had to be led*: Author interview with Lynn King, Apr. 2017.

30    *You work to get a status*: Avrel Seale, "A Rose by Any Other Name," *Texas Alcalde*, September–October 1994, 15.

30    *The relationships between the different*: Kirk Bohls, "Earl: No One Has a Rosier Future," *Austin American-Statesman*, Aug. 22, 1976, C1.

32    *They did what human beings*: Isabel Wilkerson, *The Warmth of Other Suns: The Epic Story of America's Great Migration* (New York: Random House, 2010), 14.

32    *I knew that I lived*: Richard Wright, *Black Boy* (New York: World, 1947), 147.

33    *breaks his leg this season*: Willie Morris, *The Courting of Marcus Dupree* (Garden City, NY: Doubleday, 1983), 58.

34    *And the Rangerettes remained*: Rebecca Markovits, "Texas History 101," *Texas Monthly*, Sept. 2004. The Rangerettes were founded in 1940, admitted their first black member in 1973, and elected their first black officer in 2012. Gussie Nell Davis, the founder of the Rangerettes, stated that she would be receptive to an African American member—even though she didn't take one in the first thirty-three years of the troupe; see Jeanie R. Stanley, "Davis, Gussie Nell," *Handbook of Texas Online*, June 12, 2010, tshaonline.org/handbook/online/articles/fda83.

35    *Pages of the* Southwestern Report: Frank R. Kemerer, *William Wayne Justice: A Judicial Biography* (Austin: University of Texas Press, 2008), 7.

36    *After awhile, he came*: Ibid., 116.

36    *I would not have for*: Ibid.

36    *God-dang, when he got*: Ibid.

37    *rationale apparently was that*: Joe Richard Lansdale et al. v. Tyler Junior College, 318 F. Supp. 529 (E.D. Tex. 1970). Available at Justia, law.justia.com/cases/federal/district-courts/FSupp/318/529/1480978.

37    *If someone devised a litmus test*: Burka, "Real Governor of Texas," 115.

38    *They were tickled and eager*: Maraniss, "Justice, Texas Style."

38    *discussing ways and means*: Lee Hancock, "Unfinished History: Black Tyler's Long Fight to Change the Name—and Many Other Things—at Robert E. Lee High," *The Tyler Loop*, Sept. 18, 2017, thetylerloop.com/unfinished-history-black-tylers-long-fight-to-change-the-name-and-many-other-things-about-robert-e-lee-high.

38    *each other like fortresses*: Burka, "Real Governor of Texas," 114.

38    *A cousin wrote a letter*: Ibid., 192; see also Denise Gamino, "A Giant of Texas History," *Austin American-Statesman*, Oct. 15, 2009, A1; Douglas Mar-

tin, "William Wayne Justice, Judge Who Remade Texas, Dies," *New York Times*, Oct. 15, 2009, B11.

38    *It was a great way*: Martin, "William Wayne Justice."

38    *as wide as the goal posts*: Hancock, "Robert E. Lee High School." I also reviewed Williams's testimony as part of a University of North Texas oral-history project: Minnie Mosley Gram and Rostell Williams, oral history interview by Moisés Acuña-Gurrola, June 29, 2015, video, The Portal to Texas History, texashistory.unt.edu/ark:/67531/metapth836718.

39    *Teacher, teacher*: Bettye Mitchell and Katherine Bynum, "Oral History Interview with Bettye Mitchell," July 1, 2015, video, The Portal to Texas History, texashistory.unt.edu/ark:/67531/metapth836696.

39    *It is unbelievable that we*: *Tyler Morning Telegraph*, Nov. 22, 1971.

39    *If the black students had been*: Hancock, "Robert E. Lee High School."

40    *There's a difference between*: Burka, "Real Governor of Texas," 190.

40    *would make the circle*: Marilyn Covey, "Justice is Done," *Tyler Courier-Times-Telegraph*, May 24, 1998, 1.

40    *How's my friendly neighborhood*: Burka, "Real Governor of Texas," 189.

40    *I like Tyler*: R. D. Faubion, "Passing Judgement," *Tyler Today*, Summer 1992, 10; Marilyn Covey, "Justice Plans to End Active Duty Career," *Tyler Courier-Times-Telegraph*, 1.

40    *was bucking for sainthood*: Molly Ivins, "Of Law and Lowlife," *Los Angeles Times Book Review*, Oct. 27, 1991, 1.

41    *Tyler hosted a homecoming*: Details about the celebration, parade, and banquet come from an "Earl Campbell Day" brochure, available at the Smith County Historical Society.

41    *Running Back Campbell*: Kirk Bohls, "Scramble for Campbell: Earl's Sitting Cool as NFL Teams Fight for Draft Rights," *Austin American-Statesman*, April 23, 1978, C1.

41    *We have, as I look out*: "'Earl Campbell Day' Sets Tributes Flowing," Associated Press, Feb. 2, 1978.

41    *The organizers had made sure*: Burka, "Real Governor of Texas," 192.

41    *according to Campbell family lore*: In addition to members of the Campbell family, Tiffany Wright (SCHS), Scott Fitzgerald (East Texas Genealogical Society), and Ancestry.com were helpful resources for tracing the Campbell family's genealogy. Interviews with A. C. Flynn, Charles Clark, Donald Hamilton, and Mike Trope also provided details about the history and home life of the Campbells, as did Earl Campbell's autobiography and Newman, "Roots of Greatness."

43    *taste for white lightning*: Author interviews with Herbert and Willie Campbell (Dec. 2015) and Donald Hamilton (Apr. 2017).

44    *Enough thorns stick you*: Tyler Rose Museum, introductory video.

44    *As recently as the late nineteenth century*: Valuable information about roses in Tyler, including area soils and the shipment of roses, was provided by Brent Pemberton, "The Texas Rose Industry," *Combined Proceedings, International Plant Propagators' Society* 42 (1992), and Roger Harris, "Rose Industry," *Handbook of Texas Online*, tshaonline.org/handbook/online /articles/drr01.

44    *But disaster lurked*: Background details on the San Jose scale are available from Leo Shapiro, "*Diaspidiotus perniciosus*: San Jose Scale," *The Encyclopedia of Life*, eol.org/pages/835588/details, and C. L. Marlatt, "The Discovery of the Native Home of the San Jose Scale in Eastern China and the Importation of Its Natural Enemy," *Popular Science Monthly* 65, Aug. 1904.

45    *We never was lazy*: Thordis Simonsen, ed., *You May Plow Here: The Narrative of Sara Brooks* (New York: Norton, 1986), 39.

47    *He was always the laziest*: Mark Wangrin, "Making of a Legend," *Austin American-Statesman*, July 28, 1991, E1.

47    *The Campbell kids earned*: Information about budding comes from the Texas Rose Museum and interviews with Martha and Margaret Campbell. H. Brent Pemberton, professor at the Texas A&M AgriLife Research and Extension Center in Overton, provided me with the article "Roses" (1933) by the horticulturalist J. C. Ratsek, Texas Agricultural Experiment Station, Substation No. 2, Tyler; the 1967 "Guidelines for the Production of Roses in Smith County" by the TAMU Agricultural Extension Service; an undated Tyler Chamber of Commerce "History of the Texas Rose-Growing Industry" by E. W. Lyle; and "The Historical Geography of the Rose Industry in Smith County, Texas" by Darrel L. McDonald, presented at the 93rd Annual Meeting of the Association of American Geographers in Fort Worth in April 1997.

47    *I've been on this corner*: Newman, "Roots of Greatness," 98.

48    *A 1988 Tyler newspaper story*: Dianne Strahan, "Budding Business Ties Two Families Together," *Tyler Courier-Times-Telegraph*, June 12, 1988, 5.1.

48    *If I had to say one thing*: Texas Rose Museum, video.

49    *You'd walk through that house*: Author interview with Lynn King, Apr. 2017.

49    *The bathroom was an outhouse*: Campbell, *Earl Campbell Story*, 2.

49    *I'd bust out of the locker room*: Phillips, *Earl Campbell*, 22.

50    *he opted to take a taxi*: Paddy Joe Miller, *The Tyler Rose: The Earl Campbell Story* (Spring, TX: Schuromil, 1997), 110.

50    *I have to be honest*: Wangrin, "Making of a Legend."

50    *She had all of two dollars*: Newman, "Roots of Greatness," 98.

50    *not much to somebody*: Harvey, "He Was Never Promised."

50     *he purposely gave her wrong directions*: Campbell, *Earl Campbell Story*, 11.

51     *In many ways, the life*: Information about median income in the South in the 1970s comes from "Money Income and Poverty Status in 1975 of Families and Persons in the United States and the South Region, by Divisions and States (Spring 1976) Survey of Income and Education," US Department of Commerce, Bureau of the Census, P-60, no. 112, June 1978, 224–227, and Ray Marshall, *Employment of Blacks in the South: A Perspective on the 1960s* (Austin: University of Texas Press, 1978).

51     *When God took that rib*: Campbell, "Ann Campbell Wins."

52     *Earl Campbell was always a big kid*: Material about Campbell's schoolboy football days comes from interviews with the Campbell family, Thorndyke Lewis, J. B. Smith, David Barron, Phil Hicks, Leon Van Alstine, and Lynn King.

52     *watching Earl Campbell play*: Miller, *Tyler Rose*, 11.

53     *no reputation*: Author interview with unidentified man on the Cut, Dec. 2016.

53     *these different things within me*: Vincent Mallozzi, *Doc: The Rise and Rise of Julius Erving* (Hoboken, NJ: Wiley, 2010).

53     *When I got to the ninth grade*: Seale, "Rose by Any Other Name."

53     *Earl Campbell got me interested in golf*: A. C. Flynn told me the story about Andy Dillard and golf. At five-eight and around 220 pounds, Dillard grew to be nearly Campbellian in girth. A fellow pro once observed, "Andy could stand in front of the sun and cause a solar eclipse." See Walter Bingham, "One and Only," *Sports Illustrated*, June 12, 2000.

53     *My cousin kind of liked him*: Don McLeese, "Hooking a Heisman," *Austin American-Statesman*, Dec. 12, 1999, F1.

54     *At Moore he started learning*: Miller, *Tyler Rose*, 17.

54     *But in 1971, Campbell's ability*: Jeff Miller, "The Earl of East Texas," ESPN.com, Nov. 22, 2011, espn.com/dallas/ncf/story/_/page/heisman-dallas-week10/earl-campbell.

54     *felt a lack of passion*: "Earl Campbell: The Tyler Rose," thetylerrose.com/early-years.

54     *In the heart of north Tyler*: Miller, "Earl of East Texas."

54     *two years of what you might call*: Mark McDonald, "Team Unity," *Dallas Morning News*, Dec. 14, 1994, 1B.

54     *We had our little boat*: Constance Curry, *Silver Rights* (Chapel Hill, NC: Algonquin, 1995), 130.

55     *he would intentionally fumble*: Miller, *Tyler Rose*, 28.

56     *Campbell and some teammates*: David Barron, "Blossoming of Earl Campbell," *Houston Chronicle*, July 21, 1991.

57    *If you score a touchdown*: Annie Oeth, "Football Legend Campbell: 'Just Keep Going,'" *Jackson (MS) Clarion-Ledger*, Dec. 14, 2014, F2.

57    *Earl later said he considered*: Kevin Sherrington, "Coach's Tyler Days Are Stuff of Legend," *Dallas Morning News*, Nov. 23, 2014, C2.

58    *Lynn King was the epitome*: McDonald, "Team Unity."

59    *A strong bond developed*: Ibid.

59    *He would body-slam*: Author interview with David Barron, Sept. 2017.

60    *He couldn't score points*: John Spong, "The Great Terquasquicentennial Road Trip," *Texas Monthly*, March 2011, 122.

60    *I didn't like Corky before*: Pat Turner, "Earl Returns Home to Dedicate John Tyler Gym," *Tyler Morning Telegraph*, March 3, 1979, 3.

60    *Earl left; Earl right*: Author interview with Sam Kidd, Dec. 2016.

60    *I'd be so wide open*: Miller, "Earl of East Texas."

60    *run straight at Campbell*: Author interview with Tim Alexander, Mar. 2018.

60    *developed his passing accuracy*: Ron Martz, "Bay Bucs Sign Ex-Raider Quarterback Blount," *St. Petersburg (FL) Times*, Sept. 7, 1977.

61    *People in deep East Texas*: Kemerer, *William Wayne Justice*, 115.

61    *the 1973 John Tyler squad*: Details about the John Tyler playoff victories in 1973 can be found in David Casstevens, "As a Runner, Earl Was King of Them All," *Dallas Morning News*, Aug. 19, 1986.

61    *can't read, can't write* and *My mother asks me if* and *[Academics] didn't always interest me*: Harvey, "He Was Never Promised."

62    *carried six Plano players*: Clifford Broyles, "Clifford Broyles," *Bryan–College Station Eagle*, Jan. 27, 1974.

62    *to ignore the pass* and *he carried my whole team*: Jack Gallagher, "Campbell Acts like Superman," *Austin American-Statesman*'s Earl Campbell clipping file, undated—"Spring 1974" scribbled on clipping; also see Robert Salas, "Working: A Way of Life, Labor, of Love for Campbell," *Tyler Morning Telegraph*, Dec. 9, 1977, 6.

63    *Mike hesitated for a moment*: Dale Robertson, "Never a Rookie Like Earl," *Dave Campbell's Texas Football*, Winter 1979, 63.

64    *A bull stepped on my head*: McDonald, "Team Unity."

64    *I looked up into the stands*: Campbell, *Earl Campbell Story*, 21.

64    *Mayberry on steroids*: Author interview with Clyde Nelson IV (Apr. 2017).

65    *We got used to a bunch of white women*: The Joan Brooks comment comes by way of Phil Hicks.

65    *We even had some beer*: Sam Blair, *Earl Campbell: The Driving Force* (Waco, TX: World Books, 1980), 50.

65    *Among the scouts and coaches*: McLeese, "Hooking a Heisman."

## PART II: AUSTIN

Interviewees for this section included Tim Alexander (Mar. 2018), Fred Akers (Oct. 2017), Henry Bell III (Dec. 2016, April 2017), Gary Bledsoe (July 2017), John Sibley Butler (June 2017), Ken Dabbs (July 2017), Douglas Daniels (Nov. 2017), Betty Fine (Mar. 2017), Gary Gallagher (Oct. 2017), Pamelya Herndon (July 2017), John Holmes (Oct. 2017), Michael Hurd (Nov. 2017), Rick Ingraham (July 2017), Alfred Jackson (July 2017), Nick Kralj (July 2017), Bill Lyons (Feb. 2018), Wales Madden (Dec. 2017), Jenna Hays McEachern (Nov. 2017), Randy McEachern (June 2017), Mo Olian (Aug. 2017), Jim Phillips (Aug. 2017), Kirby Sams (May 2018), Wally Scott (Mar. 2018), Erna Smith (July 2017), Tom Swinnea (Apr. 2017), Barry Warner (Nov. 2018), Ron Wilson (August 2017), and Elmo Wright (July 2017). Quoted material from these interviews is generally not documented further in the notes.

69 *I'd love to go to*: The story of the half recruitment of Elmo Wright comes chiefly from interviews with Ken Dabbs and Elmo Wright.

71 *high-stepping his way*: Bob Glauber, "Elmo Wright, End-Zone Dance Originator, Says Cam Newton Has Right to Celebrate," *New York Newsday*, Feb. 6, 2016.

72 *integration of Longhorn football*: For the history of integration at the University of Texas, see Dwonna Goldstone, *Integrating the 40 Acres: The Fifty-year Struggle for Racial Equality at the University of Texas* (Athens: University of Georgia Press, 2006), and Tom Russell, "'Keep Negroes Out of Most Classes Where There Are a Large Number of Girls': The Unseen Power of the Ku Klux Klan and Standardized Testing at the University of Texas, 1899-1999," *South Texas Law Review* 52 (Fall 2010).

74 *to the men and women of the Confederacy*: The information about the Confederate plaque was on display at UT's Dolph Briscoe Center for American History as part of a 2017 exhibition on the removal of the Jefferson Davis statue from campus.

74 *George Allen, a black life insurance*: Neil Foley, *Quest for Equality: The Failed Promise of Black-Brown Solidarity* (Cambridge, MA: Harvard University Press, 2010), 119. Foley writes that the *Austin Statesman* reported the "'dark-complexioned Austin youth' told the professor he was of French-Jewish ancestry. When an investigation revealed Allen was 'of the Negro race,' the dean returned his admission fee and barred Allen from attending the class."

75 *shall not be used for*: The regents resolved on Sept. 29, 1944, that buildings on campus had to be segregated; UT Chancellor's Office Records, 1941–1971 (mostly 1950-1970), box 9, folder "Negroes," DBCAH. This set of

archives is hereafter cited as "Chancellor's Records," with a box number and folder name.

75    *There is not the slightest danger*: Goldstone, *Integrating the 40 Acres*, 17.

75    *It is fairly obvious*: Theophilus Painter to D. K. Woodward Jr., Jan. 31, 1948, UT President's Office Records, 1907–1968, box VG 20/B.a., folder "Negroes in Colleges, 1939–1954," DBCAH. This set of archives is hereafter cited as "President's Records," with a box number and file name.

75    *never darken the door*: Erna Smith, "Blacks Fought to Get into UT," *Austin American-Statesman*, Mar. 30, 1975, UT News and Information Service Records, box CDL2/G45b, folder "Black Studies, 1969–1978," DBCAH. This set of archives is hereafter cited as "UT Information Records," with a box number and file name.

75    *But in 1950, the US Supreme Court*: The details about the *Sweatt* case are from Russell, "'Keep Negroes Out,'" and Gary M. Lavergne, *Before Brown: Heman Marion Sweatt, Thurgood Marshall, and the Long Road to Justice* (Austin: University of Texas Press, 2010).

76    *Upon Sweatt's enrollment*: Russell, "'Keep Negroes Out,'" 18.

76    *a wooden cross*: Lavergne, *Before Brown*, 275.

76    *so that his blackness wouldn't*: Joe Frantz, *The Forty-Acre Follies* (Austin: Texas Monthly Press, 1983), 205.

76    *from others of similar age*: *Brown v. Board of Education of Topeka*, 347 U.S. 483 (1954), 494. Text of the decision is available from the Legal Information Institute, law.cornell.edu/supremecourt/text/347/483.

76    *keep Negroes out of most classes*: H. Y. McCown, registrar and dean of admissions, to President Logan Wilson, memo, May 26, 1954, Chancellor's Records, box 9, folder "Negroes."

77    *That June, Marion Ford*: Documents regarding the Ford episode—including his rushee card; his correspondence with McCown (and McCown's correspondence with UT officials); the newspaper article "Houston Negro Seeks Grid Tryout at Texas," *Houston Chronicle*; letters among the regents and the state attorney general; and the letter from Shanklin to McCown—can be found in President's Records, box VF20/B.a., folder "Negroes in Colleges, 1939–1954."

80    *Committee on Selective Admissions*: The June 1955 report on Selective Admissions can be found in Chancellor's Records, box 34, folder "Committees—Standing, Admissions Committee."

80    *But the report, laying the*: The details on standardized testing at UT are from Russell, "'Keep Negroes Out.'"

80    *In October 1954, UT was*: The Washington State episode is laid out in Goldstone, *Integrating the 40 Acres*, 115; Richard B. Fry, *The Crimson and the*

*Gray: One Hundred Years with the WSU Cougars* (Pullman: Washington State University Press, 1998); "Record of Understanding with President Clement French, of Washington State College, Concerning the Football Game Scheduled at the University of Texas between That Institution and This One on Oct. 2, 1954 in Austin," Chancellor's Records, box 34, folder "Desegregation"; and correspondence from Clement French to Logan Wilson, Sept. 22, 1954, in the Clement French Records, 1948–1956, at Washington State University.

82   *entire student section rose*: Willie Morris, *North Toward Home* (Jackson: University of Mississippi Press), 1999, 170.

82   *One can visualize*: The USC memo from Lanier Cox is in Chancellor's Records, box 34, folder "Desegregation."

83   *"Ed," Ford said*: John Maher, "Different Walks of Life: Experience with Racial Barrier Shaped Futures of Curry, Ford," *Austin American-Statesman*, March 21, 1995, C1.

83   *I was a cocky son of a bitch*: Goldstone, *Integrating the 40 Acres*, 119.

83   *feels that the coaches*: McCown to Wilson, memo, Sept. 19, 1956, Chancellor's Records, box 53, folder "Desegregation 9/1/56–8/31/58."

83   *Wilson issued a confidential memorandum*: "Concerning the Participation of Negro Students in Intercollegiate Athletics," Oct. 13, 1956, in ibid.

83   *not directly educational in character*: This became an overriding approach of UT administrators who dealt with integration over the next fifteen years. "Directly educational in character" is a key phrase, parroting some of the language in the *Brown* ruling. In June 1961, for example, UT president Joseph Smiley wrote in a draft of a letter to one alumnus that "steady progress has been made with dignity and wisdom with the result that all educational facilities of the University have been open to all qualified students without regard to race or religions permission." But UT chancellor Harry Ransom, a politically savvy former English professor, reviewing the draft of the seemingly innocuous letter, handwrote a note on the bottom: "Football, etc. dorm contacts, etc., etc., etc. *are* educational." At Ransom's suggestion, Smiley replaced the word "educational" with "academic" in the final version of the letter. The exchange can be found in J. R. Smiley to Jim Dunnington, draft letter, June 15, 1961, President's Records, box VF 32/B.b, folder "Integration 1960–61."

84   *Clinton Givans, an Air Force enlisted man*: UT Dean of Students Records Collection, box CDL 2/E.32, folder "Negro Students," DBCAH. This set of archives is hereafter cited as "Dean of Students Records," with a box number and file name.

84     *neither of which will permit*: D. X. Bible to Clinton A. Givans, Oct. 3, 1954, Dean of Students Records, box CDL 2/E.32, folder "Negro Students."

84     *concerning Negro participation*: Goldstone, *Integrating the 40 Acres*, 119; H. Y. McCown to C. P. Boner, Oct. 11, 1956, Dean of Students Records, box CDL2/E.32, folder "Integration, 1961–62."

84     *Provincialism, of which total exclusion*: Goldstone, *Integrating the 40 Acres*, 121.

85     *demanded that lab partners*: Chancellor's Records, box 53, folder "Deseg-regation 9/1/56–8/31/58"; H. Y. McCown to Logan Wilson and C. P. Boner, May 21, 1957, Chancellor's Records, box 102, folder "Desegregation"; Mc-Cown to Wilson and Boner, Sept. 21, 1956, Chancellor's Records, box 102, folder "Desegregation."

85     *Do you favor allowing participation*: For details on the student referendum, I interviewed Mo Olian (Aug. 2017) and John B. Holmes Jr. (Oct. 2017).

85     *Coffey said he wouldn't mind*: Associated Press, "Coffey Prefers Texas," *Austin Statesman*, Mar. 5, 1961, C-1, clipping in President's Records, box VF 32/B.b, folder "Integration 1960–61."

86     *passed the referendum*: Joey Holley, "Ernest Goldstein, 89; Pushed for In-tegration at U. of Texas in '50s," *Washington Post*, May 29, 2008. The give-and-take around the students' vote can be found in Chancellor's Records, box 102, folder "Desegregation 9/1/60–8/31/62."

87     *should not take unilateral action*: President's Records, box VF 32/B.b., fold-er "Integration 1960–61."

87     *tawdry and suffocating*: Morris, *North Toward Home*, 170.

87     *He had grown up poor*: Biographical details on Darrell Royal are from Jenna Hays McEachern, *DKR: The Royal Scrapbook*, with Edith Royal (Austin: University of Texas Press, 2012); Darrell Royal, *Darrell Royal Talks Foot-ball* (Englewood Cliffs, NJ: Prentice-Hall, 1963); Jimmy Banks, *The Darrell Royal Story* (Austin: Eakin, 1994); John Maher and Kirk Bohls, *Bleeding Or-ange: Trouble and Triumph Deep in the Heart of Texas Football* (New York: St. Martin's, 1992); and Denne H. Freeman, *Hook 'Em Horns: A Story of Texas Football* (Huntsville, AL: Strode, 1974). Also, the Darrell Royal Papers at the DBCAH and Darrell Royal vertical file at the Stark Center hold clip-pings that proved helpful.

87     *The K in Darrell K Royal*: John Maher says he heard that Darrell Royal start-ed using the middle initial *K* on the advice of Lyndon Baines Johnson. In the era of JFK and RFK, LBJ told him he needed to be known by three initials, for headline writers if for no other reason.

89     *Last Saturday a Negro*: Cooksey's letter is in Dean of Students Records, box CDL2/E.32, folder "Negro Students."

89　*the feeling of our coaches*: McCown to Wilson, memo, Nov. 10, 1959, in ibid.

89　*Syracuse tackle John Brown*: Ben Cosgrove, "LIFE at the 1960 Cotton Bowl: 'Battle of the Hard-Noses,'" *Time*, Jan. 2, 2014, time.com/3878581/cotton -bowl-1960-when-syracuse-whipped-texas-for-the-national-title.

90　*Oh, they were bad*: Jeff Merron, "'The Express' in Real Life," ESPN.com, Oct. 13, 2008, espn.com/nhl/story/_/id/3634484.

90　*some pretty uncomplimentary things*: Joe Banham, "Racial Dispute Not Called For," *Monroe (LA) News-Star*, Jan. 6, 1990, 11-A.

90　*unanimously agreed that they*: W. W. Heath to Thornton Hardie, Nov. 5, 1962, Chancellor's Records, box 102, folder "Desegregation, 9/1/62– 8/1/64."

91　*Heath admitted that he*: Ronnie Dugger, *Our Invaded Universities: Form, Reform, and New Starts* (New York: Norton, 1974), 71.

91　*Under our oaths of office*: Press Release, Nov. 9, 1963, Chancellor's Records, box 102, folder "Desegregation, 9/1/62–8/1/64."

91　*asked whether he was currently*: Jeff Miller, *The Game Changers: Abner Haynes, Leon King, and the Fall of Major College Football's Color Barrier in Texas* (New York: Sports Publishing, 2016), 154.

92　*is an ambitious young man*: Mielly to Ransom, Nov. 19, 1963, and Ransom to Mielly, Dec. 16, 1963, both in Chancellor's Records, box 102, folder "De-segregation 9/1/62–8/1/64."

93　*Just how soon the backfield*: Miller, *Game Changers*, 154.

93　*that splendid assortment of dentists*: Gary Cartwright, "Orange Peril," *Texas Monthly*, Nov. 1976, texasmonthly.com/articles/orange-peril.

94　*was like handing Royal an anchor*: McEachern, *DKR*, 108.

94　*When I first came here*: Jan Reid, "Coach Royal Regrets," *Texas Monthly*, December 1982, texasmonthly.com/articles/coach-royal-regrets.

94　*could have had the courage*: Scott Cobb and Daniel Rodriguez, "Royal Pain: Allegations Still Surround Legendary Coach," *Austin Chronicle*, Oct. 4, 1996, austinchronicle.com/news/1996-10-04/524684.

94　*The same year that he privately*: Almetris Marsh Duren, *Overcoming: A History of Black Integration at the University of Texas at Austin* (Austin: University of Texas Press, 1979), 15.

94　*Orange and White Lack Black* and *Bevo Needs Soul*: Author interviews with Bill Lyons and Harriet Murphy, Feb. 2018; see also, "Black Activism Surfaces in '60s," *Austin Statesman*, Mar. 30, 1975, clipping in UT Information Records, box CDL2/G45b, folder "Black Studies, 1969–1978."

95　*In a devastating 1972 series*: Banks, *Darrell Royal Story*, 156–159.

95　*a linebacker named Leon O'Neal*: Darren D. Kelly, "Paying the Price for

'Slow Integration': A History of Race and Football at the University of Texas at Austin from 1954 to 1972" (master's thesis, University of Texas at Austin, 2009).

95　*In 1969, a student questionnaire*: Margaret Berry Papers, box 3D122, folder "Black Student Questionnaire," DBCAH.

95　*The journalist (and, later*: James Toback, "Longhorns and Longhairs," *Harper's*, Nov. 1970, 70. Additional material quoted from this article in the next several pages is not documented separately.

96　*One of the players pointed*: The story of Erwin and the tree cutting has been told many times, including in Asher Price, "UT's Many Trees Have an Arborist Rooting for Them," *Austin American-Statesman*, Oct. 4, 2006, A1.

98　*The proper thing*: Darrell Royal, *Coach Royal: Conversations with a Texas Football Legend*, with John Wheat (Austin: University of Texas Press, 2005), 33.

99　*He was still reeling*: McEachern, *DKR*, 118.

100　*Nothing out in the open*: Jack Keever and Robert Heard, "Racism: Royal's 'Image' Bad among Blacks," *Austin Statesman*, Nov. 16, 1972, B3.

100　*Shaw, if you keep playing*: Gary Shaw, *Meat on the Hoof* (New York: Dell, 1972), 209.

102　*two separate, unlabeled windows*: Author interview with John Pope, summer 2017.

102　*Bear Bryant was big enough*: Howell Raines, "Goodbye to the Bear," *New Republic*, Jan. 23, 1983, newrepublic.com/article/71262/goodbye-the-bear.

102　*Bryant was a football coach*: The comments by Keith Dunnavant, Don Keith, and John Papadakis are from the documentary *Against the Tide*, directed by Mark Davis, released on Showtime in 2003.

102　*never face a black player*: John Maher, e-mail to author, June 2018.

103　*Everything starts with winning*: Banks, *Darrell Royal Story*, 186.

103　*Let's face it*: McEachern, *DKR*, 108.

103　*become a stigma*: Maher and Bohls, *Bleeding Orange*, 33.

103　*Mean Joe Greene*: Miller, *Game Changers*, vii.

104　*Darrell, what are you doing*: John Maher to the author, July 2017.

105　*This has hurt me in recruiting*: Freeman, *Hook 'Em Horns*, 157.

105　*Whittier said that his teammates*: Whittier's experience at UT is told in Maher and Bohls, *Bleeding Orange*, 190–191.

105　*Senior years are*: Billy Dale, e-mail to author, Feb. 2018.

105　*How can he say that*: Jack Keever and Robert Heard, "Racist Image Puzzles Royal," *Austin Statesman*, Nov. 17, 1972, 44.

105　*These newspapers have faith*: "The Longhorns and Racism," *Austin Statesman*, Nov. 18, 1972, 4.

105   *We batted zero last year*: Lou Maysel, "AP Black Series Didn't Hurt Texas," *Austin Statesman*, Feb. 25, 1973, C1.

106   *He couldn't tell you who*: Author interview with Larry Temple, Sept. 2017.

106   *recommending Royal for vice president*: The correspondence between Walter Jenkins and the Houston attorney Billy Goldberg, Jan. 2 and 6, 1964, as well as correspondence about the exchanges of gifts and the invitations aboard Air Force One, are in the Darrell Royal file at the LBJ Presidential Library.

107   *I think I've always had*: Banks, *Darrell Royal Story*, 149–150.

107   *Staving off chest pains*: Michael Beschloss, "In His Final Days, LBJ Agonized over His Legacy," *PBS NewsHour*, Dec. 4, 2012, pbs.org/newshour/politics/lbjs-last-interview.

108   *Yesterday it was commonly said*: "Remarks by Former President Lyndon Johnson at a Civil Rights Symposium, 12/12/72," video posted on YouTube by the LBJ Library, Feb. 8, 2013, youtube.com/watch?v=RJKq18m00Ys.

109   *A few weeks later, Royal*: Banks, *Darrell Royal Story*, 150.

110   *more than 250 scouts*: Author interview with Leon Van Alstine, Apr. 2017; Lou Maysel, *Here Come the Texas Longhorns*, vol. 2, *1970–1978* (Austin: Burnt Orange, 1978), 15.

110   *goodies offered to players*: Morris, *The Courting of Marcus Dupree*, 97 and Blair, *Earl Campbell*, 55.

110   *any sold black boy*: Randy Harvey, "He Was Never Promised a Rose Garden: JT Superstar, Campbell," *Austin Statesman,* Jan. 13, 1974, C3.

112   *And he was persistent*: Kirk Bohls, "Dabbs Worthy of UT Honors," *Austin-American Statesman*, Nov. 7, 2014, C1.

114   *scorned passing because it was art*: Reid, "Coach Royal Regrets." Some people also attribute the remark to Woody Hayes of Ohio State.

114   *the black coach has not reached*: Jones Ramsey and Bill Little, press release, Jan. 24, 1970, University of Texas Sports News Service, copy in Darrell Royal folder, Stark Center.

114   *Such thoughts are not in my heart*: Ibid.

115   *Every black athlete that Royal*: Gary Cartwright, "Royal Still Rules in Texas," publication and date not included with clipping, Darrell Royal folder, Stark Center. Even into the late 1980s, when a star San Antonio high schooler named Johnny Walker was considering where to go to college, his father tried to steer him away from UT. "He told me Texas had a reputation as a racist institution. He was very upset when I announced I was going to Texas." (Maher and Bohls, *Bleeding Orange*, 199)

115   *I understand you don't like* and *No, Earl, that's wrong* and *I asked simply that they*: Blair, *Earl Campbell*, 54–55.

116    *UT recruiters had one rule*: Author interview with Bill Lyons, Feb. 2018.

116    *if this is a factor*: Blair, *Earl Campbell*, 55.

116    *my people were bought and sold*: Campbell, *Earl Campbell Story*, 17; Harvey, "He Was Never Promised."

116    *"Mrs. Campbell," Royal told her* and *We're coming to Texas*: Royal, *Coach Royal*, ix and author interview with Mickey Herskowitz, Nov. 2018.

116    *The atmosphere was cold*: Blair, *Earl Campbell*, 54.

118    *God, if it's your will*: Miller, *The Tyler Rose*, 41.

118    *Henry Bell, and his wife, Nell*: In 1976, Nell Bell, described by her son Henry as fitting to a T the no-nonsense football-loving mother played by Sandra Bullock in the film The Blind Side, was awarded a spot by the University of Texas on the Cotton Bowl Association's board of directors.

118    *I liked what I saw*: Lou Maysel, "Bell Cow Likes Longhorns: Campbell Headed for Texas," *Austin Statesman*, Feb. 9, 1974.

119    *He will get a fair chance*: Robert Salas, "Campbell Signs with Longhorns," *Tyler Morning Telegraph*, Feb. 13, 1974, 1.

119    *Royal handed Campbell his pen*: Blair, *Earl Campbell*, 58.

119    *Here at home there has been*: Salas, "Campbell Signs with Longhorns."

120    *ask for a ten-dollar loan*: Paddy Joe Miller, *The Tyler Rose: The Earl Campbell Story* (Spring, TX: Schuromil, 1997), 192.

120    *Red Man chewing tobacco*: Ibid., 39.

120    *When school started, I*: Avrel Seale, "A Rose by Any Other Name," *Texas Alcalde*, September–October 1994, 12.

120    *If it touched your head*: Dan Zehr, "A Separated city," *Austin American-Statesman*, Jan. 18, 2015, A1.

121    *And a gentleman's agreement*: Ken Herman, "Council's Politics Loses One Identity," *Austin American-Statesman*, Dec. 11, 2016, E1.

121    *known for refusing service*: "Station Owner, Ex-Target of Rights Protesters, Dies," *Austin American-Statesman*, Nov. 21, 1981, B4.

121    *He looked surprised after getting hit*: Thorne Dreyer, Alice Embree, and Richard Croxdale, eds., *Celebrating The Rag: Austin's Iconic Underground Newspaper* (Austin: New Journalism Project, 2016), 78–79. *Celebrating The Rag* also includes a reprint of Gary Thiher, "32 Jailed in Don Weedon Conoco Protest," *Rag*, May 6, 1968.

122    *It was a clash of two Austins*: Details of life around Austin in the mid-1970s are based on advertisements and articles in Dreyer, Embree, and Croxdale, *Celebrating the Rag*.

123    *affirmative action program gone berserk*: Jason Mellard, *Progressive Country: How the 1970s Transformed the Texan in Popular Culture* (Austin: University of Texas Press, 2013), 164.

123  *The whole approach they're into*: Toback, "Longhorns and Longhairs."

123  *He liked to hang out*: Freeman, *Hook 'Em Horns*, 165.

124  *like nothing better than to turn*: Toback, "Longhorns and Longhairs," 70.

125  *In 1964, the Court found*: Anthony Lewis, "Court Says Texas Must Redistrict," *New York Times*, Mar. 3, 1964, nytimes.com/1964/03/03/court-says-texas-must-redistrict.html?src=DigitizedArticle. And yet even as the hue of the Texas Legislature was changing, the old guard clung, in ugly ways, to power. After Eddie Bernice Johnson, an African American woman who represented Dallas, filed a complaint with the Equal Employment Opportunity Commission, claiming that the state comptroller, Robert S. Calvert, was discriminating against women and minorities in his hiring, Calvert explained that he would not hire a woman because "we wouldn't be about to send her down to one of those nigger or Mexican neighborhoods." A statewide elected official, he added that Johnson was "nothing but a stupid nigger woman who doesn't know what she's talking about." Based on Calvert's own comments, the federal agency found, in a bit of understatement, that "it is reasonable to infer that discrimination because of race is taking place in respondent's hiring practices." The back-and-forth between Robert Calvert and Eddie Bernice Johnson is in *Jet*, Oct. 11, 1973, 10.

125  *UT's entering law school class*: Steve Wisch, "New Law Class Has No Blacks," *Daily Texan*, June 11, 1971.

125  *We have found continued lip-service*: John L. Warfield to Representative Senfronia Thompson, Oct. 23, 1973, John L. Warfield Papers CDL3-2005-08412, Correspondence / Texas Black Legislative Caucus, 1973–1979, DBCAH (hereafter cited as Warfield Papers).

126  *out of 1,600 faculty*: Cascell Noble, "A Report on Black Faculty at the University of Texas at Austin," 1979, copy in Warfield Papers. At the start of Campbell's senior year, September 1977, UT had 1,641 white and 24 black faculty members. By the summer of 1978, a half year after he won the Heisman, three black UT faculty members resigned, including the history department's only black professor. That professor, Douglas Daniels, told me in November 2017 that he took a pay cut to join the University of California system. "The University's priorities do not lie in the area of Afro-American Studies, nor do they make much of a pretense of attempting to benefit the Afro-Americans who live in the state," Daniels told the *Daily Texan* (Debbie Wormser, "UT Racist, Warfield Says," Sept. 21, 1978). "When you get large numbers of whites in positions of power, they hire large numbers of whites," Daniels continued. "The question is not one of

finding qualified blacks, but rather of finding people who are qualified to recognize their merits."

126 *there were only 600 black students out of 41,000*: Chuck Kaufman, "Racial Imbalance Worries Blacks," *Daily Texan*, March 7, 1975.

126 *Out of more than 1,500 students at UT's law school*: Duren, *Overcoming*, 32.

126 *Sometimes I get the feeling*: Ibid., 27.

126 *Social Life Called Deficient*: Derby Bay and Henry Wells, "Social Life Called Deficient; UT Blacks Afforded Little Mixing," *Daily Texan*, Apr. 13, 1971.

126 *Gary Bledsoe, a law student*: Erna Smith, "UT Association Wants More Black Grad Student Requirements," Mar. 30, 1975, UT Information Records, box CDL2/G45b, folder "Black Studies, 1969–1978"; see also "Black Students Describe UT," 1975, in the same folder.

126 *$500,000 to resurface*: Craig Collisson, "The Fight to Legitimize Blackness: How Black Students Changed the University" (PhD diss., University of Washington, 2009), 259.

126 *UT's new president, Lorene Rogers*: Anna Marie Pena, "Rogers Opposes 7 Demands," *Daily Texan*, April 18, 1975; Duren, *Overcoming*, 18.

127 *Coming to UT was a sort of*: "Black Students Describe UT," 1975, UT Information Records, box CDL2/G45b, folder "Black Studies, 1969–1978."

127 *hoping the next class*: Erna Smith, "Psychological Obstacles at UT," *Austin Statesman*, Mar. 30, 1975, clipping in ibid.

128 *One black senior spoke*: Goldstone, *Integrating the 40 Acres*, 111.

129 *chiseled from stone* and *ran into the end zone*: Brad Buchholz, "Rock of Ages," *Austin American-Statesman*, Dec. 9, 2007, A1. The chiseled remark was said by Doug English; Brad Shearer remembered how Earl ran into the end zone.

129 *He's got a lot of tools* and *might have gone straight*: Maysel, *Here Come the Texas Longhorns*, 56.

129 *Royal ran the wishbone*: Jenna Hays McEachern, *100 Things Longhorns Fans Should Know and Do Before They Die* (Chicago: Triumph, 2008), 196.

130 *a discovery more pleasing*: Morris, *Courting of Marcus Dupree*, 46.

130 *would sit on the curb*: Seale, "A Rose by Any Other Name."

130 *Put that ole gray suit*: Marty Akins, "Our Lovely Dixie," Darrel K Royal Papers, box 3J14, folder 82–236, "Poems and Works of Players," DBCAH.

131 *has provided an image*: McEachern, *100 Things Longhorns Fans*, 86. Leaks was the first African American inducted into the university's Hall of Honor—but only in 1985, thirty-five years after the tradition of honoring its athletes began (Maher and Bohls, *Bleeding Orange*, 190).

131 *Plans after college*: UT Athletics Media, Men's Hall of Fame, Earl Campbell folder, 1974-2006, Stark Center.

131  *During practice I was*: John Maher and Kirk Bohls, *Long Live the Longhorns: 100 Years of Texas Football* (New York: St. Martin's, 1993), 186.

131  *That shows how smart*: Mickey Herskowitz, "Campbell Earned Respect of All," *Houston Post*, July 28, 1991, Earl Campbell folder, Stark Center.

132  *He's the only one*: Maysel, *Here Come the Texas Longhorns*, 65.

132  *He got up on a bench*: Bob Galt, "The Rose Grows on Steer Soil," *Dallas Times Herald*, Apr. 22, 1975.

132  *Lord Don't Let It Rain*: Steve Pate, "A Rose Is a Rose to Momma," *Dallas Morning News*, Nov. 3, 1977, 1B.

132  *There once was a Texan*: "Chitter Chatter," undated, Earl Campbell folder, Stark Center.

132  *More black students*: Author interview with Gary Bledsoe, July 2017.

134  *are content to identify*: Erin Tarver, "College Football Is Here; But What Are We Really Cheering?" *New York Times*, Aug. 21, 2017, nytimes .com/2017/08/21/opinion/college-football-black-athletes.html.

134  *You might hear things*: Tom Cushman, "Game of the Week," *Philadelphia Daily News*, Oct. 15, 1975, 43.

134  *working, of all places*: Author interviews with Bill Lyons (Feb. 2018) and Wally Scott (Mar. 2018).

135  *If a guy works in*: Jim Lefko, "Brain Coach," *Daily Texan*, Dec. 7, 1977, DBCAH.

136  *I was sitting in front*: Seale, "Rose by Any Other Name," 13.

136  *determined not to return*: Author interview with Barry Warner, Nov. 2018.

136  *He began sitting*: Campbell, *Earl Campbell Story*, 33.

136  *Bob Hope offered to send*: McEachern, *100 Things Longhorns Fans*, 67.

138  *It was kind of strange*: David Maraniss, "Dear Earl: Campbell Runs On, Only Now He's Carrying Advice," *Washington Post*, June 12, 1990, C6.

138  *Despite its impersonal nature*: Shaw, *Meat on the Hoof*, 196.

138  *We sure never went*: Reid, "Coach Royal Regrets."

139  *I lost my mom three years ago*: Earl Campbell, "Darrel Royal, 1924–2012," *Sports Illustrated*, Nov. 19, 2012, 20.

139  *I just remember people saying*: Maher and Bohls, *Bleeding Orange*, 194.

139  *it is a relief to have*: Dale Robertson, "This Year the Real No. 20 Will Stand Up," *Dave Campbell's Texas Football*, July 1977, 109.

139  *I kept reinjuring it*: Ibid.

140  *He was running under wraps*: Ibid.

140  *Darrell, we brought you down here*: Royal, *Darrell Royal*, from the foreword by Cactus Pryor, ix.

141  *Some coaches don't want*: David Barron, "Rank and Style," *Houston Chronicle*, Oct. 5, 2001, Sports, 9.

141   *I don't care if a coach*: Reid, "Coach Royal Regrets."

141   *the final straw came*: Author interview with Ken Dabbs, July 2017.

142   *This is Secret Agent Aught-aught-six*: Reid, "Coach Royal Regrets."

142   *build a university the football team*: Morris, *Courting of Marcus Dupree*, 359.

142   *The Night It Rained Furniture*: Ibid., 356.

143   *They are like tribes*: Ibid., 357.

143   *easily the most bizarre*: Stephen Ross, "One More Time: Why This Game is Special," SB Nation, Sept. 30, 2010, barkingcarnival.com/2010/09/29/one-more-time-why-this-game-is-special.

143   *Coach Royal, I want you*: McEachern, *DKR*, 121.

144   *We finally have Earl*: Reid, "Coach Royal Regrets."

144   *I wanted everything to go*: Robertson, "This Year the Real No. 20," 109.

144   *spent the entire frustrating*: Ibid.

145   *Everyone from the Black Muslims*: Gary Cartwright, "The Lonely Blues of Duane Thomas," *Texas Monthly*, February 1973, texasmonthly.com/the-culture/the-lonely-blues-of-duane-thomas.

145   *Even the criticisms of his*: Morris, *Courting of Marcus Dupree*, 80.

146   *Whatever you say anywhere* and *For all his bluster*: Dugger, *Our Invaded Universities*, 130.

146   *Shivers's differences with Royal*: Details on the Shivers-Royal dynamic and the layout of Royal's home are in Roy Edwards, "Darrell Royal: Sad End of an Era in UT Athletics," *Texas Sports*, April 1980, clipping in Allan Shivers Papers, box 2.325/C66, folder "Athletics," DBCAH.

147   *You brought me more*: Author interview with Jim Phillips, Aug. 2017.

147   *all walks of life*: Edwards, "Darrell Royal: Sad End."

147   *It wasn't his interest*: Maher and Bohls, *Bleeding Orange*, 34.

148   *The only Longhorn to stay*: Earl Campbell, thetylerrose.com/the-college-years.

149   *I'm leaving Earl Campbell*: Miller, *Tyler Rose*, 90.

149   *Every morning at precisely 6:30*: Kirk Bohls, "Earl: A Trip with a Star," *Austin American-Statesman*, Dec. 4, 1977, D1.

149   *even gamblers, posing as journalists*: Ron Hutcheson, "Bookies, Gamblers Savor OU Clash," *Daily Texan*, Oct. 8, 1976, 1.

150   *his dark crusading face*: Shaw, *Meat on the Hoof*, 82.

150   *customarily described in old press releases*: The University of Texas Off Season Football Training Program Press Release, UT-Austin Sports News Service, June 1976.

150   *smutty or foul talk*: Jack Gallagher, "Medina, UT's Antiseptic Atmosphere," *Houston Post*, Nov. 20, 1968, Frank Medina folder, Stark Center.

150   *he called all of them "Mr. Man"*: McEachern, *100 Things Longhorns Fans*, 53.

150    *It was like a little bitty man*: David Flores, "Tiny Trainer Medina Was Giant in UT Football Heyday," *San Antonio Express-News*, Feb. 3, 1989, 1-B.

150    *divided players into their Christian denominations*: McEachern, *100 Things Longhorns Fans*, 54.

150    *now and then dole out cookies*: "Background Information on Frank Medina," University of Texas at Austin Athletics Media Relations Men's Hall of Honor Collection, Frank Medina folder, 1954–1993, Stark Center.

150    *The all-American hurdler Ray Cunningham, You didn't want to go, and When you're in two-a-days*: Billy Dale, "Frank Medina," Texas Longhorn Support Network, texaslsn.org/frank-medina-1.

151    *I heard him hollering*: "The Earl Campbell Story: Winning Personality," 31, unidentified clipping (possibly a 1978 UT Sports program) included in Earl Campbell folder, Stark Center. The exchange also appears in Blair, *Earl Campbell*, 84–85.

151    *Akers, like Royal* and *I figured since Ford*: Kevin Sherrington, "Farm Couldn't Hold Sharecropper's Boy," *Dallas Morning News*, Apr. 24, 2016, C2; various articles, Fred Akers folder, University of Texas at Austin Athletics Media Relations, Former Coaches Files Collection, Stark Center.

152    *By his own count, Akers*: Kenny Hand, "Royal Mess: Despite Solid Achievements, Akers' Job on the Line at UT," *Houston Post*, Nov. 22, 1986, 1F.

152    *his sole hobby, he said*: Kirk Bohls, "The Final Days," *Austin American-Statesman*, Dec. 22, 1976, E1.

152    *inaugural UT press conference*: Mike Jones, "Akers Has Cool Emotions," *Dallas Morning News*, Dec. 1, 1977, 1B; Kirk Bohls, "Horns Believed in Akers—and Themselves," Nov. 28, 1977, D1; Kirk Bohls, "Akers Meets the Press," *Austin American-Statesman*, Dec. 29, 1976; Kirk Bohls and George Breazeale, "It's Wyoming's Akers for UT Coach," *Austin American-Statesman*, Dec. 16, 1976, A1.

153    *But the hiring committee*: Lou Maysel, "Mike Campbell: 'I Guess I'll Get Another Job . . . ,'" *Austin American-Statesman*, Dec. 17, 1976, E1.

153    *We haven't had a confrontation*: Edwards, "Darrell Royal: Sad End."

153    *When I come back*: Hand, "Royal Mess."

153    *I don't think this can*: James Walker, "Texas Wishbone Pulled," Dec. 30, 1976, Fred Akers folder, Stark Center. No publication information included with clipping.

153    *uninvited to appear on*: Denne H. Freeman, "Akers Surviving Pressure," *Bryan–College Station (TX) Eagle*, Nov. 13, 1977, 1B.

154    *We're so young we hold hands*: Douglas Looney, "Down and Out Can Be Upsetting," *Sports Illustrated*, Oct. 16, 1977, 24.

154   *It is evident by our*: Medina, "Dear Longhorn," May 9, 1977, in Dale, "Frank Medina."

154   *When you're a wishbone fullback*: Jim Trotter, "A Heisman for Earl?," *Austin American-Statesman*, July 10, 1977, H1.

155   *A promotional tour of likely*: Kirk Bohls, "Campbell Discovers Girdles, Heisman Big Part of Future," *Austin American-Statesman*, Aug. 19, 1977, C1; David Casstevens, "The Man who Follows DKR Knows a Challenge," *Dave Campbell's Texas Football*, July 1977.

155   *It came down to Earl's* and *Earl's got a lot of obstacles*: Bohls, "Campbell Discovers Girdles."

155   *I need to know, Mr. Campbell*: Earl Campbell, thetylerrose.com/the-col-lege-years; Miller, *Tyler Rose*, 94–95.

156   *I don't know* and *I would get hot*: "The Earl Campbell Story: Winning Personality," in Earl Campbell folder, Stark Center; see also, Blair, *Earl Campbell*, 84–85.

156   *I can remember the days*: "Frank Medina," undated UT Sports Information Service press release, folder "Frank Medina, 1954–1993," Stark Center.

156   *In church the other day*: Robertson, "This Year the Real No. 20," 109.

156   *Watching Earl go through*: Miller, *Tyler Rose*, 97.

157   *I don't think I've ever been*: Trotter, "A Heisman for Earl?"

158   *Beautiful women in the Neiman-Marcus*: Morris, *Courting of Marcus Dupree*, 427.

158   *As part of the 1936 Texas Centennial*: Negro Achievement Day, cosponsored by the Dallas Negro Chamber of Commerce, was a big deal. In 1946, 115,000 African Americans attended the state fair, and black schools closed for the day. A parade to the Hall of State culminated in the presentation of the Most Distinguished Negro Citizen Award. The schedule for Negro Achievement Day in 1955, the year of Earl Campbell's birth, included performances by Louis Armstrong, a twins contest, a beauty contest, parades with marching bands, black 4-H Club demonstrations, and, the crowning event, a football game between two all-black colleges. This enthusiasm troubled Juanita Craft, a Dallas activist with the NAACP, who worried that African Americans were implicitly acquiescing in the segregation of the state fair by enthusiastically attending on the one day set aside for them. In 1951, observing how hard it was to raise money to pay for the civil rights legal struggle, she wrote to the executive director of the NAACP in New York that the 182,347 African Americans who attended the fair spent at least three dollars each for entry to an event that essentially preserved segregation, while "we have to beg for two dollars per year to fight Jim Crow." See R. N. Burrow, "Juanita Craft: Desegregating the State

Fair of Texas," *Legacies: A History Journal for Dallas and North Central Texas* 16, no. 1 (Spring 2004).

159   *intense emotional discomfort*: Foundation for Community Empowerment, "A Great Park for a Great City," July 31, 2017, available at scribd.com/document/355374502/A-Great-Park-for-a-Great-City-Final#download&-from_embed.

160   *It makes you feel like*: Ibid.

160   *Heading into the 1977 matchup*: Details of the 1977 Texas-OU game, including comments from Campbell, Akers, and McEachern, are from Looney, "Down and Out."

161   *"Randy is Dandy" T-shirts*: McEachern, *100 Things Longhorns Fans*, 214.

161   *Without taking anything away*: "News and Notes from the Southwest Conference," Oct. 11, 1977, Fred Akers folder, Stark Center.

161   *I set a couple records*: Author interview with Rick Ingraham, July 2017.

162   *The pork chops and dressing*: UT Sports Information Service press release, Oct. 16, 1977, Earl Campbell folder, Stark Center.

162   *Ann Campbell rearranged her schedule*: Bohls, "Earl: A Trip with a Star."

162   *One of her front teeth*: Newman, "Roots of Greatness," 98.

162   *I don't think she could ever*: Blair, *Earl Campbell*, 91.

163   *On the line was the*: Technically, if Texas had lost to A&M and if A&M had lost its next game, against Houston, Texas would have gone to the Cotton Bowl.

163   *All I wanted to do*: "Thousands Cheer 'Horns," *Austin American-Statesman*, Nov. 22, 1977, A1.

163   *If an Aggie and a*: The content of the racist message was reprinted in two letters to the editor printed in the *Daily Texan*'s "Firing Line," Nov. 22, 1977: Joe Feagin and Devon Gerardo Peña, "Pursue UT Racism," and E. A. Saenz, "TV or Cowboy Racism."

163   *The sign was put there*: "Investigation Clears Cowboys," *Daily Texan*, Nov. 22, 1977, 2.

163   *I feel sorry for those* and *I'm not trying to tell you*: Bohls, "Earl: A Trip with a Star."

164   *We do wonder if we're*: Some details of the 1977 matchup between UT and Texas A&M are from Douglas Looney, "What a Way to Wind It Up," *Sports Illustrated*, Dec. 5, 1977, 20.

164   *Earl, I really expect 170 yards*: Bohls, "Earl: A Trip with a Star."

164   *If you poured a cup of coffee*: Bohls, "Campbell Was Unstoppable at Texas," *Austin American-Statesman*, July 28, 1991, clipping in Earl Campbell file, Stark Center.

165 *couldn't catch a cold*: John Pirkle, *Oiler Blues: The Story of Pro Football's Most Frustrating Team* (Houston, TX: Sportline, 2000), 159.

165 *Some teammates called him* and *He never caught*: Bohls, "Campbell Was Unstoppable."

165 *How bad do we want it?*: Looney, "What a Way."

165 *If he doesn't win*: Jerry Wizig, "Aggie Says Give Campbell Heisman or Throw It Away," *Houston Chronicle*, Nov. 27, 1977, sec. 3, 7.

165 *Grab, hold on and hope for help*: Looney, "What a Way," 20.

165 *Earl is the best running back*: Dave Campbell, "The Great Tyler Rose, Texas' Man for All Seasons," *Dave Campbell's Texas Football*, Jan. 1978, 25.

165 *People Run Over*: UT News Release, undated, Earl Campbell folder, Stark Center.

166 *A group of two dozen Orangebloods*: Undated two-page list titled "People Attending the Heisman Awards," Earl Campbell folder, 1974–2006, Stark Center.

166 *was not a Madison Avenue creation* and *stigma of advertisement*: Gordon H. White Jr., "Heisman Trophy 'Show Biz,'" *New York Times*, Dec. 7, 1977, D12.

167 *Only a day before, Ann Campbell*: Jim Trotter, "Mama Campbell Has Her New York Debut," *Austin American-Statesman*, Dec. 9, 1977; author interviews with Rick Ingraham and Henry Bell III.

167 *I play football when I*: Jim Trotter, "Earl the Same in New York or Austin," *Austin American-Statesman*, Dec. 9, 1977, G1.

168 Robert Lipsyte, "Behind the Easy Smile, O. J. Was Hard to Read," *New York Times*, June 19, 1994, sec. 8, 2.

168 *I think my biggest thrill*: Buchholz, "Echoes of Earl," *Austin American-Statesman*, Dec. 12, 1998. Buchholz recounts an exchange he had with Campbell when he was a student journalist at UT.

169 *I am not a football player*: Trotter, "Earl the Same in New York."

169 *This isn't what I came*: Miller, *Tyler Rose*, 111.

## PART III: HOUSTON

Interviews for this section were conducted with David Barron (Sept. 2017), Leon Beck (Feb. 2018), Gregg Bingham (Jan. 2018), Kirk Bohls (Aug. 2018), Ken Burrough (Aug. 2017), Dave Casper (Summer 2017), Gator Conley (Feb. 2018), Curley Culp (Jan. 2018), Joel Dinerstein (Mar. 2017), Mickey Herskowitz (Nov. 2018), David Lopez (Aug. 2017), Carl Mauck (Aug. 2016), John McClain (Nov. 2018), Dan Pastorini (Aug. 2016 and Aug. 2017), Dale Robertson (Aug. 2017), Erna Smith

(July 2017), Mike Trope (Oct. 2016), and Barry Warner (Nov. 2018). Quoted material from these interviews is generally not documented further in the notes. Many of the articles cited below are from Dale Robertson's clipping file (DRCF), which consists of newspaper clippings pasted into spiral-bound notebooks. Many of these articles do not include dates or page numbers.

172    *When Satan came to Houston*: The poem was sent to the newspaper by a reader; reprinted in David McComb, *Houston: A History* (Austin: University of Texas Press, 1981).

172    *When I was in Cleveland* and *he considered the trade*: John Pirkle, *Oiler Blues: The Story of Pro Football's Most Frustrating Team* (Houston: Sportline, 2000), 108.

172    *We had no friends*: Kenneth Turan, "Bum Phillips—The Genuine Article," *Washington Post*, Dec. 21, 1980, F1.

172    *National Football League's garbage can*: Pirkle, *Oiler Blues*, 108.

172    *Team owner Bud Adams*: Background information on Adams came from some of the interviewees listed above; Pirkle, *Oiler Blues*; and Ed Fowler, *Loser Takes All: Bud Adams, Bad Football, and Big Business* (Atlanta: Longstreet, 1997).

173    *The Astrodome, which opened in 1965*: I. A. Naman, "Domed Stadium Air-Conditioning Design," *ASHRAE Journal*, June 2009.

174    *Events hosted in the dome*: Lee Hockstader, "Once the 'Eighth Wonder,' Now a Relic," *Washington Post*, June 8, 2003, A1.

174–5 *In a 1977 survey of players* and *In the condition the field*: Dale Robertson, "Dome Could Pull Rug Out from under Oilers," *Houston Post*, DRCF.

175    *If the Astrodome was*: Dale Robertson, "Oilers Agree Training Facility the Pits," *Houston Post*, Sept. 20, 1979, DRCF; Robertson, "New Facility for Oilers to Be Delayed," *Houston Post*, no date on clipping, Clipping Notebook 1978–79, DRCF.

175    *To be real honest* and *The Dolphins practiced here*: Robertson, "Oilers Agree Training Facility."

175    *I smelled a rat* and *Leon, you're gonna be*: Robertson, "New Facility for Oilers."

176    *At Cutter Bill*: Chris Lane, "A Glimpse into the Wild Ride of Cutter Bill Western World Is a Texas Time Capsule," *Houston Press*, Mar. 2, 2016, houstonpress.com/arts/a-glimpse-into-the-wild-ride-of-cutter-bill-west-ern-world-is-a-texas-time-capsule-8205931.

176    *Absolutely no one was wearing*: Joe Simnacher, "Judi Buie: Texan Kick-Started Craze for Cowboy Boots in New York," *Dallas Morning News*, Apr. 16, 2003, 5B. Simnacher's story quotes a 1982 interview with Buie.

177  *By the following November*: Jason Mellard, *Progressive Country: How the 1970s Transformed the Texan in Popular Culture* (Austin: University of Texas Press, 2013), 172–174.

177  *The man who managed to bring*: O. A. "Bum" Phillips and Ray Buck, *He Ain't No Bum* (Virginia Beach, VA: Jordan, 1979); Curry Kirkpatrick, "Hallelujah. He's. Uh. Bum," *Sports Illustrated*, Oct. 27, 1980, 70–82.

178  *Gillman, who as a nerdy kid*: Bob Wolf, "Under Sid Gillman, the Charger Era Came to Pass," *Los Angeles Times*, Aug. 16, 1989, part 3, 1.

179  *He favored hand-tooled boots*: Dale Robertson, "Boots for Bum," *Houston Post*, DRCF; the story of Phillips's boot-buying habits is filled out in Kirkpatrick, "Hallelujah."

179  *I'd like to get him into*: E. M. Swift, "Scorecard," *Sports Illustrated*, July 30, 1978, 12.

179  *Texas wasn't blocking well*: Bum Phillips and Gabe Semenza, *Bum Phillips: Coach, Cowboy, Christian* (Brenham: Lucid Books, 2010), 103.

180  *You know the old cliché*: Dale Robertson, "Oilers' Rights to Tyler Rose Come Cheaply," *Houston Post*, DRCF.

180  *just doesn't sound right*: Willie Morris, *The Courting of Marcus Dupree* (Garden City, NY: Doubleday, 1983), 357.

180  *It's not fashion*: Mellard, *Progressive Country*, 190.

180  *The spot was Gilley's*: Author interview with Gator Conley, Feb. 2018; Michael Ennis, "The Conqueror Worm," *Texas Monthly*, Aug. 1980, 122–127; Aaron Latham, "The Ballad of the Urban Cowboy: America's Search for True Grit," *Esquire*, Sept. 12, 1978; John Spong, "Urban Cowboy Turns 35," *Texas Monthly*, June 2015, texasmonthly.com/the-culture/urban-cow-boy-turns-35; Bob Claypool, *Saturday Night at Gilley's* (New York: Delilah/Grove, 1980); Billy Porterfield, *The Greatest Honky-Tonks in Texas* (Dallas: Taylor, 1983).

181  *The per capita income*: Ray Marshall, *Employment of Blacks in the South: A Perspective on the 1960s* (Austin: University of Texas Press, 1978), 11.

182  *In black barbecue joints*: Robb Walsh, "How the Texas BBQ Boom Marginalizes Its African-American Roots," *FirstWeFeast* (blog), June 17, 2016, firstwefeast.com/features/2016/06/texas-bbq-overlooks-african-ameri-can-roots; J. C. Reid, e-mail to the author, May 2018.

182  *More than 1.5 million people*: William K. Stevens, "Houston, Fastest Growing Big City, Showing Signs of Having Hit Prime Time," *New York Times*, Dec. 16, 1981, A20.

182  *The unemployed pour into town*: Jan Morris, "City of Destiny," *Texas Monthly*, Oct. 1981, 130.

183  *Pasadena, home to oil refineries*: C. David Pomeroy Jr., "Pasadena, TX,"

*Handbook of Texas Online*, June 15, 2010, tshaonline.org/handbook/on
-line/articles/hdp02.

183    *redneck end of the hippie-redneck spectrum*: Mellard, *Progressive Country*,
       178; see also Rachel Graves, "Urban Cowboy, 25 years later," *Houston
       Chronicle*, May 15, 2005, A16.

184    *carouse at the all-white Gilley's*: Details about Earl Campbell at Gilley's are
       from author interviews with Leon Beck (Feb. 2018), who handled publicity
       for the club, and Gator Conley (Feb. 2018).

184    *saloon cowboys*: Aaron Latham, *Perfect Pieces* (New York: Arbor House,
       1987), 9.

184    *escape from the overwhelming complexities*: Ibid., 16.

184    *The story was obvious*: Spong, "Urban Cowboy Turns 35."

185    *Come on over*: David Maraniss, "Dear Earl: Campbell Runs On, Only Now
       He's Carrying Advice," *Washington Post*, June 12, 1990.

185    *He, in turn, embraced*: Dale Robertson, "'Davy Crockett Wouldn't Have
       Asked for a Raise at the Alamo': Same Old Earl, One More Verse," *Houston
       Post*, Clipping Notebook July 14, 1982–June 20, 1983, DRCF.

185    *Earl was the whitest black man*: Author interview with Dale Robertson, Aug.
       2017.

186    *His grandmother could have*: Jan Reid, "Gambling on the Gamblers," *Texas
       Monthly*, Jan. 1984, 154.

186    *It probably hadn't helped*: Author interview with Mike Trope, Oct. 2016.

186    *I mean, he didn't know what*: Author interview with Witt Stewart, Oct. 2018.

186    *These black guys spend money*: M. Cordell Thompson, "Discrimination in
       Football Nothing New," *Jet*, Nov. 15, 1973, 68.

186    *the average NFL salary was $25,000*: Debra Bell, "US News Questioned
       Football's Future Nearly 45 Years Ago," *US News*, Feb. 1, 2013, usnews
       .com/news/blogs/press-past/2013/02/01/us-news-questioned-pro-foot
       -balls-future-nearly-45-years-ago.

187    *They wouldn't give another black*: Peter Gent, *North Dallas Forty* (New York:
       Morrow, 1973), 76.

187    *Through the mid-1960s, the Oilers*: Thompson, "Discrimination in Foot-
       ball," 68.

187    *But in 1966, the Oilers*: "Negro Quota System Dropped by Houston Oilers,"
       *Jet*, Nov. 23, 1967, 57.

187    *Still, into the 1970s*: Jonathan I. Brower, "The Black Side of Football: The
       Salience of Race" (PhD diss., University of California at Santa Barbara,
       1973), 115, 116, 123. The racial makeup of teams from the South was 29
       percent African American; for teams from other parts of the country, it
       was 35 percent.

188     *Even in the strict business*: George Plimpton, *Paper Lion: Confessions of a Last-String Quarterback* (New York: New American Library, 1974), 168.

188     *Fear. They all got too much*: Gent, *North Dallas Forty*, 131.

189     *If there's one thing*: UPI, "Campbell Sweeps Awards with MVP," *Brownsville (TX) Herald*, Dec. 29, 1978, 1B.

189     *driving through Palestine and Corsicana*: Avrel Seale, "A Rose by Any Other Name," *Texas Alcalde*, September–October, 1994, 12.

190     *I want it*: Brad Buchholz, "Echoes of Earl," *Austin American-Statesman*, Dec. 12, 1998, 1.

190     *Mr. Scott, I need a car*: Wally Scott gave me a copy of the notes for his father's unpublished memoir; see also Fowler, *Loser Takes All*, and Pirkle, *Oiler Blues*.

190     *Hop in my Rolls*: Kirk Bohls, "Earl: A Trip with a Star," *Austin American-Statesman*, Dec. 4, 1977.

191     *at each Pro Bowl*: Pirkle, *Oiler Blues*, 172.

191     *to build a house*: Kent Demaret, "Earl Campbell Eats Up Yards, but He and Wife Reuna Measure Their Gains in Acres," *People*, Sept. 8, 1980, people .com/archive/for-fans-earl-campbell-eats-up-yards-but-he-and-wife -reuna-measure-their-gains-in-acres-vol-14-no-10.

191     *It's going to be simple*: Pirkle, *Oiler Blues*, 131.

192     *All this money don't make*: Bruce Newman, "The Roots of Greatness," *Sports Illustrated*, Sept. 3, 1979, 98.

192     *one of the town's reservoirs*: Asher Price, "Austin as Dry as San Angelo?," *Austin American-Statesman*, May 15, 2011, B1.

192     *I'll never forget one starry night*: Kirk Bohls, "Earl to Open Up on TV on Monday," *Austin American-Statesman*, June 24, 2013, C1.

192–193     *I remember one time he* and *It was the second day of camp*: Bill Sullivan, "Former Teammates Remain in Awe," *Houston Chronicle*, July 29, 1991, 1C.

193     *A poor man's Joe Namath*: Dale Robertson, "Oiler Quarterback Scarred but Remains Confident," *Houston Post*, Jan. 6, 1979.

193     *She may be why Pastorini*: Kevin Cook, *The Last Headbangers: NFL Football in the Rowdy, Reckless '70s—The Era That Created Modern Sports* (New York: Norton, 2013), 182.

194     *Every quarterback wants*: Dale Robertson, "Never a Rookie like Earl," *Dave Campbell's Arkansas Football*, Winter 1979, 62.

194     *If y'all think about it*: Bum Phillips, *The Best of Bum: The Quotable Bum Phillips*, with David Kaplan and Daniel Griffin (Austin: Texas Monthly Press, 1980), unpaginated.

194     *has two speeds*: Norman Chad, "Week 3," *Washington Post*, Sept. 21, 1980,

washingtonpost.com/archive/sports/1980/09/21/week-3/55e90a46-06e1-47a9-8aaa-fc978721537b/?utm_term=.ccefa4d0becd.

194    *You know what he reminds*: Barry Lorge, "The Earl of Campbell," *Washington Post*, Dec. 27, 1978.

195    *Mamma, Don't Let Your Babies*: Newman, "Roots of Greatness," 98.

195    *If you could count to three*: Thomas "Hollywood" Henderson, *Out of Control: Confessions of an NFL Casualty* (New York: Putnam, 1987), 263.

195    *Your blue pen is for*: Ibid., 83.

195    *The Oilers' style*: Dale Robertson, "NFL Record to Define Oiler's Image," *Houston Post*, Clipping Notebook July 14, 1982–June 20, 1983, DRCF.

196    *Dallas players are made*: Dale Robertson, "It's Bum and Tom and Never the Twain Shall Meet," *Dave Campbell's Texas Football*, Mar. 1979, 19.

196    *Everybody makes fun of*: Phillips and Buck, *He Ain't No Bum*, 21.

196    *Thursdays were beer-keg days*: Kirkpatrick, "Hallelujah," 76.

197    *You won't fight for anyone*: Author interview with Dan Pastorini, Aug. 2017.

197    *People said I was too easy*: Robertson, "It's Bum and Tom."

197    *I approached my first tackle*: Frank Luska, "To Tackle Earl Was to Tackle a Superman," *Dallas Times Herald*, Aug. 19, 1986.

198    *three-piece-suit football*: Robertson, "It's Bum and Tom."

198    *One o'clock*: Dale Robertson, "Dollars Make Sense to Oilers," *Houston Post*, DRCF.

199    *There was a caravan*: Author interview with Gregg Bingham, Jan. 2018.

199    *Perhaps they had in mind*: Michael May, "The Freedom Files," *Texas Observer*, Mar. 20, 2014, texasobserver.org/freedom-files; author correspondence with Michael May, May 2018.

199    *not welcome after sunset*: James W. Loewen, *Sundown Towns: A Hidden Dimension of American Racism* (New York: New Press, 2005); see also the associated website, sundown.tougaloo.edu/sundowntowns.php.

199    *"drive-through" county*: Patricia J. Ruland, "Parks, Wildlife, and Racism," *Austin Chronicle*, Aug. 10, 2012, austinchronicle.com/news/2012-08-10/parks-wildlife-and-racism/all.

200    *He bleeping ran over him* and *I'm glad that cat's*: Dale Robertson "LA Dumps Oilers," *Houston Post*, Sept. 25, 1978, 1D.

200    *At times I've said*: Frank Luska, "The Bruising Truth about Earl Campbell," *Dallas Times Herald*, Sept. 4, 1982, C3.

200    *I got Earled*: Dale Robertson, "We Just Want to Hold Him under a Mile," *Houston Post*, Dec. 20, 1980, DRCF.

201    *can take his'n*: Turan, "Bum Phillips."

201    *could run for mayor*: Dale Robertson, "Oilers Sack Miami 35-30," *Houston Post*, Clipping Notebook 1977-78, DRCF.

201   *Less than a fifth*: Andrew Wiese, *Places of Their Own: African American Suburbanization in the Twentieth Century* (Chicago: University of Chicago Press, 2004), 210.

202   *when he asked Reuna's father* and *My mother said*: Demaret, "Campbell Eats Up Yards."

203   *the world's most air-conditioned city*: "History of Air Conditioning in Houston," cooldudeac.com/2014/05/19/history-of-air-conditioning-in -houston.

203   *One little thing, all by*: Nell Zink, *Mislaid* (New York: HarperCollins, 2015), 133.

203   *The Campbells' life fell*: Demaret, "Campbell Eats Up Yards."

203   *I always wanted the Rolls-Royce*: Gram Gemoets, "Barbecue Man," *Forbes*, June 6, 1994, 120.

203   *Earl isn't going to waste*: Newman, "Roots of Greatness," 104.

203   *Que pasa?*: Miller, *Tyler Rose*, 153–154.

203   *I've got a whole batch*: Demaret, "Campbell Eats Up Yards."

203   *In place of NIMBY*: Robert Bullard, "The Mountains of Houston," *Cite* 93 (Winter 2014), 28–33; quotation on 28.

205   *He began criticizing the Negroes*: Plimpton, *Paper Lion*, 168–169.

206   *When you read about white athletes*: Chris Ballard, "Mr. Everything," *Sports Illustrated*, May 17, 2016, 35.

206   *new wealth and fame*: John Maher, e-mail to author, June 2018.

206   *As the broader civil rights movement*: Douglas Hartmann, *Race, Culture, and the Revolt of the Black Athlete: The 1968 Olympic Protests and their Aftermath* (Chicago: University of Chicago Press, 2003), 241.

206   *As he had done in Tyler*: Author interview with Earl Campbell, Feb. 2016.

207   *Earl could hit the wrong*: Cox News Service, "Earl Looks Different to Foes," Dec. 8, 1982.

207   *In Campbell's rookie season*: Dale Robertson, "Earl's 'Watching' Out for Linemen," *Houston Post*, Clipping Notebook Late April 1980 to mid-April 1981, DRCF.

207   *requests for about three hundred*: Dale Robertson, "Bum Not about to Tin-ker with Earl's Style," *Houston Post*, Clipping Notebook 1978–79, DRCF.

207   *Be careful, all sportswriters*: Dale Robertson, "Oilers' Mauck Not in Mold of Low-Key Linemen," *Houston Post*, Apr. 12, 1979, 6D.

207   *"Oiler Cannonball"*: Mauck's recording of the song can be heard on You-Tube, youtube.com/watch?v=weizpfwqEEY.

208   *a chance for people of all races*: Official website of Earl Campbell, web .archive.org/web/20110521084650/http://www.earlcampbell.com/EC/Bio_-_The_Oilers.html.

208   *Joe Greene, the Steelers' famous* and *The ball didn't feel like*: Pirkle, *Oiler Blues*, 140.

209   *For all his talent* and *The behinder we got*: Dale Robertson, "Steelers Derail Oiler Express 34-5," *Houston Post*, Jan. 8, 1979, 1D, DRCF.

210   *During the summer of 1979* and *some guy who ran a doughnut shop* and *Look, used to be I*: Dale Robertson, "Camp Williams: Former Oilers Executive Helps Pro Football Players Shape Up," *Houston Post*, Clipping Notebook 1978-79, DRCF.

211   *Across town at Gilley's*: Spong, "Urban Cowboy Turns 35"; author interview with Gator Conley, Feb. 2018.

211   *I don't want you to fumble*: Fowler, *Loser Takes All*, 54.

212   *Before Earl came along*: Newman, "Roots of Greatness," 97.

212   *I have never played* and *On film, it looks like guys*: Dale Robertson, "Oilers Ride Colts 28-16," *Houston Chronicle*, Oct. 15, 1979, D1.

213   *It may be the most noticed* and *We hate them*: Dale Robertson, "Surging Oilers wa . . . [headline cut off]," *Houston Post*, Clipping Notebook 1978-79, DRCF.

213   *You think we're obnoxious now*: Pirkle, *Oiler Blues*, 139.

213   *the team up north*: Ibid., 147.

213   *He's the greatest running back*: Luska, "Bruising Truth about Earl Campbell."

213   *Remember how I told you*: Dale Robertson, "Oilers Perform like Champs When Everyone Is Watching," *Houston Post*, 1D, Clipping Notebook 1978-79, DRCF.

213   *Crocodiles like water*: Dale Robertson, "Boots for Bum," *Houston Post*, Clipping Notebook 1978-79, DRCF.

214   *We knew Earl would carry*: Frank Luska, "To Many, Campbell Was Overused and Abused," *Dallas Times Herald*, Aug. 20, 1986.

214   *Last year was a nightmare* and *I saw it*: Pirkle, *Oiler Blues*, 156.

214   *One year ago we knocked*: Turan, "Bum Phillips."

215   *Well, I was hanging out*: Cantrell's rendition of "Bum's Promise" can be heard on SoundCloud, soundcloud.com/tomcantrell/bums-promise.

215   *I'd live a lot longer*: Pirkle, *Oiler Blues*, 167.

215   *Earl's walking better*: Phillips, *Best of Bum*. Helen Phillips once said of her husband: "You've heard of men dying with their boots on. Well, I think Bum was born with 'em on."

216   *He runs with a lot*: Robertson, "Bum Not about to Tinker."

216   *If I ran that way*: Dale Robertson, "Dorsett Utilizes His Talents," *Houston Post*, Clipping Notebook 1978-79, DRCF.

216   *This perception of abuse*: Miller, *Tyler Rose*, 157.

# NOTES

216 *It's the hitter versus*: "Campbell Attacks with Vigor," *New York Times*, Nov. 23, 1980, sec. 5, 13.

216 *Many of y'all have questioned*: Phillips, *Best of Bum*.

216 *He's the kind of guy*: Dale Robertson, "Workhorse: Oilers' Game Plan Includes 25 Carries for Campbell," *Houston Post*, Clipping Notebook 1978–79, DRCF.

216 *Earl Campbell is the best*: Miller, *Tyler Rose*, 164.

217 *I never felt like he carried*: Bum Phillips, in "A Football Life—Earl Campbell," published by Online Documentaries on YouTube, Apr. 28, 2018, youtube.com/watch?v=vS4jMv-VuoM.

217 *the day cowboy chic ended*: Ennis, "Conqueror Worm," 124; also see Spong, "Urban Cowboy Turns 35," and Craig Hilavaty, "Looking Back on the Houston Premiere of 'Urban Cowboy' 35 years later," *Houston Chronicle*, May 20, 2015, chron.com/entertainment/slideshow/Looking-back-on-the-Houston-premiere-Urban-110153.php.

218 *It was as if Gilley's*: Ennis, "Conqueror Worm," 126.

218 *You can make a career*: Ibid., 125.

219 *And, well, once Travolta*: Andy Warhol, *The Andy Warhol Diaries*, ed. Pat Hackett (New York: Warner, 1991), 292.

220 *I was madly stalking Houston*: Henderson, *Out of Control*, 257.

220 *The peer pressure for me*: Maraniss, "Dear Earl."

220 *now controls and corrupts*: Don Reese, "I'm Not Worth a Damn," *Sports Illustrated*, June 14, 1982, 66.

221 *I wouldn't think anybody*: Dale Robertson, "Players May Shun Oiler Drug Consultant," *Houston Post*, July 1982.

221 *The* Washington Post *reported in 1986*: All quoted material in this paragraph comes from Gary Pomerantz, "Drug Problem in NFL Raises Racial Issues," *Washington Post*, May 7, 1986, B1.

221 *There's two kinds of coaches*: Phillips, *Best of Bum*.

222 *known to study his playbook*: Author interview with Leon Beck, Feb. 2018.

222 *kindergarten level*: Mark Newman, "DuPree, Casper Are Blue," *Miami Herald*, Aug. 3, 1982, D3.

222 *something out of the 1940's*: William N. Wallace, "Raiders Found Flaw in Oilers' Offense," *New York Times*, Dec. 30, 1980, B11.

222 *It's got to be a joke*: William N. Wallace, "Phillips Is Discharged by Oilers after Controversy over Offense," *New York Times*, Jan. 1, 1981, sec. 1, 25.

223 *football at the OK Corral*: Dale Robertson, "NFL Record to Define Oiler's Image," *Houston Post*, Clipping Notebook July 14, 1982–June 20, 1983, DRCF.

223 *Campbell asked for a raise*: Associated Press, "Campbell Is Seeking $1 Mil-

lion a Season," *New York Times*, Jan. 8, 1981, B15; Hal Lundgren, "Lines Drawn," *Houston Chronicle*, Jan. 7, 1981, sec. 2, 1.

223　*Everything for Earl*: Author interview with Witt Stewart, Oct. 2018.

223　*We won't be blackmailed*: Lundgren, "Lines Drawn."

223　*We're bigger than the Ayatollah*: Author interview with Witt Stewart, Oct. 2018.

224　*still doesn't have the security*: Lundgren, "Lines Drawn."

224　*who made $95,000 in 1980*: UPI, "Average N.F.L. Salary is $90,102, Survey Says," *New York Times*, Jan. 29, 1982, A22.

224　*Heroes don't act that way*: Robertson, "Same Old Earl."

224　*The agency had infiltrated*: Author interview with Witt Stewart, Oct. 2018.

224　*You want to make slaves*: UPI, "Man Kills Son in Football Argument," Jan. 8, 1981, upi.com/Archives/1981/01/08/Man-kills-son-in-football-argu -ment/6302347778000; UPI, "Doc Says Son's Slaying during Football Spat Was Self-Defense," July 15, 1981.

225　*Ultimately the Oilers held fast*: AP, "Campbell, in Reverse, Says He Won't Press Demands," *New York Times*, June 4, 1981, D21.

226　*You taught him well*: According to Stewart, Adams told him that Campbell demanded $50,000 as an appearance fee.

226　*the first woman to win*: William K. Stevens, "The Houston That Was Loses Its Hold," *New York Times*, Nov. 22, 1981, sec. 4, 5.

226　*Less than 150 years earlier*: Howard Beeth and Cary D. Wintz, eds., *Black Dixie: Afro-Texan History and Culture in Houston* (College Station: Texas A&M University Press, 1992), 15.

227　*One member called them "oddwads"*: William K. Stevens, "Houston Accepts New Political Force," *New York Times*, Nov. 2, 1981, A16.

227　*The year of Whitmire's run*: Roxanna Asgarian, "Timeline: The History of HIV/AIDS in Houston," *Houstonia*, Feb. 28, 2018, houstoniamag.com /articles/2018/2/28/hiv-aids-timeline-houston.

227　*city is the most diverse*: Leah Binkovitz, "Within Houston's Diversity, a Complicated Story Still Being Told," *Kinder Institute Research*, Apr. 23, 2018, kinder.rice.edu/2018/04/19/within-houstons-diversity-complicat -ed-story-still-being-told.

227　*There's room for diversity*: William K. Stevens, "Woman in the News: Feminist Mayor for Houston," *New York Times*, Nov. 19, 1981, A24.

227　*come out and fight*: Sharon Herbaugh, "Mayoral Candidates Feud over Debate," Associated Press, Nov. 14, 1981.

228　*Until recently she wore*: Stevens, "Woman in the News."

228　*I'm a mayor who*: Ibid.

228　*What can we do to keep*: Fowler, *Loser Takes All*, 153.

229    *The video was booed*: "Oilers Summary," *Houston Chronicle*, Sept. 17, 1991, Sports sec., 5.

229    *He never got the best*: Luska, "Campbell Was Overused and Abused."

229    *Yeah, I'm frustrated*: Dale Robertson, "Frustration for Campbell," *Houston Post*, n.d., DRCF.

229    *Up in New York, the NFL*: Richard Sandomir, "Ed Garvey, who Took on the N.F.L. and then Conservatives, Dies at 76," *New York Times*, Feb. 23, 2017, B15.

230    *I don't understand how Garvey*: Bill Brubaker, "Campbell Blames Garvey, Donlan for Long Strike," *Miami Herald*, Oct. 12, 1982, C1.

231    *is a company whore*: Allen Abel, "Strike Watchers Settle In for Siege," *Toronto Globe and Mail*, Nov. 16, 1982.

231    *What really hurt was seeing*: Dale Robertson, "Bethea: Push to Settle Hurt Players' Position," *Houston Post*, Clipping Notebook July 14, 1982–June 20, 1983, DRCF.

232    *the CBS affiliate in Houston*: Pirkle, *Oiler Blues*, 179.

232    *In the I-formation*: William N. Wallace, "For Campbell, It Is Not a Good Season," *New York Times*, Oct. 28, 1981, B8.

232    *Coming out of the I* and *Earl set an NFL record* and *He isn't the same Earl* and *I don't think it's* and *I really don't know why* and *It gets harder all the time*: Cox News Service, "Earl Looks Different to Foes," Dec. 8, 1982.

234    *is only a shoddy imitation*: Dale Robertson, "Campbell, Brazile Feel Heat," *Houston Post*, 1C, Clipping Notebook July 14, 1982–June 20, 1983, DRCF.

234    *When the county judge who*: Brad Buchholz, "Astrodome Recalls Texas of Yesteryear," Cox News Service, *Chicago Tribune*, Oct. 3, 1999, C6.

234    *The nation's drilling rig count*: Colin Eaton, "1980s Oil Bust Left a Lasting Mark," *Houston Chronicle*, Aug. 31, 2016, chron.com/local/history/econ-omy-business/article/The-1980s-oil-bust-left-lasting-mark-on-Hous-ton-9195222.php.

234    *A Houston dentist reported*: Michael White, "Oil Our Yesterdays," *Guardian Weekly*, April 13, 1986, 7.

234    *And by 1983, the mills*: Barbara Canetti, "One of the Nation's Largest Steel Mills Closing," UPI, Jan. 26, 1984, upi.com/Archives/1984/01/26/One-of-nations-largest-steel-mills-closing/5550443941200.

234    *This came just as Gilley's*: Graves, "Urban Cowboy, 25 Years Later."

234    *Federal agents raided Cutter Bill*: Lawrence Wright, "Rex Cauble and the Cowboy Mafia," *Texas Monthly*, Nov. 1980, 173.

235    *Earl, you didn't get where*: Robertson, "Campbell, Brazile Feel Heat."

235    *The franchise's management and coaches*: Michael Janofsky, "Disenchant-ment behind Campbell Trade," *New York Times*, Oct. 11, 1984, B17.

235 *the things I want to*: Brad Buchholz, "Hundreds Greet Campbell at Auto Dealer's Promotion," *Austin American-Statesman*, July 22, 1981.

236 *you're never gonna have*: Author interview with Dale Robertson, Aug. 2017.

236 *Everything seemed right*: Earl Campbell, *The Earl Campbell Story: A Football Great's Battle with Panic Disorder*, with John Ruane (Toronto: ECW, 1999), 69.

237 *you gave them a good fight*: Kirk Bohls, "God Only Made One Earl," *Austin American-Statesman*, Aug. 9, 1987, D8.

237 *Everything changes except what*: Associated Press, Aug. 18, 1986, no byline or headline.

237 *10,000 yards weren't going to* and *If I had it to do all over*: Bohls, "God Only Made One Earl."

## Epilogue

Interviewees for this section included Sam Biscoe (summer 2017), Gregg Bingham (Jan. 2018), Gary Bledsoe (July 2017), Verlin Callahan (Nov. 2018), Earl Campbell (Dec. 2015, Feb. 2016), Herbert Campbell (Dec. 2015), Ben Carrington (Jan. 2017), Cedric Golden (May 2017), Rick Ingraham (July 2017), Caesar Martinez (Oct. 2016), Jenna Hays McEachern (Nov. 2017), Alberta Phillips (May 2018), and Witt Stewart (Oct. 2018). Quoted material from these interviews is generally not documented further in the notes.

240 *I never felt so bad* and *Earl has done far more* and *I think at this point* and *There had been several racist*: Maraniss, "Dear Earl: Campbell Runs On, Only Now He's Carrying Advice," *Washington Post*, June 12, 1990.

241 *not academically competitive with whites* and *I think that the University*: Brian Davis, "Third and Long: Earl Campbell Continues to Recruit Minority Athletes despite Anger at Graglia's Comments," *Daily Texan*, Oct. 9, 1997.

242 *Ahead of a home game*: Michael Hall, "We Love the Westlake Chaps. No, Really," *Texas Monthly*, Oct. 1989, 116.

242 *It was at about this time*: Details of Campbell's worsening medical problems come from the following sources: William Nack, "The Wrecking Yard," *Sports Illustrated*, May 7, 2001, 78; Jan Reid, "Earl Campbell," *Texas Monthly*, Sept. 2001, 107; and Brad Buchholz, "Rock of Ages," *Austin American-Statesman*, Dec. 9, 2007.

244 *I stay focused and prayerful* and *biggest, baddest player*: Chip Brown, "Toll of Glory: Earl Campbell Paying Price for Punishing Running Style," *Dallas Morning News*, June 30, 2007, 1C.

244 *It reached the point*: "Earl Campbell: Addiction to Painkillers and His Campaign to Help Others," ThePostGame (blog), Oct. 29, 2013, thepostgame

.com/blog/men-action/201310/earl-campbell-fighting-painkiller-addic-tion-football-vicodin-oxycontin-spinal; see also Jim Vertuno, "Heisman Winner, Hall of Fame Player Campbell Says NFL Should Do More," Associated Press, June 30, 2017, and Dave Anderson, "Football Legend Speaks Out about Toughest Opponent," *Westlake (TX) Picayune*, Apr. 18, 2013, statesman.com/news/local/football-legend-speaks-out-about-toughest -opponent/cUGvJc41tcDxBz84PPhTOI.

244   *He wasn't communicating clearly*: Stan Jones, in "A Football Life—Earl Campbell," published by Online Documentaries on YouTube, Apr. 28, 2018, youtube.com/watch?v=vS4jMv-VuoM.

244   *Do whatever you want to*: Campbell's rehab journey is told in David Barron, "Wistful Thinking: Campbell One of NFL's Greats Who Never Got to the Big Game," *Houston Chronicle*, Jan. 30, 2017, C1, and Barron, "Earl Campbell: UT Icon Proud of Sobriety, Royal's Guidance," *Houston Chronicle*, Nov. 10, 2012, Sports, 4; see also, Bucky Gleason, "Pushing Drugs in the Locker Room," *Buffalo News*, Sept. 7, 2014, A1; Melissa Rohlin, "Football: Taking on the Pain, Campbell Tells Tale of Alcohol, Pill Addictions," *San Antonio Express-News*, May 20, 2016, C1; and Michael Barnes, "Longhorn Legends Praised off the Field," *Austin American-Statesman*, Apr. 4, 2013, D1.

245   *The most serious injury*: Brown, "Toll of Glory."

245   *Jack Tatum, nicknamed the Assassin*: Lee Jenkins, "Life's Roses (and Sausages)," *Sports Illustrated*, July 9, 2012, 70.

245   *I guarantee I have CTE*: Rob Trucks, "Former NFL Player: I Guarantee I Have CTE," *Deadspin*, Jan. 28, 2014, deadspin.com/former-nfl-player-i -guarantee-i-have-cte-1509813582.

246   *I will 100 percent tell you*: Author interview with Gregg Bingham, Jan. 2018.

246   *I can't play because I've*: Josh Peter, "Campbell's Hard Knocks," *USA Today*, Jan. 31, 2017, 1C.

247   *Sometimes I tell my wife*: Nack, "The Wrecking Yard," 78.

247   *Ann Campbell died, age eighty-five*: *Tyler Morning Telegraph*, Aug. 7, 2009, obituaries.tylerpaper.com/obituaries/tylerpaper/obituary.aspx -?n=ann-l-campbell&pid=131030365&fhid=6714.

247   *Everybody in the world has*: Dale Robertson, "Oilers' Earl Campbell: 'We Just want to Hold Him under a Mile,'" *Houston Post*, Dec. 12, 1980.

248   *As for the fiftieth reunion*: Bettye Mitchell and Katherine Bynum, "Oral History Interview with Bettye Mitchell," July 1, 2015, video, The Portal to Texas History, texashistory.unt.edu/ark:/67531/metapth836696.

249   *the district served a student population* and *We'll forever say this*: Adam Russell, "Desegregation Order: Tyler ISD Looks to Move On," *Tyler*

*Morning Telegraph*, July 18, 2015, tylerpaper.com/news/local/desegre
-gation-order-tyler-isd-looks-to-move-on/article_8d8c0174-1998-5872-
8635-76b507b9e618.html.

250    *might as well use their diplomas*: Tasneem Raja, "To Be Black at Robert E.
Lee High School," *New Yorker*, Sept. 19, 2017, newyorker.com/news/news
-desk/what-is-it-like-to-be-a-black-student-at-robert-e-lee-high-school.

250-1  *unthinkable for a black person*: Author interview with Sam Biscoe (summer
2017).

251    *University of Texas running back*: Ricky Williams discussed the events in
Tyler on the *Dudley and Bob with Matt Show*'s daily podcast, Austin radio
station KLBJ, Jan. 18, 2017, klbjfm.com/media/podcasts/2017-1-18-pt2
-former-nfl-player-ricky-williams.

251    *A dash-cam video shows Williams*: The video was posted to YouTube by
KTBC Fox 7 Austin, Jan. 19, 2017, youtube.com/watch?v=LBgO_MR-
G7uM.

252    *We both reached out to*: Roy Maynard, "Heisman Trophy Winner Ricky
Williams Questions Police Stop in Tyler, Texas," *Tyler Morning Telegraph*,
Jan. 18, 2017, tylerpaper.com/sports/pro/heisman-trophy-winner-ricky
-williams-questions-police-stop-in-tyler/article_d184fa59-9829-508b-
8f17-86f61c559a7d.html.

252    A black guy walking during daytime: *Dudley and Bob with Matt Show*'s daily
podcast, Jan. 18, 2017.

254    *his sole line was scratched*: Author interview with Witt Stewart, Oct. 2018.

255    *But in his own quiet*: Juan R. Palomo, "Affirmative Action Takes Athletic
Twist," *USA Today*, Apr. 10, 1997, 14A; "Bill May Hamper University Athletics, Some Say," *Dallas Morning News*, May 17, 1997, 4A.

255    *Obviously,* Hopwood *means that a lot*: "Capitol Notebook," *Houston Chronicle*, Mar. 7, 1997, 37.

258    *he once had such momentum*: Jason Cohen, "Earl Campbell's Third Act,"
*Texas Monthly*, Jan. 21, 2013, texasmonthly.com/articles/earl-campbells
-third-act.

259    *For a long time everything*: Reid, "Earl Campbell," 144.

259    *This state wants to see you*: Author interview with Rick Ingraham, July 2017.

259    *It fell to Caesar Martinez*: Author interview with Caesar Martinez, Oct.
2016.

259    *I really want it bad*: "Earl Campbell Press Availability transcript," Sept. 9,
2012, TexasSports.com, texassports.com/news/2012/9/9/090912aaa_732
.aspx.

# INDEX

early years in football, 54, 56–57;
Campbell's friends from, 168;
Campbell's senior year, 58–65;
and college recruitment of
Campbell, 116–117, 119; and
desegregation of Tyler school
system, 28, 33, 34–35, 37–38;
football state championship, 9,
99, 110; regional final against
Conroe, 62, 240
Jones, Jim, 230
Jones, Mike, 152
Jones, Stan, 244
Jordan, Barbara, 4–5, 113, 125
Joyce, Edmund P., 166
Juneteenth, 18
Justice, William Wayne, 33–34, 35–41,
53–54, 248

**K**

Kaepernick, Colin, 145, 188
Kansas City Chiefs, 71–72
Keith, Don, 102
Kennedy, John F., 106
Kennedy, Robert, 71
Kidd, Sam, 15, 20, 45, 61
KIKK radio station, 235
Kilgore, Texas, 34
Kilgore College, 23, 34
Killer (bouncer), 220
KILT radio station, 208
Kinder Institute, 227
Kiner, Steve, 196
King, Billie Jean, 174
King, Lynn, 57–61, 64, 65, 168
King, Martin Luther, Jr., 11, 71, 102,
121, 240, 257
Kinzie, Bill, 15, 47
Kinzie, Earl Christian, 14–17, 41, 201

KLBJ radio station, 252–253
knee injuries and surgeries, 8, 217,
235, 242, 243
Knievel, Evel, 174
Korean War, 84
Koy, Ted, 150
Kralj, Nick, 74, 103
Kristofferson, Kris, 124
KTBC radio station, 86
Ku Klux Klan, 19–20, 74, 183, 199, 224
Küntzi, Christian, 14

**L**

LaCroix, Butch, 54, 57
*LA Free Press*, 122
Laird, Bruce, 212
Lamar College, 178
Landry, Tom, 195–196
Lansdale, Joe Richard, 37
Latham, Aaron, 184, 218
Latino community, 226–227
Lauren, Ralph, 180
LBJ High School, 242
LBJ Presidential Library, 106, 109
leadership of Campbell, 156–157
*League of Denial: The NFL, Concus-
sions, and the Battle for Truth*
(Fainaru-Wada and Fainaru),
246
Leaks, Roosevelt, 119, 131, 151
Lee, Dorothy, 27
Leland, Mickey, 125
Lemon Tree Club, 121
Lewis, Jerry Lee, 180
Lewis, Thorndyke, 52
Loewen, James, 199
Lone Star Café, 177
Lonestar Nurseries, 44
Longview, Texas, 27, 55–56

Orange Coats, 93–94

*Our Invaded Universities* (Dugger), 146

*Out of Control: Confessions of an NFL Casualty* (Henderson), 220

Owens, Chachie, 138

Oxycontin, 243–244

**P**

Painter, Theophilus S., 75

Papadakis, John, 102

*Paper Lion* (Plimpton), 188, 205

Pasadena, Texas, 183

Pastorini, Dan: on Campbell's competitiveness, 4; on Campbell's talent, 200, 245; and contract negotiations, 173, 191; and Gilley's, 183–184; last game as Oiler, 214; *Monday Night Football* victories, 1–4; and racial dynamics of Oilers, 197; and successful Oilers seasons, 207, 209; toughness of, 193–194; traded, 222

Payton, Walter, 31, 204

peach growing, 44

Pearson, Drew, 213

Penders, Tom, 255–256

Penn State University (Nittany Lions), 167

*People*, 203

pep rallies, 39, 56, 163, 208

perfectionism of Campbell, 129, 259–260

Perry, Fred, 100

Peters, Robert, 37

Phillips, Alberta, 256

Phillips, Edrina, 177

Phillips, Oail "Bum": and AFC title games, 209–210, 213–215; background, 177–178, 182; on Campbell's rookie year, 11; and Campbell's trade to New Orleans, 235–236; criticisms of, 222; and drafting of Campbell, 179–180; early years with Oilers, 178–179; famous *Monday Night Football* game, 2; fired from Houston, 221–222, 225; fired from New Orleans, 236; loyalty to Campbell, 215; and Miami Dolphins game, 200–201; named Oilers head coach, 194; reliance on Campbell, 197–198, 211–212, 215–216; and signing of Campbell, 189; support of Campbell, 194; team-building efforts, 196–197

Phillips, Wade, 179–180

Phillips Petroleum, 172

PIBBY (Place in Blacks' Back Yard) policy, 203–204

*Pittsburgh Post*, 172

Pittsburgh Steelers, 103, 208–210, 213–215

*Places of Their Own: African American Suburbanization in the Twentieth Century* (Wiese), 201–202

Plano High School, 62

Plimpton, George, 188, 205

Poindexter, Albert Sidney, 19

politics in football, 188

Porterfield, Billy, 181

poverty, 25–26, 42–43, 49–52, 59, 87–88, 189

Prairie View A&M, 77, 86, 111

Preciphs, Jess, 95